# How to Navigate Today

I0801000

C O R N E L L   B O A T E R S   L I B R A R Y

# How to Navigate Today

SIXTH EDITION

by Leonard Gray

*Based on the original edition by M. R. Hart*

CORNELL MARITIME PRESS

*Centreville, Maryland*

Copyright © 1943, 1953, 1959, 1968, 1970, 1986
by Cornell Maritime Press, Inc.

All rights reserved. No part of this book may be used or reproduced in any manner whatsoever without written permission except in the case of brief quotations embodied in critical articles and reviews. For information, address Cornell Maritime Press, Inc., Centreville, Maryland 21617.

Library of Congress Cataloging in Publication Data

Gray, Leonard.
How to navigate today.

Rev. ed. of: How to navigate today / by M. R. Hart.
5th ed. 1970.
Bibliography: p.
Includes index.
1. Navigation. I. Hart, M. R. (Marion Rice),
1891- How to navigate today. II. Title.
VK555.G6995 1986 623.89 86-47711
ISBN 0-87033-353-4

Manufactured in the United States of America
First edition, 1943. Sixth edition, 1986; second printing, 1994

# Contents

# Preface

MARION RICE HART, THE AUTHOR OF THE FIRST edition of *How to Navigate Today,* was trained as a chemical engineer and geologist and has been a research physicist, miner, surveyor, sculptor, painter, photographer, sailboat skipper, instructor, aviator, author, and radio operator. She has never been a noisy rebel flouting the conventions for women of her generation (she was born in 1891); she has just quietly done what she felt like doing, avoiding publicity and making a fuss only when she had to, to cut through red tape (without which flying and international travel would not be what they are) or to take a poke at pretension or stupidity.

Mrs. Hart bought a boat in England in 1936—not so much a yacht as an enormous (90-foot, 50-ton) tub—and, after hiring and then firing in turn four variously incompetent captains, took over the skipper's job herself and sailed around the world, in three years, with a crew of young men. *How to Navigate Today* can be considered a by-product of that experience and of her conviction that existing navigation texts were too complicated and confusing.

During World War II she tried to join the Merchant Marine, as a radio operator or navigator, but was rejected (for being a woman) and had to settle for a prosaic job with the Signal Corps.

In 1946, Mrs. Hart (then a mere 55) became a student pilot, and was soon flying around, solo, to various countries. Seven years later she flew across the Atlantic in a single-engine lightplane with an off-duty airline pilot as her co-pilot. But why carry an extra 160 pounds in an already overloaded airplane? So she made six or seven subsequent Atlantic flights by herself. She was not a flying grandmother—"I'm divorced and childless," she'd say (although she does wear tennis shoes)—and records of any kind were not important to her, although she continued flying (and passing the biannual physicals) until she was in her mid-eighties, before retiring—temporarily, at least—to California.

The first edition of *How to Navigate Today* helped to train many Air Force and Navy navigators during World War II. It was concise and practical. But even such ancient fields of study as navigation change over the years, and repeated minor revisions can go only so far. This latest edition is meant to bring to the book all of the new navigation methods while preserving Mrs. Hart's commonsense approach.

# Acknowledgments

LARGE DRAWINGS ARE BY BILL TINKER. SMALL CUTS are from *Transportation—A Pictorial Archive from Nineteenth-Century Sources,* selected by Jim Harter; *Harter's Picture Archive for Collage and Illustration,* edited by Jim Harter; *Picture Sourcebook for Collage and Decoupage,* edited by Edmund V. Gillon, Jr.; *Goods and Merchandise—A Cornucopia of Nineteenth-Century Cuts,* compiled and arranged by William Rowe; and *Women—A Pictorial Archive from Nineteenth-Century Sources,* selected by Jim Harter—all from Dover Publications.

Excerpts from the *Nautical Almanac* are courtesy of the Nautical Almanac Office, U. S. Naval Observatory. Excerpts from Publication No. 249 are courtesy of the Defense Mapping Agency.

# How to Navigate Today

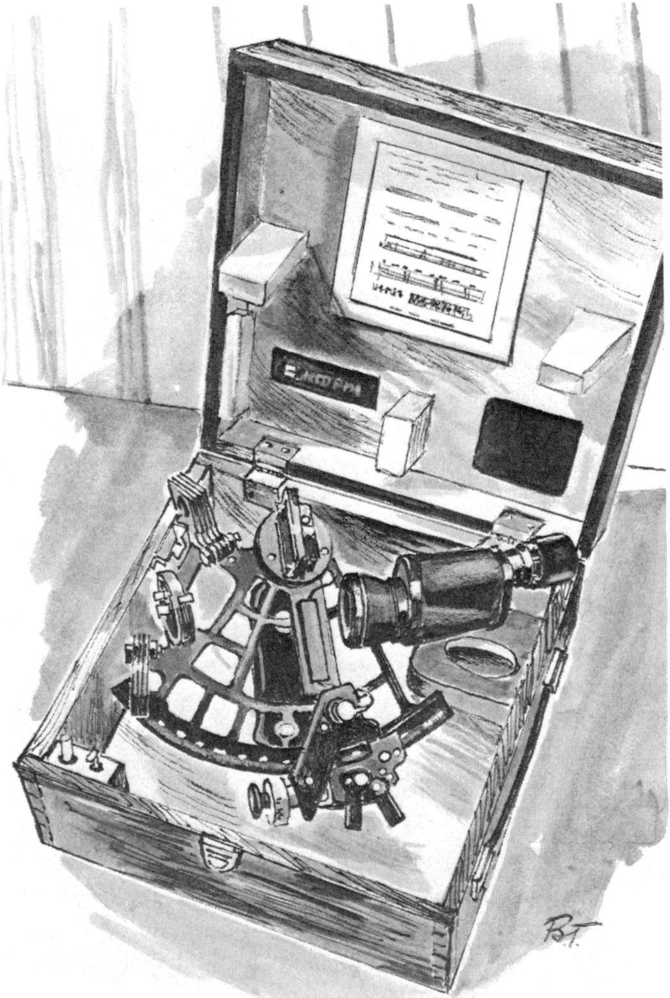

CHAPTER 1

# Getting Started

IT IS 10:15 A.M. LOCAL TIME (1415 GMT) MAY 3, AND we are approaching Bermuda in a 37-foot ketch. The sky is clear, and the wind is from the southwest at 15 knots. Lively music from a Bermuda station is coming in clearly on the radio, hinting at what it's like there, and everyone is anticipating showers and good food in St. Georges Harbour—maybe by tomorrow—after being at sea for a week. Our loran fixes have been very close to our DR positions, and no one foresees any problems.

But now Dale turns the radio off and, looking worried, peers out of the companionway and says, "There's something wrong with the loran—or our DR. I just got a loran fix 35 miles from the DR." Lee tries the loran set and gets the same result, and then there's a heated discussion among the crew about which position is correct—or are they both wrong? Everyone is worried about the reefs around Bermuda. While the argument is going on, Sandy (who isn't even supposed to be the navigator) takes the sextant forward, gets half a dozen sun sights, then goes below and reduces them.

Sandy comes up the ladder and explains how a line can be drawn parallel to the sun's line of position so that it intercepts Gibbs Hill Light (or whatever point we would like to get to). Then, at the proper time, we can turn to the course represented by the line, and follow it to our landfall. And if we haven't arrived within sight of land in three or four hours, another sun LOP will give us a running fix. No one else understands celestial navigation—we thought it wouldn't be necessary to learn it, with a good loran set—but we don't know anything else to do, so after more discussion we decide to try Sandy's method. (The boat has no electronic navigation equipment except for loran.) Six and a half hours later, Lee yells, "Lighthouse off the port bow!"

Not every celestial-navigation success is so dramatic, but it is true that electronic systems sometimes fail (and loran accuracy deteriorates offshore as you approach the transmission limit—for example, nearing Bermuda). Another reason to learn celestial navigation is that if you go on a cruise without any special knowledge, you're likely to be given difficult or unskilled non-nautical jobs that no one else wants: cooking, washing dishes—maybe worse.

## Uses of Celestial Navigation

Celestial navigation is used, these days, as just one means of position fixing for boats and ships that are out of sight of land. It was once important for long-range air navigation, but is no longer, except for special purposes such as polar flying and some military flying. Even for marine navigation, it is now more often a back-up method than a primary one. But, as in the Bermuda-landfall example, the ability to use celestial navigation is still essential for ocean sailors. This will still be true even when the new Global Positioning System (GPS) is fully operational and GPS receivers are reasonably priced. Equipment can fail, and batteries can go dead. Also, not all boats have electronic navigation equipment.

Our purpose here is to explain, to those who understand Mercator charts and plotting, how to use the simplest and most reliable tabular celestial-navigation methods and either want to teach themselves celestial navigation from the beginning or want to learn more about it. *Nautical Almanac* and H. O. 249 excerpts in the back of this book include the pages needed to see how the examples were worked.

The best tabular methods for small boats are H. O. 249 Vol. 1, for stars, and H. O. 249 Vols. 2 and 3, for the sun, moon, and planets. (The official name is now Defense Mapping Agency Pub. No. 249 [AP3270 in the United Kingdom], but most navigators still call it H. O. 249.) These methods were originally designed for air navigation, but are still published by DMA, and are excellent for small boats. They have two limitations:

First, they show angles just to the nearest 1′ of arc, rather than to the nearest 0′.1, as in some other methods, such as H. O. 229. This feature is actually an advantage, because rounding off to the nearest minute simplifies the computations (thus reducing the chances for error) but gives all the accuracy that is needed. Second, Vols. 2 and 3 accommodate only those bodies with declinations not over 30°. Luckily, this is not a serious limitation, because Vols. 2 and 3 cover all the bodies in the solar system, and for the remainder—the stars—a navigator seldom needs more than those given in Vol. 1, which lists the best seven for a particular place and time. Vols. 2 and 3 can be used to work sights for any stars with declinations not over 30° (this includes 30 of the 57 navigational stars), but there is hardly ever any need for this.

Celestial navigation is not difficult—a navigator can work effectively without using geometry or any other mathematics beyond addition and subtraction and occasional multiplication and division—but it requires good judgment, some knowledge, and a lot of practice. Inexperienced celestial navigators are usually astonished at how many errors they make—even though the work is not difficult. It's just that there are so many opportunities for error. There's a cure for this: work everything a second time—preferably by a different method.

### Recommendations

1. Learn the H. O. 249 method first; then, if you desire, get a navigation calculator (see Chapter 8) to do the computations automatically—but don't stop prac-

ticing with H. O. 249. You will probably need it some day. Use a simple pocket calculator to do the adding and subtracting. Check all computations, even though the repetition is boring.

2. Buy the three volumes of H. O. 249 (Vol. 1 needs to be replaced every five years, Vols. 2 and 3, never) and the *Nautical Almanac* (which must be replaced every year). The *Air Almanac* or *Reed's Almanac* could be used instead, but the *Nautical Almanac* is recommended.

3. Practice identifying the important navigational stars, even though you will learn how to plan twilight sights to make it easy to find the best stars to sight.

4. Keep working problems, to stay in practice, even after you have learned H. O. 249, and keep a notebook on what you want to remember. Use a sight-reduction form, like the one shown in Fig. 3, Chapter 3, with its explanatory notes.

5. Practice twilight sights, sun sights, and moon sights on a beach, when you can, using an inexpensive plastic sextant (which can also be a back-up sextant at sea) or a more sophisticated one.

6. Plot your practice sights on small-area plotting charts, which can be bought from the Defense Mapping Agency or nautical-supply stores.

7. Time your sights with a digital watch ashore, and take three digital watches to sea, so that if one fails you will still have accurate time. (Cheap ones can be as precise as expensive ones, even though they don't have the same features.) Check them by listening to the WWV time signal—at any time of the day or night—on 2.5, 5, 10, 15, or 20 MHz on a shortwave radio, or (ashore) by calling the time number.

28

CHAPTER 2

# How Celestial Navigation Works

IMAGINE AN ANT ON A FLAT CONCRETE SURFACE 100 feet from a flagpole (Fig 1). From where the ant is, the angle from the "horizon" (the concrete surface) up to the brass ball on top of the flagpole is, let's say, 40°. If the ant moves a number of feet closer to the flagpole, the angle from the horizon to the brass ball will increase to, say, 50°. (If the ant moves all the way to the flagpole, the angle becomes 90°.) A circle with the flagpole at its center could be drawn on the concrete through the ant's first position to represent the locations of all the places from which the angle up to the brass ball is 40°; likewise, a circle through the second position would mark all the places where the angle up to the ball is 50°.

## Sextant Altitude

In a similar way, someone with a sextant can measure the angle from the horizon up to a star or other body. If the observer moves one nautical mile closer to a point directly under the star, the angle will increase by 1′ (1/60 of a degree), and if the observer moves a mile farther away the angle will decrease by 1′. Directly under the star, the angle is 90°.

The reason the angle changes by exactly one minute when the observer moves one mile can be thought of in this way: at a point one-fourth of the way around the

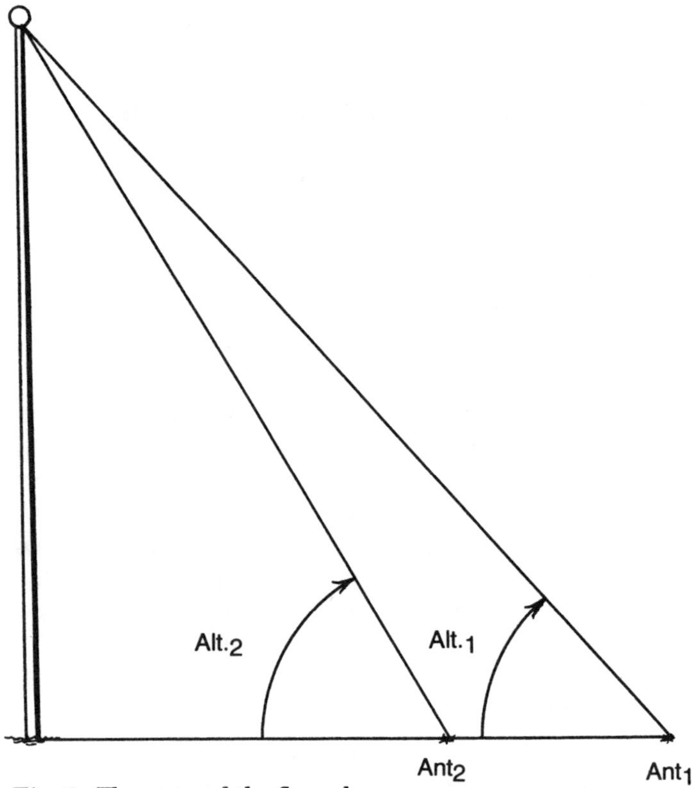


*Fig. 1.* The ant and the flagpole

earth from the point just under the star, the altitude of the star (the angle from the horizon up to the star) is 0°—in other words, the star is seen on the horizon. Directly under the star, the altitude is 90°. Between the two places, the altitude has changed 90° × 60 minutes/degree = 5,400 minutes, while the observer was moving 90° × 60 miles/degree = 5,400 nautical miles. (A nautical mile is defined as one minute of the arc of a great circle on the earth.) Therefore, if the observer moves one nautical mile, the observed altitude changes by one minute of arc.

### Positions of Navigational Bodies

The positions of the sun and moon, the four navigational planets, and the 57 navigational stars are calculated in advance and listed in the *Nautical Almanac*. Therefore, we can find the point on the earth over which each body is located at any moment. Celestial positions are defined by declination (d), which is the same as latitude (measured north or south from the equator to the pole); and Greenwich hour angle (GHA), which is measured from the meridian of Greenwich, England, like longitude, but goes all the way around 360°, measured to the west. From the GHA, we can get the local hour angle (LHA), which is needed to look up data in tabular methods such as H. O. 249. LHA equals GHA minus west longitude (or plus east longitude).

### The Assumed Position

In celestial navigation, we select a point close to the dead reckoning (DR) position (where we think we are) but at a whole degree of latitude, and at a longitude that will make the LHA also a whole degree. (Chapter 3 describes how this works in practice.) Using only whole numbers for latitude and LHA allows the tables to be more compact. The point we have selected is called the assumed position (AP).

### Computed Altitude and Azimuth

H. O. 249 gives the computed altitude (Hc) and azimuth (Zn) that would exist at the AP for the latitude (of the AP), declination (of the body we sighted), and LHA (at the time of the sight) that we entered the tables with. (The azimuth is the angular direction, measured clockwise from north.)

### The Intercept, LOP, and Fix

The difference (in minutes) between the Hc and the observed altitude (Ho) is called the intercept, and this distance, in miles, is laid off from the AP toward the Zn if Ho is greater than Hc, or away from it if Hc is greater than Ho. (If the observed altitude is 5′ greater than the computed altitude, for example, that means we are 5 miles closer, so we measure 5 miles toward the body from the AP.) At that point, we draw a perpendicular line, and that is the LOP—the line of position (see Fig. 2). If everything has been done precisely, the observer is located somewhere on the LOP. (Although the LOP is drawn as a straight line, it is actually a curve, with its center at the point directly under the body. But the difference between the curve and a straight line is so slight, for such a short line, that the error is negligible.)

So we end up with an LOP, on which we presume we are located. An LOP for another body shot at the same time (or, better, several LOPs) should intersect in a point, where we conclude we are—a fix. And that, minus a few details, is the essence of celestial navigation. You will probably find it interesting to learn more theory,

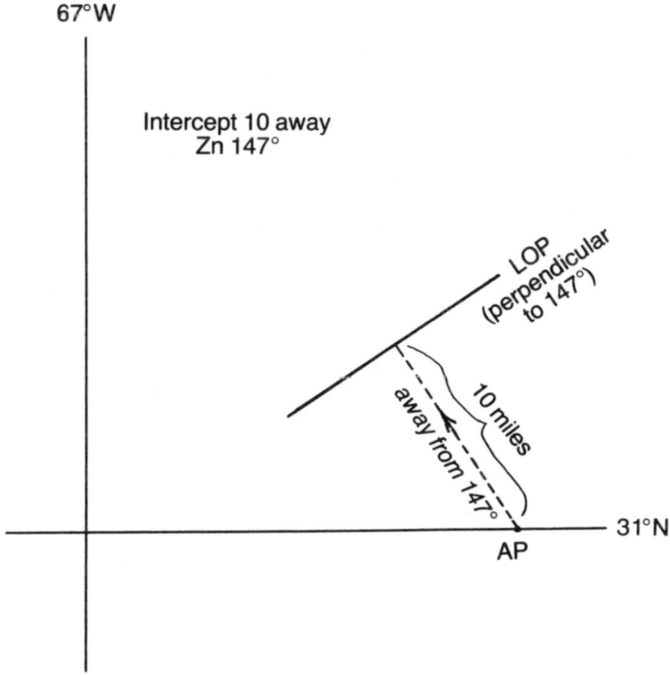


*Fig. 2.* Plotting an LOP

sooner or later, but this is all the background you need to be a capable celestial navigator.

### Time and Longitude

Time is important in navigation because the apparent positions of the stars, sun, moon, and planets are constantly changing. There are several kinds of time. Greenwich mean time (GMT) is the local zone time (LZT) and also the local mean time (LMT) at the zero meridian, which runs through Greenwich, England. For each 15° of longitude, going away from the zero meridian, the zone time changes 1 hour—minus for west, plus for east longitude. To say it the other way, to convert from zone time to GMT, add 1 hour for each 15° of west longitude or subtract 1 hour for each degree of east longitude. For example, Philadelphia is at 75°W, so to get GMT from Philadelphia time (EST), we add 5 hours (75° ÷ 15°/hour = 5 hours). If we had started with daylight saving time, we would add only 4 hours. The +5 hours time zone extends from 67°.5 to 82°.5, with its center at 75°—except that on land the line sometimes follows a crooked path that generally coincides with state borders.

### LMT, LZT, and GMT

LMT, like LZT, changes with longitude, but LMT changes gradually, rather than in steps, as LZT changes. For example, Miami Beach is at about 80°W, in the EST zone. When it's noon (zone time) in Miami Beach, it's 5:00 P.M. GMT—or, stated in the 24-hour system, 1700—but the LMT in Miami Beach is 1720. (The time equivalent of 80° is 5 hours, 20 minutes.)

Changing from LZT or LMT to GMT, or vice versa, sometimes results in a change in the date, so look out for this. Also, when you're shooting some sights before and some after midnight, don't neglect the date change when you enter the *Nautical Almanac.*

### Summary

1. The sextant altitude increases 1′ for each 1 mile the observer moves toward the body.

2. The *Nautical Almanac* gives positions of bodies stated in declination (like latitude) and GHA (like longitude, but 0° to 360°).

3. The navigator selects an assumed position at the nearest whole degree of latitude, and with a longitude that makes the LHA a whole degree. (GHA − W longitude, or + E longitude, = LHA.)

4. H. O. 249 gives Hc and Zn at the AP.

5. The intercept (difference between Hc and Ho) is the number of miles from the AP that the LOP is to be drawn perpendicular to the Zn—toward the Zn (if Ho is greater) or away from the Zn (if Hc is greater).

6. To convert from zone time (LZT) to GMT, add (if in W longitude) or subtract (if in E longitude) 1 hour for each 15° of longitude, measured to the center of the time zone. For example, 9 A.M. EST is 9 + 5 = 1400 GMT. Note that on land the zone boundaries are not always straight. Also remember that standard time equals daylight saving time minus 1 hour.

These ideas and routines will become clearer in the next chapter, where their use in practical navigation is explained.

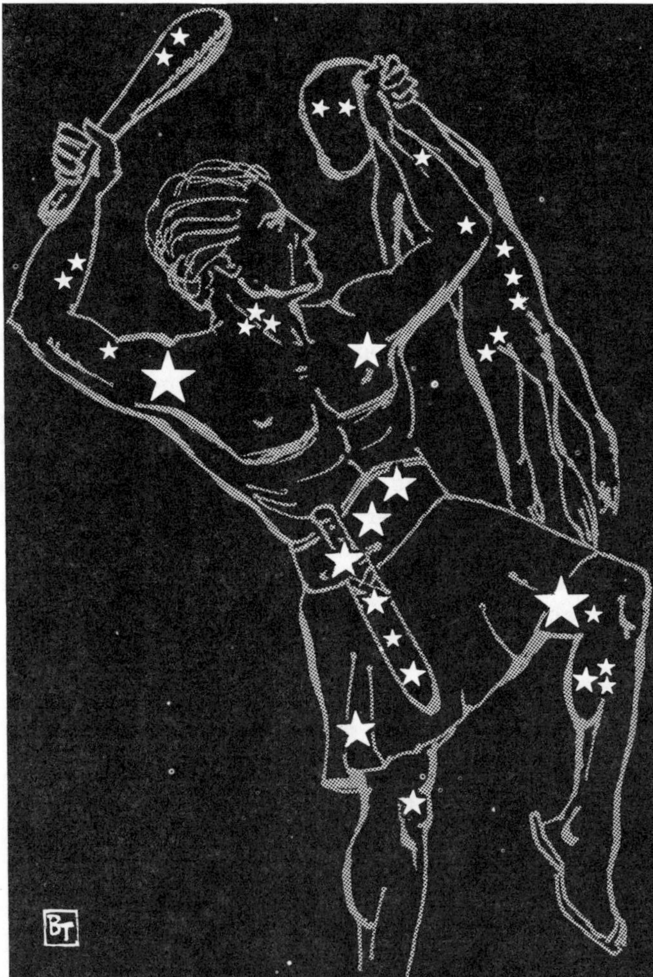
BT

CHAPTER 3

# Star Sights

STARS ARE THE MOST DIFFICULT BODIES TO SIGHT with a sextant, because the sights must be taken during twilight, when the stars are fading as the horizon brightens (at A.M. twilight), or vice versa (at P.M. twilight). But a round of star sights can result in the most accurate fix, because there are usually enough stars available to get several LOPs to cross for the fix, so that random errors tend to cancel out.

To show how it works, we will make up a plan for the stars to be sighted during A.M. twilight January 7, 1987; then, after sighting, we will find the LOP for each sight—using the *Nautical Almanac* and H. O. 249 Vol. 1 for both procedures. Our DR position at 1100 GMT is 31°12′N, 65°53′W.

## The Twilight Plan

1. The first step is to find, from the *Nautical Almanac* right-hand daily page, the times of A.M. nautical twilight (the approximate time to begin sighting), civil twilight (the middle of the sighting period), and sunrise (end of sighting). The A.M. twilight tables are the upper set, and they are entered with the DR latitude. We can either take the figures listed for 30°N—0601, 0631, and 0657, respectively—or, for more accuracy, interpolate (mathematically or by eye) to get 0603, 0633, and 0700.

These times are not labelled in the almanac, but they are LMT, and we need to convert them to GMT by adding (because we are in west longitude) the time equivalent of the longitude: 0424. (In east longitude we would subtract the time equivalent.) This is found in the table CONVERSION OF ARC TO TIME, on p. i, the first yellow page in the back of the *Nautical Almanac*. Adding 0424 in each case gives 1027 for nautical twilight, 1057 for civil twilight, and 1124 for sunrise (all GMT).

2. Next we get LHA♈ (the local hour angle of Aries) at 0633 LMT, the time of civil twilight. The easiest way to do this (if you can keep the instructions straight) is to enter the almanac's left-hand daily page GMT column with the LMT, and from the column headed ARIES, GHA, take out the LHA♈. For 06 hours we get 196°16′. Then from the almanac's yellow pages, ARIES column, for 33m, 00s, we get 8°16′ more. This (rounded) gives 205° for the LHA♈ at 0633 LMT.

3. We find the predicted altitudes and azimuths of the best seven stars to sight by entering H. O. 249 Vol. 1 with the assumed latitude (31°N) and the LHA♈ at the predicted time of civil twilight (205°). We find the magnitude of each star in the INDEX TO SELECTED STARS, 1987, on the *Nautical Almanac* page marker, and list the stars from dimmest to brightest (because that's the order in which we will sight them at A.M. twilight). The result is the A.M. twilight plan:

| | | *Predicted* | |
|---|---|---|---|
| *Mag.* | *Body* | *Alt.* | *Az.* |
| 2.2 | Kochab | 46° | 007 |
| 2.1 | Rasalhague | 33° | 095° |

| | | | |
|---|---|---|---|
| 2.0 | Dubhe | 50° | 332° |
| 1.3 | Regulus | 38° | 261° |
| 1.2 | Spica | 48° | 186° |
| 1.2 | Antares | 20° | 140° |
| 0.1 | Vega | 30° | 060° |

Chapter 10 tells how to add planets and the moon to the list, when they are available, by using a star finder, which can be set up using the same LHA♈ that was used to enter H. O. 249 Vol. 1.

### Taking the Sights

At sighting time, all we need to do is get ready at the time of nautical twilight, 1027 GMT, set the sextant to 46°, turn toward 007°T (the variation and deviation will of course have to be applied to get the compass direction), and, when the horizon becomes light enough, locate and shoot Kochab. Then we repeat the process for the other stars. The navigator should get as many sights as possible during twilight—either by taking two of each of the seven stars or by going through the list with one sight each, then repeating the list.

### Reducing the Sights to Get Intercept and Zn

For the sight reduction, we will enter the same page of H. O. 249 Vol. 1 that we used for the twilight plan, but this time we will use a more precise LHA♈ for each star. First, we fill out the sight-reduction form (Fig. 3).

**Top of the Sight-Reduction Form.** Our DR course is 010°, speed 7.8 knots. Our height of eye was 6 feet when we took the sights. We add this information, and the data already noted, to the top of the form, then list the name of each star and the GMT when it was sighted.

## Sight-Reduction Form for H. O. 249 or H. O. 229

C: 010° Date: JAN. 7, 1987 Assumed lat.: 31° N *
S: 7.8 DR pos: 31° 12′N, 65°53′W. LHA♈ at: 0633 LMT 205°
at 1100 GMT Ht. of eye: 6 ft.

| | LMT | GMT |
|---|---|---|
| Naut. Twi. | 0603 | 1027 |
| Civil Twi. | 0633 | 1057 |
| Sunrise | 0700 | 1124 |

| Body | KOCHAB | RASALHAGUE | DUBHE | REGULUS | ANTARES | VEGA |
|---|---|---|---|---|---|---|
| GMT | 11-00-03 | 11-02-19 | 11-04-13 | 11-06-15 | 11-08-01 | 11-15-22 |
| hs | 46°11′ | 34°09′ | 49°45′ | 36°01′ | 21°08′ | 33°44′ |
| IC | −1′ | −1′ | −1′ | −1′ | −1′ | −1′ |
| dip | −2′ | −2′ | −2′ | −2′ | −2′ | −2′ |
| R/~~LL/UL~~ | −1′ | −1′ | −1′ | −1′ | −2′ | −1′ |
| Ho | 46°07′ | 34°05′ | 49°41′ | 35°57′ | 21°03′ | 33°40′ |
| | | | | | | |
| GHA (h) \| v | 271°29′ | 271°29′ | 271°29′ | 271°29′ | 271°29′ | 271°29′ |
| SHA☆ | — | — | — | — | — | — |
| GHA (m/s) | 0°01′ | 0°35′ | 1°03′ | 1°34′ | 2°01′ | 3°51′ |
| v corr. (moon, planets) | — | — | — | — | — | — |
| GHA (total) | 271°30′ | 272°04′ | 272°32′ | 273°03′ | 273°30′ | 275°20′ |
| long. −W or ~~+E~~ | 65°30′ | 66°04′ | 65°32′ | 66°03′ | 65°30′ | 66°20′ |
| LHA | 206° * | 206° * | 207° * | 207° * | 208° * | 209° * |
| | | | | | | |
| Dec. \| d | | | | | | |
| d corr. (not for stars) | | | | | | |
| Dec. (total) | * | * | * | * | * | * |
| | | | | | | |
| Altitude \| d | | | | | | |
| d corr. | | | | | | |
| Hc | 45°58′ | 34°07′ | 49°17′ | 35°57′ | 21°31′ | 33°22′ |
| Ho | 46°07′ | 34°05′ | 49°41′ | 35°57′ | 21°03′ | 33°40′ |
| Intercept | 9 t | 2 a | 24 t | 0 | 28 a | 18 t |
| | | | | | | |
| Z | | | | | | |
| Zn | 006° | 096° | 331° | 262° | 143° | 061° |
| Miles to move AP | 2.0 | 1.7 | 1.4 | 1.2 | 1.0 | |

*Table entry

MOVE FIX 1 MILE TOWARD 120°

*Fig. 3A.* Sight reduction form—seven stars

## Notes for Sight-Reduction Form

| Form Entry | H.O. 249 Vol. 1 Stars | H.O. 249 Vol. 2 or 3; H.O. 229 | | | |
|---|---|---|---|---|---|
| | | Sun | Moon | Planet | Star |
| GHA (h) | GHA♈ (hour) | ← GHA of the body (hour) → | | | |
| *v* | – | – | *Nautical Almanac* white pages | | – |
| SHA ☆ | – | – | – | – | *Naut. Alm.* white pages |
| GHA (m/s) | ← *Nautical Almanac* yellow pages: 1st, 2nd, or 3rd column → | | | | |
| *v* corr. | – | – | *Nautical Almanac* yellow pages | | – |
| GHA (total) | GHA♈ | GHA sun | GHA moon | GHA planet | GHA star |
| – Long. W / + Long. E | ← Use a figure close to the DR long. that will result in a whole degree of LHA → | | | | |
| LHA | LHA♈ | LHA sun | LHA moon | LHA planet | LHA star |
| Dec. | – | ← *Nautical Almanac* white pages; Dec. (hr.) → | | | |
| *d* | – | ← *Nautical Almanac* white pages → | | | – |
| *d* corr | – | *Nautical Almanac* yellow pages: dec. inc. ← for min. and sec. (show + or – ) → | | | |
| Dec. (total) | – | ← Total declination → | | | |
| Altitude | – | ← Called "Hc" in H.O. 249 Vols. 2 and 3, and H.O. 229 → | | | |
| d | – | ← H.O. 249 Vols. 2 and 3, or H.O. 229: "d", main table (show + or – ) → | | | |
| d corr. | – | ← H.O. 249 Vols. 2 and 3, Table III, or H.O. 229 Interpolation Table (show + or – ) → | | | |
| Hc | Tabulated | ← "Alt." ± "d corr." → | | | |
| Ho | ← From the upper section of the form → | | | | |
| Intercept | ← Difference between Hc and Ho ("computed greater away") → | | | | |
| Z | – | ← H.O. 249 Vols. 2 and 3, or H.O. 229 main table → | | | |
| Zn | Main table<br>Also use Table 5, p. 322 | ← Computed from Z, following the rules on each page of H.O. 249 Vols. 2 and 3, or H.O. 229 → | | | |

*Fig. 3B.* Notes for sight-reduction form

**Sextant Corrections.** For the first star, Kochab, the sextant reading (hs) was 46°11′. The sextant index correction (IC) for all the sights was −1′. (At the end of the round of sights, when the horizon was bright, we sighted it and found that the sextant reading was not 0°00′, but 0°01′, so the IC is −1′.) The rounded-off dip correction for a height of eye of 6 feet, from the inside cover of the *Nautical Almanac*, is −2′. Be sure you enter the "ft." column (not the "m" column, which is meters) if you measured the height of eye in feet. The rounded-off refraction correction, R (also from the inside cover), which compensates for the atmosphere's bending of the light rays from the star, is −1′ for Kochab's altitude of 46°11′. Applying all these corrections gives us an observed altitude (Ho) of 46°07′. Table A4, in the front of the *Nautical Almanac,* gives additional refraction corrections for non-standard temperature and pressure conditions. These are seldom needed, except for very low altitudes.

**Rounding Off Numbers.** We need a few words here about rounding off numbers. One way to do this is to change the final digit to zero if it's less than 5, otherwise increase the previous digit by one. Thus, 36.4 rounds to 36 and 36.5 rounds to 37. There is a better method, which works the same way except for numbers that end in 5. For these numbers, we round *up* if the previous digit is *odd,* but round *down* if the previous digit is *even.* Therefore, 31.5 rounds to 32, 32.5 rounds to 32, 33.5 rounds to 34, etc. This method is better, because it gives the errors more of a tendency to cancel out than to build up.

**GHA♈ and LHA♈.** Now we enter the left-hand daily page of the almanac with the whole number of hours

(11, in this case) and take out the GHA♈, which we round to the nearest minute (271°29′) and record on the form. Next, still working on the Kochab sight, we turn to the yellow page for 0m 03s, in the ARIES column, and take out the increment, which we round to 0°01′. We add these, to get 271°30′. Now we need to subtract a figure for the longitude (if it were east longitude, we would be adding), as close as possible to the DR longitude, that will make the result—the LHA♈—a whole number. Because 65°30′ is closer to the DR longitude than 66°30′ is, that's what we subtract, getting an LHA♈ of 206°. Note that 65°30′ is the longitude of our assumed position (AP) for Kochab.

**Finding Hc and Zn.** Now we enter H. O. 249 Vol. 1 with the assumed latitude (31°N) and LHA♈ for Kochab (206°), and take out the Hc (45°58′) and Zn (006°).

**Getting the Intercept.** We copy the Ho value from the top of the form, then get the intercept, which is the difference between Hc and Ho. If Hc is *greater* than Ho, the intercept is plotted in a direction *away* from the Zn; otherwise, it is plotted *toward* the Zn. In this case, it is 9 miles toward 006°.

### Getting the Fix

The form is then filled in for the other five stars that were sighted. If the shots had all been made at the same time, we could now plot the LOPs for a fix, but these shots were taken at different times.

**Advancing the LOPs.** Each LOP represents the position of the vessel at the time the sight was made. But while we were taking these sights, our vessel moved two miles, and we need to adjust for the motion. For each sight, we find the distance we traveled from the time of that sight to the time of the final sight. (The time of the fix will be the time of the final sight.) For the Kochab sight, the time was:

$$15 - 0 = 15 \text{ minutes (rounded)}$$

and the distance traveled was:

$$7.8 \times (15 \div 60) = 2.0 \text{ miles}$$

We do this for each of the stars (except, of course, the final one, Vega), getting 2.0, 1.7, 1.4, 1.2, and 1.0 miles traveled. We list these amounts at the bottom of the form. Consider the LOP for Kochab. We were (presumably) somewhere on that LOP at 11-00-03. By 11-15-22 (the time of the last sight), our vessel—and the LOP—had moved 2.0 miles toward 010°. We could advance the 11-00-03 LOP 2.0 miles toward 010°. But it's easier, and gives the same result, if we move the AP instead of the LOP.

**Plotting the Fix.** For each sight, we plot the AP on the 31° latitude line, at each of the AP longitudes we selected (65°30′, 66°04′, etc.). We move the Kochab AP 2.0 miles toward 010°, the Rasalhague AP 1.7, etc., to get a set of advanced APs. Then we plot each LOP, from its advanced AP, as shown in Fig. 4. One final step is needed, because H. O. 249 Vol. 1 gradually gets out of date. No correction was needed for 1984 or 1985, but for earlier and later years we need to use Table 5, in the back of the book. In 1987, for latitude 31°N and LHA♈ 206°, the fix position (where the LOPs crossed) must be moved 1 mile toward 120°. This puts our fix at 31°13′N, 66°04′W. (For an actual round of sights, of course, the

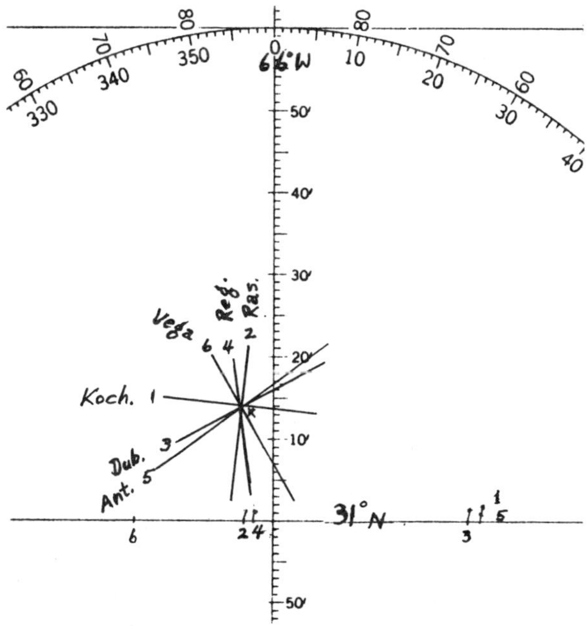


*Fig. 4.* Plot of AM star sights

LOPs would not all cross conveniently at a point, as they did here. Chapter 7 tells what to do about that.)

## Polaris Sights

Polaris is only a second-magnitude star, but it's easy to identify. Also, a Polaris LOP (which is a latitude line) is much easier to compute. The altitude of the elevated pole (the one we could see if it were visible) equals the latitude of the observer, and Polaris is close to the north pole (within 1°), so a simple correction can be made to the Ho to yield the latitude. For example, we sighted

Polaris at 11-14-43 on January 7, 1987. The hs was 30°31′. Find the latitude. Solution:

| | |
|---|---|
| hs | 30°31′ |
| IC | −1′ |
| dip | −2′ |
| R | −2′ |
| Ho | 30°26′ |
| corr. | +48′ |
| lat. | 31°14′ |

The GHA♈ was 275° and the LHA♈ was 209° (rounded). The correction (+48), found on p. 324 of H. O. 249 Vol. 1, could have been taken from the back of the *Nautical Almanac* instead, but the H. O. 249 correction is much simpler—one step instead of three—and is accurate enough (to the nearest minute). The Polaris LOP, like the others, must be advanced to the fix time. A navigator can add Polaris to the twilight plan by working the above computations (the corrections) in reverse, to get the predicted altitude. The predicted azimuth is 000°.

### Other Stars, with Vol. 2 or 3

There may be times when stars other than the ones in the plan are sighted—because of partly cloudy skies, possibly. Sights on stars other than the ones listed in H. O. 249 Vol. 1 can be reduced—if their declinations are not over 30°—by using H. O. 249 Vol. 2 or 3. (If the declination is over 30°, another method, like H. O. 229, could be used to work the sight.) Fig. 5 shows the sight reduction for Sabik (which is not listed in H. O. 249 Vol.

## Sight-Reduction Form for H. O. 249 or H. O. 229

C: 010°  Date: JAN. 7, 1987  Assumed lat.: 31° N *
S: 7.8  DR pos: 31° 12′ N, 65° 53′ W  LHA♈ at: ______ LMT ______
at 1100 GMT  Ht. of eye: 6 ft.

| | LMT | GMT |
|---|---|---|
| | | |
| Civil Twi. | | |
| | | |

| Body | SABIK | | | | | |
|---|---|---|---|---|---|---|
| GMT | 11-10-24 | | | | | |
| hs | 23°22′ | | | | | |
| IC | −1 | | | | | |
| dip | −2 | | | | | |
| R/~~LL/UL~~ | −2 | | | | | |
| Ho | 23°17′ | | | | | |
| | | | | | | |
| GHA (h) \| v | 271°29′ | | | | | |
| SHA☆ | 102°36′ | | | | | |
| GHA (m/s) | 2°36′ | | | | | |
| *v* corr. (moon, planets) | — | | | | | |
| GHA (total) | 376°41′ | | | | | |
| long. −W or ~~+E~~ | 65°41′ | | | | | |
| LHA | 311° * | * | * | * | * | * |
| | | | | | | |
| Dec. \| *d* | | | | | | |
| *d* corr. (not for stars) | | | | | | |
| Dec. (total) | S15°43′ * | * | * | * | * | * |
| | | | | | | |
| Altitude \| d | 23°72′ 24°12′ \| −42 | | | | | |
| d corr. | −30′ | | | | | |
| Hc | 23°42′ | | | | | |
| Ho | 23°17′ | | | | | |
| Intercept | 25 a | | | | | |
| | | | | | | |
| Z | | | | | | |
| Zn | 127° | | | | | |
| Miles to move AP | | | | | | |

*Table entry

*Fig. 5.* Sight reduction form—Sabik

1), using H. O. 249 Vol. 2. Altitude corrections are applied, as before, to get Ho. The GHA block on the form, as before, is GHA♈: 271°29′ (for 11 hours). But for this sight we need to fill in the blocks for SHA (102°36′)

and declination (S15°43′), from the right side of the left-hand daily page of the almanac. We add the hour-angle increment from the yellow pages (ARIES column) for 10 minutes and 24 seconds: 2°36′. There is no increment for declination, because star declinations change very little in three days.

Adding the GHA♈ for 11 hours, the SHA, and the increment for 10 minutes 24 seconds gives us the GHA of the star (not, as when using Vol. 1, the GHA♈): 376°41′ (16°41′) for 11-10-24. (It is done this way to save space in the almanac, because it would take many pages to list the GHA of each star for each hour of each day.) The remainder of the sight reduction for a star worked with H. O. 249 Vol. 2 or 3 is the same as for other sights using Vol. 2 or 3, and is explained in Chapter 4 ("Finding Hc and Zn").

### Vol. 1 vs. Vols. 2 and 3

To summarize the differences between H. O. 249 Vol. 1, and Vol. 2 or 3, for sight reduction:

**Vol. 1.** Enter with latitude (of the AP), LHA♈, and star name; take out Hc and Zn. (Used only for stars.)

**Vol. 2 or 3.** Enter with latitude (of the AP), declination, and LHA of the body; take out Hc and Z, then convert Z to Zn. (Used for sun, moon, and planets. Can be used for stars having declinations not over 30°.)

### Summary

1. Make up a twilight plan showing predicted altitude and azimuth of each of seven stars to sight (using H. O. 249 Vol. 1) at the time of civil twilight. If desired,

add any available planets and the moon, using the star finder (see Chapter 10).

2. Take the sights.

3. Reduce the sights, using H. O. 249 Vol. 1 for the seven selected stars and H. O. 249 Vol. 2 or 3 for the moon and planets. Do the work on a form (see Fig. 3).

4. Plot the APs and advance them for all but the last sight; plot the LOPs.

5. Correct or discard any erroneous LOPs, and plot the fix.

BT

CHAPTER 4

# Sun Sights

THE SUN IS USUALLY THE SIMPLEST BODY TO sight, because it is easy to locate and the horizon is normally well defined at times when the sun can be sighted. We can get a sun sight, wait several hours—or less, if the time is near local apparent noon (LAN), when the sun is at its highest altitude for the location—until the sun's azimuth has changed significantly, and get another sight. Then we advance the first LOP to the time of the second one (as we advanced the star LOPs of Chapter 3 to a common time) and cross the LOPs to get a running fix. Also, we can often get a moon LOP during the day (see Chapter 6) or, with luck and good visibility, a Venus LOP or even a Jupiter LOP during the day (see Chapter 5) to cross with the sun LOP for a fix.

## Several Sights Needed for Accuracy

One problem with such sights, however, is that a fix on two bodies (or a running fix on one body) does not include the built-in redundancy needed to expose errors. What if one sight is off by, say, 1°? How would we know? The answer is that we should take a number of sights when we shoot a single body—at least five or six (it doesn't take long)—and discard any that plot far from the others, if we can't find the error.

## Reduction of Sun Sights

Sun sights are reduced using the *Nautical Almanac* and H. O. 249 Vol. 2 (for latitudes 0° to 40°) or Vol. 3 (for latitudes 40° to 89°). We will work a series of sun sights (Fig. 6) and, about five hours later, another series (Fig. 7), then advance all but the last sight and plot a running fix (Fig. 8).

**Altitude Corrections for the Sun.** The IC and dip corrections are the same as for any other bodies, but the refraction correction is combined with the other sun-sight corrections, and listed in Tables A2 and A3, inside the front cover of the almanac. The tables give the total correction for refraction, parallax (the error caused by the observer's not being at the center of the earth—a significant error only for the sun and moon), and semi-diameter (the error caused by shooting the lower limb [LL] or the upper limb [UL] instead of the center). Normally, the lower limb is observed unless it is hidden by clouds. Both the LL and the UL corrections are in Tables A2 and A3 in the almanac. If you ever have non-standard temperature and pressure, also use Table A4.

For the 14-01-09 sight, we have an IC of −1′, dip correction of −2′, and lower limb correction of +14′. Applied to the hs of 25°37′, this results in an Ho of 25°48′. We record all of this on the form, Fig. 6.

**Sun's GHA and LHA.** For sun sights, we get the GHA and LHA of the sun—not of Aries, as we did for the star sights worked with H. O. 249 Vol. 1. We get the GHA from the right-hand daily page of the almanac, and add the increment for minutes and seconds from the yellow

## Sight-Reduction Form for H. O. 249 or H. O. 229

C: 335° Date: JAN. 7, 1987 Assumed lat.: 31° N *

S: 5.2 DR pos: 30°42′ N, 65°58′ W LHA♈ at: ______ LMT ______

at 1400 GMT Ht. of eye: 6 ft.

| | LMT | GMT |
|---|---|---|
| | | |
| Civil Twi. | | |

| Body | SUN → | | | | | |
|---|---|---|---|---|---|---|
| GMT | 14-01-09 | 14-03-19 | 14-06-01 | 14-08-03 | 14-10-24 | 14-14-22 |
| hs | 25°37′ | 25°47′ | 26°14′ | 26°26′ | 26°46′ | 27°14′ |
| IC | −1′ | −1′ | −1′ | −1′ | −1′ | −1′ |
| dip | −2′ | −2′ | −2′ | −2′ | −2′ | −2′ |
| ~~R~~/LL/~~UL~~ | +14′ | +14′ | +14′ | +14′ | +14′ | +14′ |
| Ho | 25°48′ | 25°58′ | 26°25′ | 26°37′ | 26°57′ | 27°25′ |
| GHA (h) \| v | 28°27′ \| | 28°27′ \| | 28°27′ \| | 28°27′ \| | 28°27′ \| | 28°27′ \| |
| SHA☆ | — | — | — | — | — | — |
| GHA (m/s) | 0°17′ | 0°50′ | 1°30′ | 2°01′ | 2°36′ | 3°36′ |
| v corr. (moon, planets) | — | — | — | — | — | — |
| GHA (total) | 388°44′ 28°44′ | 389°17′ 29°17′ | 389°57′ 29°57′ | 390°28′ 30°28′ | 391°03′ 31°03′ | 392°03′ 32°03′ |
| long. −W or ~~+E~~ | 65°44′ | 66°17′ | 65°57′ | 65°28′ | 66°03′ | 66°03′ |
| LHA | 323°* | 323°* | 324°* | 325°* | 325°* | 326°* |
| Dec. \| d | S22°24′ \| −0.3 | \| | \| | \| | \| | \| |
| d corr. (not for stars) | — | | | | | |
| Dec. (total) | S22°24′* | S22°24′* | S22°24′* | S22°24′* | S22°24′* | S22°24′* |
| Altitude \| d | 25°73′ 26°13′ \| −49 | 25°73′ 26°13′ \| −49 | 26°45′ \| −50 | 26°76′ 27°16′ \| −50 | 26°76′ 27°16′ \| −50 | 27°46′ \| −50 |
| d corr. | −20′ | −20′ | −20′ | −20′ | −20′ | −20′ |
| Hc | 25°53′ | 25°53′ | 26°25′ | 26°56′ | 26°56′ | 27°26′ |
| Ho | 25°48′ | 25°58′ | 26°25′ | 26°37 | 26°57′ | 27°25′ |
| Intercept | 5a | 5t | 0 | 19a | 1t | 1a |
| Z | | | | | | |
| Zn | 142° | 142° | 142° | 143° | 143° | 144° |
| Miles to move AP | 27.2 | 27.0 | 26.8 | 26.6 | 26.4 | 26.1 |

*Table entry ADVANCED TO 1915 GMT

*Fig. 6.* Sight reduction form—sun

pages as we did for stars, but being careful to use the SUN-PLANETS column. Then we subtract west longitude (or add east longitude) of the AP, to get the sun's LHA (see Fig. 6).

**Sun's Declination.** From the same line as the GHA on the right-hand daily page, we get the sun's declination, which we list on the form. We put the *d* value, from the foot of the declination column, on the same line of the form. Also, we have to determine the sign: plus if the declination is increasing with time, minus if it's decreasing. For this sight, *d* is listed as 0.3, and we label it "−" because the sun's declination for 1400 is S22°23′.7, and for 1500 is 22°23′.4. The *d* value is the amount by which the declination increases or decreases in an hour, and it is used to interpolate to get the declination change for minutes and seconds of time. To find the amount to add to or subtract from the hourly declination value from the daily page, we enter the "*v* or *d* Corrn" column of the yellow page with the *d* value and minutes and seconds, and take out the increment. In this case, there is nothing to be added or subtracted, because the declination for 14-01-09 rounds off to the same value as the declination for 1400: S22°24′.

**Finding Hc and Zn.** Now we turn to H. O. 249 Vol. 2 and find the page for LAT. 31°, DECLINATION (15°-29°) CONTRARY NAME TO LATITUDE. We enter the table with declination 22° (temporarily ignoring the 24′) and LHA 323°, and take out Hc 26°13′, *d* −49, and Z 142°. (Note that the + or − sign for *d* is not listed on every line. You may have to look up or down.) What is called "Hc" in the book is not quite Hc. We list it (26°13′), under "Alt.," and also list the *d* value (−49). We have to add or (as in this case) subtract an increment. We turn to Table III, enter with −49 (the *d* value) and 24′ (the minutes of declination) and take out the increment: −20′. This table performs the interpolation to the altitude value for minutes of declination. The table did the same thing that this equation would do:

$$(-49 \div 60) \times 24 = -20'$$

We apply the $-20'$ to the tabulated altitude value of 26°13′ to get Hc = 25°53′, which we show on the form. Now we take the difference between Hc and Ho, as for stars, and get the intercept: 5 miles away from 142° (away, because Hc is greater than Ho).

You will remember that H. O. 249 Vol. 1 gave the azimuth (Zn) directly. But Vols. 2 and 3 show azimuth angle (Z), which must be converted to Zn by applying the rules at the top (for N lat.) or bottom (for S lat.) of the page. In this case (N lat., LHA greater than 180°), Zn = Z, or 142°.

### Later Sun Sights

We work the other five sun sights from this series, as shown in Fig. 6; then, several hours later—when the sun has moved far enough across the sky to form an angle of at least 45° (ideally close to 90°) between an LOP from the first series and one from the second series—we take the second series of sun sights (Fig. 7).

**Advancing Earlier Sights.** Now we advance all the earlier sights to the time of the final one (19-15-24), as we did in Chapter 3 for the star sights. This time, the amounts to advance the earlier series of sights (bottom of Fig. 6) are much greater: 27.2, 27.0, 26.8 miles, etc. The amounts to advance those in the later series (bottom of Fig. 5) are only 0.9, 0.7, 0.5, 0.4, and (too small to bother with) 0.2 miles.

## Sight-Reduction Form for H. O. 249 or H. O. 229

C: 335 Date: JAN. 7, 1987 Assumed lat.: 31°N *
S: 5.2 DR pos: 31°12′N, 66°12′ W LHA♈ at: ____ LMT ____
at 1915 GMT Ht. of eye: 6 ft.

| | LMT | GMT |
|---|---|---|
| | | |
| Civil Twi. | | |

| Body | SUN→ | | | | | |
|---|---|---|---|---|---|---|
| GMT | 19-05-17 | 19-07-03 | 19-09-12 | 19-11-17 | 19-13-20 | 19-15-24 |
| hs | 24°47′ | 24°34′ | 24°12′ | 24°16′ | 23°39′ | 23°22′ |
| IC | −1′ | −1′ | −1′ | −1′ | −1′ | −1′ |
| dip | −2′ | −2′ | −2′ | −2′ | −2′ | −2′ |
| ~~R~~/LL/~~UL~~ | +14′ | +14′ | +14′ | +14′ | +14′ | +14′ |
| Ho | 24°58′ | 24°45′ | 24°23′ | 24°27′ | 23°50′ | 23°33′ |
| | | | | | | |
| GHA (h) \| v | 103°26′ | 103°26′ | 103°26′ | 103°26′ | 103°26′ | 103°26′ |
| SHA☆ | — | — | — | — | — | — |
| GHA (m/s) | 1°19′ | 1°46′ | 2°18′ | 2°49′ | 3°20′ | 3°51′ |
| *v* corr. (moon, planets) | — | — | — | — | — | — |
| GHA (total) | 104°45′ | 105°12′ | 105°44′ | 106°15′ | 106°46′ | 107°17′ |
| long. −W or ~~+E~~ | 65°45′ | 66°12′ | 66°44′ | 66°15′ | 65°46′ | 66°17′ |
| LHA | 39° * | 39° * | 39° * | 40° * | 41° * | 41° * |
| | | | | | | |
| Dec. \| *d* | S22°22′ \| -0.3 | | | | | |
| *d* corr. (not for stars) | — | | | | | |
| Dec. (total) | S22°22′* | S22°22′* | S22°22′* | S22°22′* | S22°22′* | S22°22′* |
| | | | | | | |
| Altitude \| d | 24°68′ 25°08′ \| -48 | 24°68′ 25°08′ \| -48 | 24°68′ 25°08′ \| -48 | 24°35′ \| -48 | 23°61′ 24°01′ \| -48 | 23°61′ 24°01′ \| -48 |
| d corr. | −18′ | −18′ | −18′ | −18′ | −18′ | −18′ |
| Hc | 24°50′ | 24°50′ | 24°50′ | 24°17′ | 23°43′ | 23°43′ |
| Ho | 24°58′ | 24°45′ | 24°23′ | 24°27′ | 23°50′ | 23°33′ |
| Intercept | 8t | 5a | 27a | 10t | 7t | 10a |
| | | | | | | |
| Z | 360° −140° | 360° −140° | 360° −140° | 360° −139° | 360° −138° | 360° −138° |
| Zn | 220° | 220° | 220° | 221° | 222° | 222° |
| Miles to move AP | 0.9 | 0.7 | 0.5 | 0.4 | 0.2 | |

*Table entry

*Fig. 7.* Sight reduction form—sun (continued)

### The Running Fix

When we plot these sights (first advancing each AP by the proper amount), we find—as in actual navigation—that some are more accurate than others, and one

(19-11-17) plots so far from the others that we should ignore it (see Fig. 8). Taking the estimated center of the other LOPs, we find that the running fix is at about 31°19′N, 66°24′W.

Now we can see the need for taking a number of sun sights. If we had taken only two, and the second one had happened to be our 19-11-17 sight, the fix would have been grossly in error.

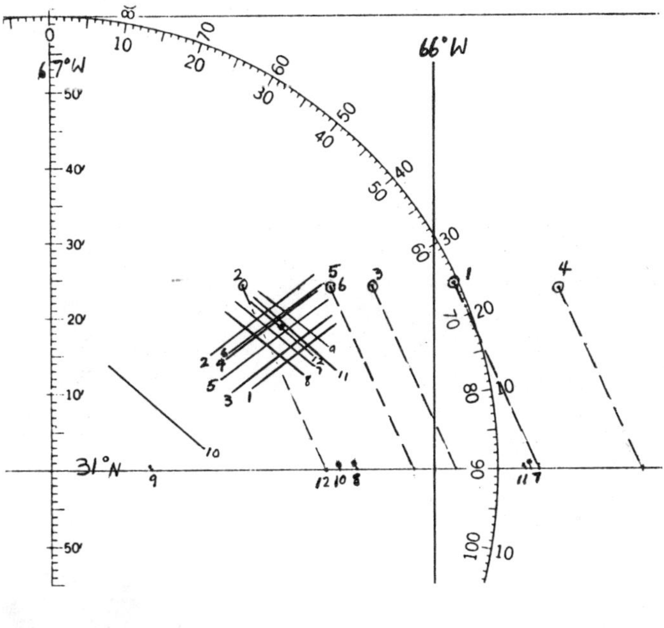


*Fig. 8.* Plot of running fix—sun

### The Noonsight

The noonsight was useful before accurate time was available at sea. It is still performed by some navigators—possibly for the sake of tradition—but is no longer needed. To get a noonsight, the navigator starts shooting before LAN (local apparent noon—the time of the sun's highest altitude), continues until after LAN, and then works out the vessel's latitude from the highest observed altitude (using only the approximate time). The computations are somewhat easier than ordinary sight reduction, but the sighting itself takes longer. It's better to take sun sights as usual and work them with H. O. 249 Vol. 2 or 3.

CHAPTER 5

# Planet Sights

PLANETS ARE VERY USEFUL TO THE NAVIGATOR. They are easy to locate during the dark part of twilight, because they are seen as something out of place in the pattern. Also, Saturn, Jupiter, or (especially) Venus, if properly placed, can usually be sighted early at evening twilight or late at morning twilight, when the stars are not visible but the horizon is well defined—sometimes even before the sun has set or after it has risen. Therefore, planets should always be included in the twilight plan when they are available (see Chapter 10). Even more important, sometimes Venus and Jupiter can be sighted during the day, if they are far enough from the sun and the sky is clear.

## Identification of Planets

The PLANET NOTES, on p. 8 of the *Nautical Almanac,* give good narrative information for spotting the planets throughout the year, and the diagram on p. 9 shows graphically how far from the sun each planet is (see excerpts). The table in the lower right-hand corner of the left-hand daily page gives the time (in LMT) of meridian passage of each planet, which can be thought of in relation to the meridian passage of the sun (roughly at noon, LMT) to get a general idea, quickly, of where each planet is—or at least whether it's visible at A.M. or P.M. twilight.

### Sight Reduction for Planets

Fig. 9 shows how a Saturn sight is reduced. The altitude corrections for planets are like those for stars, except that there is sometimes an additional minor correction for Venus or Mars, given inside the front cover of the *Nautical Almanac*. It is usually very small, but at some times it's enough to round off to a minute.

The GHA and declination of each navigational planet are found on the left-hand daily page, and each one has a value shown at the bottom—*v* for GHA and *d* for declination—because the planets' positions change rapidly. The corrections for the *v* and *d* values are given on the right sides of the yellow pages, and the *v* correction is in addition to the regular increment for minutes and seconds shown on the left sides of these pages. (Note that *v* for Venus is sometimes minus.)

The rest of the sight-reduction procedure is the same for planets as for stars. H. O. 249 Vol. 2 or 3 is used, as for other bodies of the solar system.

### Venus and Jupiter in Daylight

Some people, even experienced navigators, are surprised to learn that Venus and (less often) Jupiter can be sighted in daylight—not always, but often enough to be very helpful. It's entirely possible to get an occasional two-body fix or—with rare luck—a three-body (sun-moon-Venus) fix during the day. Venus is easier, because it's so much brighter (−3 to −4 magnitude), but Jupiter should not be ignored.

# Sight-Reduction Form for H. O. 249 or H. O. 229

C: ______ Date: JAN. 7, 1987 Assumed lat.: 31° N *

S: ______ DR pos: 31°12′ N, 65°53′ W LHA♈ at: ______ LMT ______

at 1100 GMT Ht. of eye: 6 ft.

| | LMT | GMT |
|---|---|---|
| | | |
| Civil Twi. | | |
| | | |

| Body | | SATURN | | | | | |
|---|---|---|---|---|---|---|---|
| GMT | | 11-06-00 | | | | | |
| hs | | 20°15′ | | | | | |
| IC | | −1′ | | | | | |
| dip | | −2′ | | | | | |
| R/~~LL/UL~~ | | −3′ | | | | | |
| Ho | | 20°09′ | | | | | |
| | | | | | | | |
| GHA (h) | v | 16°25′ 2.2 | | | | | |
| SHA☆ | | — | | | | | |
| GHA (m/s) | | 1°30′ | | | | | |
| *v* corr. (moon, planets) | | 0 | | | | | |
| GHA (total) | | 377°55′ 17°55′ | | | | | |
| long. −W or ~~+E~~ | | 65°55′ | | | | | |
| LHA | | 312° * | * | * | * | * | * |
| | | | | | | | |
| Dec. | *d* | S21°14 0 | | | | | |
| *d* corr. (not for stars) | | — | | | | | |
| Dec. (total) | | S21°14′* | * | * | * | * | * |
| | | | | | | | |
| Altitude | d | 20°33′ -45 | | | | | |
| d corr. | | −10′ | | | | | |
| Hc | | 20°23′ | | | | | |
| Ho | | 20°09′ | | | | | |
| Intercept | | 14 a | | | | | |
| | | | | | | | |
| Z | | | | | | | |
| Zn | | 132° | | | | | |
| Miles to move AP | | | | | | | |

*Table entry

*Fig. 9.* Sight reduction form—Saturn

**Necessary Conditions.** There's a catch to this. Conditions have to be just right:

1. The planet must not be too close to the sun. The bodies should be separated by at least 25° or 30° in GHA. Another way to check for sufficient separation is by using the PLANETS diagram on p. 9 of the almanac. If observing conditions are good, Venus (or Jupiter) can be seen in daylight if its line on the diagram is at least two hours from the sun's middle line (not the shaded band on the diagram). The greater the separation, the better. For example, in 1987 Venus can be observed in daylight from January 1 to about April 15, and from about December 15 through the end of the year. The best times are around the first of January and the last of December.

2. The sky must be clear. A thin haze of cirrus may keep you from seeing a planet in daylight.

3. You have to know where to look. Use the star finder (see Chapter 10) or work a preliminary sight reduction of the planet, to get Hc and Zn, using the expected sighting time and DR position. Then set the sextant to the Hc and point it toward the Zn and look for the planet. The sextant optics should be clean, and you should use a sighting telescope.

4. You should pick the best times for taking sights. A good time to do this is near the meridian transit of the planet (shown, in the lower right corner of the left-hand daily page of the almanac, as LMT, which must be converted to GMT), because then the change in altitude is slow, so spotting should be easier. There is a psychological advantage in knowing you can see the planet. You may think it's invisible until you spot it, then you can see it, shining brightly, and could find it again if you had to.

Fig. 10 shows an example of the sight reduction for a Venus-sun fix during daylight, and Fig. 11 shows the

## Sight-Reduction Form for H. O. 249 or H. O. 229

C: 045° Date: JAN. 7, 1987 Assumed lat.: 31° N *

S: 4.5 DR pos: 31°25'N, 66°01'W LHA♈ at: ______ LMT ______

at 1500 GMT Ht. of eye: 6 ft.

| | LMT | GMT |
|---|---|---|
| | | |
| Civil Twi. | | |
| | | |

| Body | VENUS | SUN | | | | |
|---|---|---|---|---|---|---|
| GMT | 15-09-13 | 15-14-02 | | | | |
| hs | 34°33' | 32°56' | | | | |
| IC | −1' | −1' | | | | |
| dip | −2' | −2' | | | | |
| R/~~LL~~/UL | −1' | +15' | | | | |
| Ho | 34°29' | 33°08' | | | | |
| | | | | | | |
| GHA (h) \| v | 92°49' \| 0 | 43°27' \| | \| | \| | \| | \| |
| SHA☆ | — | — | | | | |
| GHA (m/s) | 2°18' | 3°30' | | | | |
| *v* corr. (moon, planets) | 0 | — | | | | |
| GHA (total) | 95°07' | 406°57' 46°57' | | | | |
| long. −W or ~~+E~~ | 66°07' | 65°57' | | | | |
| LHA | 29° * | 341° * | * | * | * | * |
| | | | | | | |
| Dec. \| *d* | S16°34' \| +0.5 | S22°23' \| -0.1 | \| | \| | \| | \| |
| *d* corr. (not for stars) | — | — | | | | |
| Dec. (total) | S16°34' * | S22°23' * | * | * | * | * |
| | | | | | | |
| Altitude \| d | 34°82' 35°22' \| -52 | 33°57' \| -56 | \| | \| | \| | \| |
| d corr. | −29' | −21' | | | | |
| Hc | 34°53' | 33°36' | | | | |
| Ho | 34°29' | 33°08' | | | | |
| Intercept | 24 a | 28 a | | | | |
| | | | | | | |
| Z | 360° − 145° | | | | | |
| Zn | 215° | 159° | | | | |
| Miles to move AP | 0.4 | | | | | |

*Table entry

*Fig. 10.* Sight reduction form—Venus and sun

plot. Note that the crossing angle of the two LOPs in this instance is only 56°—just above the minimum. But regardless of the crossing angle, it was not good practice to get only one sight of each body. We should have shot at least six sights of each body, to minimize errors.

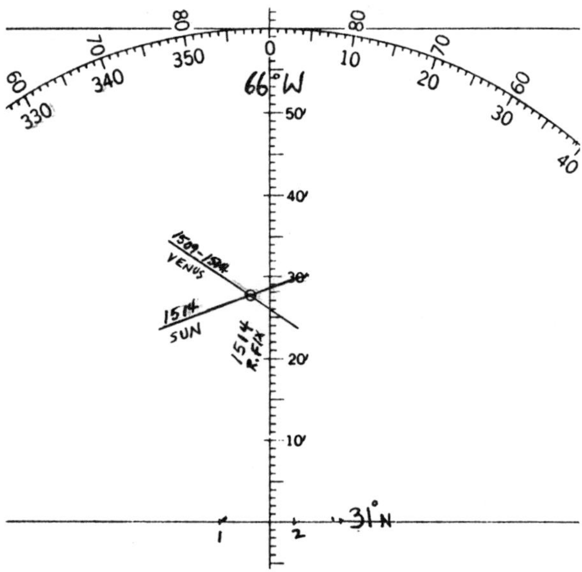


*Fig. 11.* Plot of Venus-sun fix

CHAPTER 6

# Moon Sights

THE AUTHOR ONCE HAD A PROFESSOR OF nautical astronomy (during wartime, when his preparation for the course was probably rushed) who told his class that the moon was useless for navigation because "it wanders all over the place." The professor was wrong. The moon could be described as wandering, but its movements are precisely predicted in the *Nautical Almanac*.

In some ways, the moon is the most useful body for navigation. It can be sighted often at morning or evening twilight, and, like the bright planets, is sometimes visible when the stars have faded (at A.M. twilight) or are not yet visible (at P.M. twilight). Best of all, for a number of days each month before, during, and after first and last quarters, the moon is visible during daylight, and a moon LOP can be crossed with a sun LOP for a fix. (The moon is visible when its GHA is about 25° or more from the GHA of the sun.)

There are some disadvantages to moon sights. When the moon is not full, sometimes only the top is illuminated, so only upper-limb sights can be made, but that causes no trouble for most navigators. Altitude corrections for the moon are more involved than for other bodies, but are not difficult.

### Sighting a Thin Crescent

Just before and after new moon, when the moon is a thin crescent, there are times when neither the lower nor the upper limb is lighted. Care is needed near new moon to ensure that the lower or upper limb—not just the bottom or top point—is being brought to the horizon. (See Fig. 12.) But this is not much of a disadvantage, because when this situation occurs the moon is usually so close to the sun that a moonsight would not be very useful.

### Altitude Corrections

IC and dip corrections for the moon are the same as for other bodies. The remainder—combined corrections for refraction, parallax, and semidiameter—for either the lower limb or the upper limb are given on the two pages inside the back cover of the almanac. The horizontal parallax (HP), from the daily page, is one of the entering arguments for the bottom table. HP is the value of the parallax at 0° altitude, and changes from hour to hour. (Parallax is the error caused by observing the altitude from the surface of the earth, rather than from its center. It is slight for the sun and practically zero for other bodies.)

Directions for using the tables are printed next to them, and are clearly stated, except for one sentence: "All corrections are to be **added** to apparent altitude, *but* 30′ *is to be subtracted from the altitude of the upper limb.*" This means that if you have observed the upper limb, you should add the corrections from the tables and

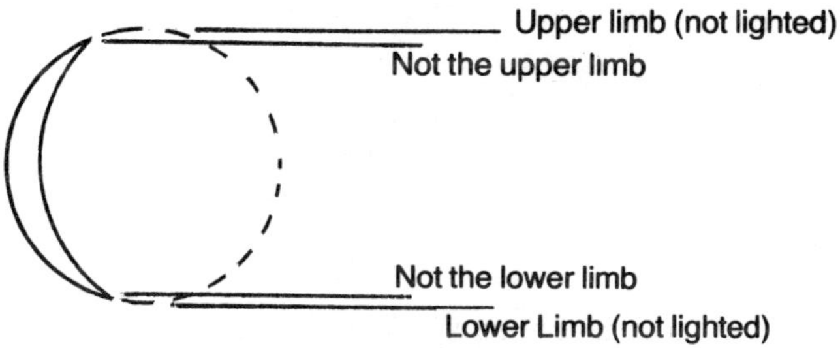


a. Neither limb is lighted. No sight possible.

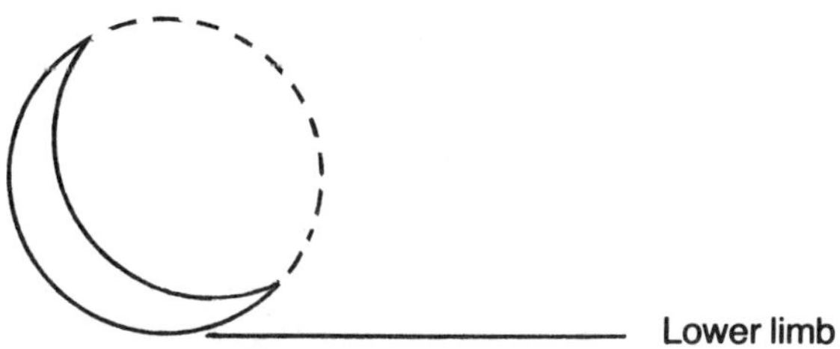


b. Lower limb is lighted.

*Fig. 12.* Sighting a crescent moon

apply a further correction of $-30'$. If you ever have non-standard temperature and pressure, also use Table A4.

## Sight Reduction for the Moon

After the altitude corrections are made, the sight reduction for the moon is about the same as for planets. (Note that the *v* and *d* corrections can be very large.) An example of sun and moon sights for a fix is shown in Figs. 13 and 14.

## Sight-Reduction Form for H. O. 249 or H. O. 229

C: 250° Date: JAN. 7, 1987 Assumed lat.: 31° N *
S: 6.7 DR pos: 31°08′N, 65°32′W LHA♈ at: ______ LMT ______
at 1800 GMT Ht. of eye: 6 ft.

| | LMT | GMT |
|---|---|---|
| | | |
| Civil Twi. | | |
| | | |

| Body | SUN → | | | 55.8 MOON UPPER LIMB → | | |
|---|---|---|---|---|---|---|
| GMT | 18-00-13 | 18-02-18 | 18-03-08 | 18-06-12 | 18-09-21 | 18-12-08 |
| hs | 31°59′ | 31°46′ | 31°44′ | 20°58′ | 21°41′ | 22° 18′ |
| IC | −1′ | −1′ | −1′ | −1′ | −1′ | −1′ |
| dip | −2′ | −2′ | −2′ | −2′ | −2′ | −2′ |
| R/LL(S)/UL(M) | +15′ | +15′ | +15′ | −30′ +2′ +62′ | −30′ +2′ +62′ | −30′ +2′ +62′ |
| Ho | 32°11′ | 31°58′ | 31° 56′ | 21°29′ | 22°12′ | 22°49′ |
| | | | | | | |
| GHA (h) \| v | 88°26′ | 88°26′ | 88°26′ | 352°44′ \| 14.9 | 352°44′ \| 14.9 | 352°44′ \| 14.9 |
| SHA☆ | — | — | — | — | — | — |
| GHA (m/s) | 0°03′ | 0°34′ | 0°47′ | 1°26′ | 2°14′ | 2°54′ |
| v corr. (moon, planets) | — | — | — | 2′ | 2′ | 3′ |
| GHA (total) | 88°29′ | 89°00′ | 89°13′ | 354°12′ | 355°00′ | 355°41′ |
| long. −W or +E | 65°29′ | 66°00′ | 65°13′ | 65°12′ | 66°00′ | 65°41′ |
| LHA | 23° * | 23° * | 24° * | 289° * | 289° * | 290° * |
| | | | | | | |
| Dec. \| d | S22°22′ \| −0.3 | S22°22′ \| −0.3 | S22°22′ \| −0.3 | N10°57′ \| +13.8 | N10°57′ \| +13.8 | N10°57′ \| +13.8 |
| d corr. (not for stars) | — | — | — | +2′ | +2 | +3 |
| Dec. (total) | S22°22′* | S22°22′* | S22°22′* | N10°59′* | N10°59′* | N11°00′* |
| | | | | | | |
| Altitude \| d | 32°36′ \| −56 | 32°36′ \| −56 | 32°13′ \| −55 | 21°22′ \| +29 | 21°22′ \| +29 | 22°43′ \| +29 |
| d corr. | −21′ | −21′ | −20′ | +29′ | +29′ | 0 |
| Hc | 32°15′ | 31°75′ 32°15′ | 31°53′ | 21°51′ | 21°51′ | 22°43′ |
| Ho | 32°11′ | 31°58′ | 31°56′ | 21°29′ | 21°72′ 22°12′ | 22°49′ |
| Intercept | 4 a | 17 a | 3 t | 22 a | 21 t | 6 t |
| | | | | | | |
| Z | 360° −155° | 360° −155° | 360° −154° | | | |
| Zn | 205° | 205° | 206° | 091° | 091° | 091° |
| Miles to move AP | 1.3 | 1.1 | 1.0 | 0.7 | 0.3 | |

*Table entry

*Fig. 13.* Sight reduction form—sun and moon

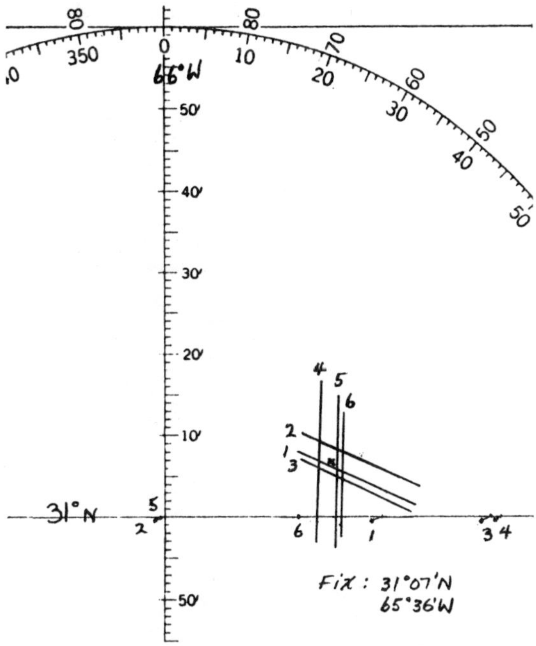


*Fig. 14.* Plot of sun-moon fix

## Guarding against Errors

Moon sights are usually easy, and can be crossed with sun sights for a fix, even sometimes when the weather is so rough that a round of star sights is impossible. But the additional altitude corrections provide more chances for error, so the practice of taking five or six sights, instead of just one, is even more important for the moon than for the sun.

B.T.

CHAPTER 7

# The Navigator's Day

SMALL BOATS CRUISING IN OPEN WATER DO NOT customarily provide short working hours for their crews—mainly because there are rarely enough crew members. But there is a strong argument for assigning the navigator to fewer watches and other duties, or—for a lucky minority cruising in larger boats—none. A navigator who is doing the job properly can spend most of the working day on navigation and related matters, such as getting weather information by radio.

## The Navigator's Daily Routine

Unless bad weather or something else interferes, the navigator should be doing the following every day:

1. Planning A.M. twilight sights, as described in Chapter 3. The best time to do this is the previous afternoon. After a plan is worked out, the one for the following day is much easier. The previous plan should be compared with the new one, to check for gross errors, and in an emergency it can be used instead of a new plan (with the navigator expecting slight differences).

2. Taking A.M. twilight sights. There will probably not be an assistant to record the time of each sight, but the navigator can do it by counting off seconds between the time of the sight and the reading of the watch. A fairly common problem is forgetting to record the

time—another reason to take as many sights as possible, at least two of each body.

3. Reducing sights and plotting. It's best to reduce and plot one sight of each body, keeping the others in reserve in case something doesn't look right.

4. Getting weather reports by radio. This is important to the navigator, because of the occasional need to change course to avoid a storm, and because there is probably no one else on the boat who will record the broadcasts. Also, the navigator knows that there is a brief but very useful storm warning every hour on station WWV (see "Keeping Time at Sea" below), on the 8th, 9th, and sometimes 10th minutes after every hour for the Atlantic, and on the 48th, 49th, and sometimes 50th minutes for the Pacific.

5. Taking sun sights for a running fix. The navigator should get a series of sun sights in midmorning, to be crossed with afternoon sun sights or, if possible, moon or Venus sights. If only one sight of a body can be taken (instead of five or six, as desired), the navigator should work the sight a second time, without looking at the first effort, as a check against errors.

6. Taking sights on other bodies. The navigator should keep track of where the moon and Venus are, and should always shoot them during the day, for a fix with the sun, when the bodies are positioned so that their LOPs make a suitable crossing angle (not less than about 45°).

7. Taking P.M. twilight sights. The plan, sighting, reduction, and plotting are similar to those of A.M. twilight, except that identification is more difficult, because the pattern of stars cannot be seen before the

bright ones appear and are sighted. That makes the plan even more important for P.M. than for A.M. twilight. Here is the plan for P.M. twilight January 7, 1987, for DR position 31°15′N, 66°03′W. The LHA♈ was 12° at 1740 LMT. Note that, as for A.M. twilight, the bodies are listed in sighting order—which for P.M. twilight is brightest to dimmest.

P.M. Twilight Plan

| | | *Predicted* | |
|---|---|---|---|
| *Mag.* | *Body* | *Alt.* | *Az.* |
| 0.2 | Capella | 37° | 053° |
| 0.9 | Altair | 18° | 270° |
| 1.1 | Aldebaran | 37° | 092° |
| 1.3 | Fomalhaut | 24° | 206° |
| 1.3 | Deneb | 41° | 305° |
| 2.2 | Kochab | 17° | 352° |
| 2.2 | Diphda | 41° | 182° |

## Keeping Time at Sea

The navigator should have three quartz digital watches, each of which has been rated (checked for error) before leaving shore. At least once a day, they should be checked against the WWV time signal, on 2.5, 5, 10, 15, or 20 MHz—or a signal from another station, such as CHU, Ottawa, on 3.33, 7.335, or 14.67 MHz—and the results recorded. These watches are inexpensive, highly accurate, shock resistant, and very reliable—one of the best bargains of the twentieth century.

The navigation watches should be set to GMT, preferably in the 24-hour mode, and not reset. Meals, watch standing, and other daily affairs will be regulated by boat time, which should be kept on a separate watch—or even an alarm clock. This timepiece will be set ahead (if the boat is eastbound) or back (if westbound) as each time zone is crossed, but the navigation watches will not be changed. Timing of navigation events should be in GMT—not, as used to be done, in LZT, which was then converted to GMT for sight reduction (resulting in occasional errors).

### Selecting the Fix Point

For a round of sights, the LOPs will of course not all cross at a point. Unless the sighting conditions have been very bad, an LOP should be rejected (after an attempt to correct it) if it lies more than four or five miles from where the fix will be. Then the center of the others should be determined by eye for the fix. The desired result is that the sum of the distances of the LOPs from the fix point be a minimum. Some specialized calculators do this mathematically, but a navigator using good judgment can do almost as well by eye.

### Using a Single Celestial LOP

There are times when only one celestial LOP is available—for example, when an overcast moves in (precluding a running fix) after the navigator has gotten a sun sight—but that LOP can be very useful.

**Sun LOP Crossed with Radio Bearing.** For example, we are approaching Bermuda January 7, 1987, and were able to get only one quick sun sight before the sky was

*Fig. 15.* Radio bearing crossed with sun LOP

obscured with clouds. The sight was at 19-27-42, our DR position was 31°05′N, 66°20′W, and the intercept was 10 miles away from 224°. We need a fix before we get near the reefs around Bermuda. What should we do?

The navigator tunes in the Gibbs Hill radio beacon, BDA, 295 kHz, at 32°15′N, 64°50′W, range about 120 miles, and gets a bearing of 054°. After the rhumb-line correction is made, using Table 1 of *Bowditch* (see Reading List), this becomes 055°. We plot the sun LOP and the radio bearing, and get a fix, at 31°17′N, 66°28′W. Fig. 15 shows the plot.

**Landfall from a Single LOP.** Even with nothing to cross with it, a single LOP can often be used for a landfall.

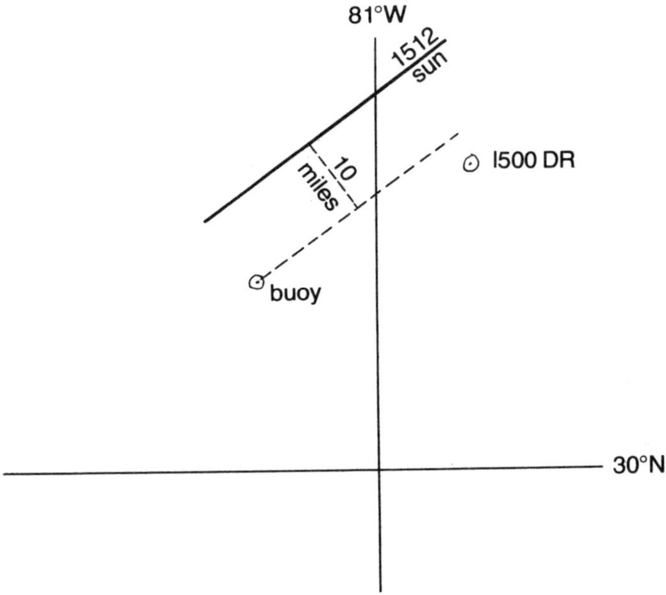


*Fig. 16.* Landfall from a single LOP

Now we are approaching the coast of Florida, with a DR position of 30°35′N, 80°51′W, intending to head for the lighted whistle buoy off the St. Johns River inlet at 30°24′N, 81°20′W (Fig. 16). We get a sun sight and plot the LOP, with a Zn of 144°. We draw a dotted line parallel to the LOP, through our destination, the buoy. This shows that the line we are actually on (the LOP) is northwest of the line we want to be on (the dotted line), and 10 miles from it. We turn to a course of 144° (perpendicular to the LOP, heading toward the dotted line) and sail for 10 miles, then turn right 90° (to 234°), and we are headed for the buoy. We don't know how long it will take, but we maintain our heading until we get there. If possible, we will get a running fix later, but we can do without it.

H.O. No 208
NAVIGATION TABLES
FOR
MARINERS AND AVIATORS
SIXTH EDITION
DREISONSTOK
UNITED STATES NAVY
HYDROGRAPHIC OFFICE
COMPACT
SIGHT REDUCTION
TABLE

CHAPTER 8

# Other Sight-Reduction Methods

THE BEST TABULAR SIGHT-REDUCTION METHODS for small boats are H. O. 249 Vol. 1 and Vols. 2 and 3. (They are two different, but complementary, methods.) They are inexpensive, simple to use, more versatile than other methods (because of the suitability of Vol. 1 for planning), and as accurate as necessary, considering the limitations of sextant accuracy. They are used by experts as well as beginners. But there are other methods that the navigator should know about.

## H. O. 229

The official name is *Sight Reduction Tables for Marine Navigation,* Pub. No. 229 (NP401 in the United Kingdom). It comes in six hardbound volumes, each covering 16° of latitude. It covers all latitudes and declinations, rather than being limited to declinations less than 30°, as are Vols. 2 and 3 of H. O. 249. It is used like those two volumes, except that the table arrangement is different.

H. O. 229 gives data to the nearest tenth of a minute of arc (compared to the nearest minute for H. O. 249). This makes it more time-consuming to use (especially its more complicated interpolation table for minutes of declination), with more chances for error, unless the figures in the book are rounded off to the nearest minute. The complete set is well suited to vessels with plenty of storage space for books and a large navigator's station. However, a navigator who uses H. O. 249 may want to take along one volume of H. O. 229, to have all the declinations covered (for the occasional sight of a star not included in H. O. 249 Vol. 1 and with a declination greater than 30°). Anyone who understands H. O. 249 can learn to use H. O. 229 with a little study.

### Davies Star Tables

These are in a single large paperback volume, and are similar in use to H. O. 249 Vol. 1, except that they have the unique feature of using the observed altitude (Ho) for table entry, instead of the star name. This means that the navigator does not need to know the name of the star that was sighted, so there is no problem of identification.

This method is not as widely used as H. O. 249, and is more complicated, so it's mainly for experienced navigators who prefer its special features.

### Davies Sun, Moon, and Planet Tables

These are in another large paperback volume, and complement the Davies Star Tables (in the same way that H. O. 249 Vols. 2 and 3 complement H. O. 249 Vol. 1). They are used for solar-system bodies and for those stars not included in the Davies Star Tables. They have the same advantages and disadvantages as the Star Tables.

### Navigation Calculators

There are several types of navigation calculators. The simplest ones, which do just basic arithmetic and are very inexpensive, are handy for the adding and subtracting in tabular-method sight reduction and other jobs, and should be on every boat. The solar-powered ones (which work also in artificial light) are especially good.

Those of the second type perform the sight reduction automatically after the navigator has found and entered into the calculator the latitude, declination, and LHA (or GHA and longitude). These are not of much value—because they only duplicate what the tabular methods do, and save little or no time—except that they allow computations from the DR position, rather than requiring a separate assumed position for each sight. This is a small advantage.

Those of the third type have a built-in long-term almanac for the sun and stars, besides the sight-reduction programs, so they save time (and errors) for sight reductions of those bodies. Since they do not work sights of the moon or planets, their use is limited. But, when reasonably priced, this kind of calculator is a good supplement to H. O. 249.

The fourth kind of calculator has a built-in almanac for all bodies, so it can be used for all sight-reduction problems. It can also compute fix points from several LOPs, and work problems such as great-circle computations (as do some of the second type). The price is high: over $500. For anyone who doesn't mind paying the money, this kind of instrument can be very useful, but the disadvantages should be considered.

**Disadvantages of Specialized Calculators.**

1. A navigator should buy a specialized calculator only after becoming proficient in at least one tabular

method, such as H. O. 249. The tabular method will always be needed as back-up, in case the batteries go dead, the instrument corrodes in salt air, or something else happens to it. It would be risky to rely on the calculator alone.

2. Operation of the calculator is usually not difficult, but must be learned—and practiced, on all kinds of problems—before it can be relied on.

3. Calculators, like other electronic devices not designed for use in salt air, must be protected at sea. The best method is to keep the instrument in a sealed plastic bag when it isn't being used—or even when it *is* being used, by punching the keys through the bag.

4. Several sets of batteries should be taken on the cruise—also sealed in a plastic bag.

5. The navigator should continue to work problems regularly with H. O. 249 or another tabular method (they can be checked with the calculator), to avoid getting out of practice.

## Emergency Methods

If the vessel must be abandoned in an emergency, the navigator should try to take along in the lifeboat all the necessary equipment: sextant, charts, almanac, regular tabular method, etc., besides the food and water. But there should also be an abbreviated tabular method, preferably stowed inside the sextant case, to be used only in an emergency. These tables are about pamphlet size, cover all navigational bodies, and are inexpensive. Computations are tedious, but there is plenty of time in a lifeboat. There are several suitable methods:

**Davies Concise Tables.** This system is different from the others in using degrees for its computations, instead of numbers that represent logarithms of functions. (This is unusual, but not a disadvantage.) It is the most useful, because it contains long-term almanacs for the sun and stars, and Polaris-correction and altitude-correction tables. Instructions are included.

**Bayless Modified H. O. 211.** This is an improved version of an old method, and includes good instructions. (The original H. O. 211, a small, flat, hardbound book, is out of print, but can be used if found. The instructions are difficult. Work some sights with it before you stow it with the lifeboat equipment.)

**H. O. 208.** This is another out-of-print publication, but it's sometimes reprinted in navigation texts (with improved instructions).

### GHA♈ in H. O. 249 Vol. 1

H. O. 249 Vol. 1 has an emergency feature, on pp. 320 and 321: tables that give GHA♈ at any time in any of the years covered (1981 to 1989, for example). The procedure is more complicated than using the *Nautical Almanac*, but these tables make it possible to work star sights with only H. O. 249 Vol. 1, if the almanac is lost.

CHAPTER 9

# Using the Sextant

THE SEXTANT IS AN ATTRACTIVE-LOOKING PRECISION instrument. It feels good in the hand, and is an antique design that still serves a need. It is not easy to use.

## Locating the Body

The first problem is locating the star (or other body) in the right side of the telescope field while the horizon is seen in the left side. You can set the scale to zero, point the scope at the star, and smoothly move the index arm away from you as you lower the sextant, keeping the star in the right of the field, until the star comes to the horizon. If you jerked a little moving the index arm, you probably lost the star.

A better way is to set the scale to zero, turn the sextant upside down, point to the star, and move the index arm away from you until the horizon is seen to come up to the star. (This way, you keep pointing directly at the star, and are less likely to lose it.) Then turn the sextant right side up, point to the horizon, in the direction of the star (which will now be easy to find), and take the sight.

The best method is to make up a twilight plan in advance (see Chapter 3), and at sighting time just set the sextant to the predicted altitude, turn to the predicted azimuth (remembering to convert from true to compass direction first) and see the star—with little or no searching.

### Swinging the Arc

When you take the sight, you must "swing the arc" to be sure you're holding the sextant vertical at the moment of coincidence. (If it's tilted, you will be measuring a bigger angle than the one you want, which is the shortest distance from the star to the horizon.) The way to swing the arc is to rotate the sextant slightly, back and forth, around an imaginary axis from you to the star (or other body), and stop swinging when the star is seen at its lowest point. (Fig. 17 shows how this looks for the sun.) Then turn the fine-adjustment knob until you get coincidence of the star with the horizon, and read the time.

### The Sextant Telescope

Always use a sextant telescope for sighting any body. Some navigators like a 6-power scope for the sun and a 3- or 4-power one for stars. But the more your vessel is being tossed around by the sea, the lower the magnification you can get by with. A 3-power, or even 2.5-power scope can give good results for all bodies.

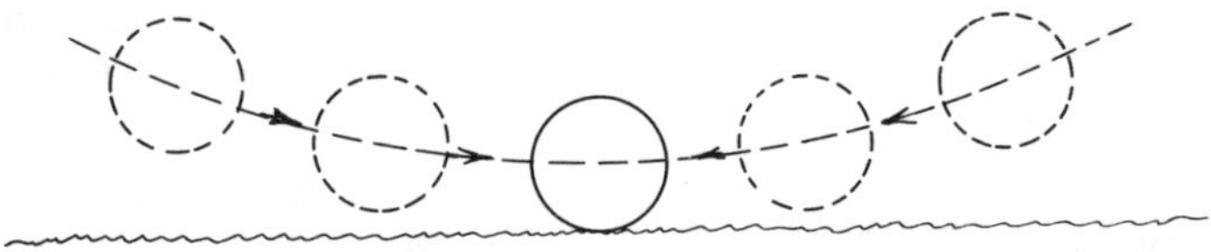

*Fig. 17.* Swinging the arc

### The Sextant Scales

Reading the sextant scales is not difficult, but it takes practice for new navigators. Beware of making an error of exactly 1°, 5°, or 10°. It's a good idea, when reading either a vernier or a micrometer-drum scale, to make a rough estimate by eye, before getting the precise reading, to avoid gross errors.

### Using Sun Filters

When you're preparing to shoot the sun, separate one of the filters from the others (a dark one, to begin with) and look at the sun through just the filter. If it isn't the right density, select another one. Then choose a horizon filter, looking at the horizon under the sun, before you start shooting.

### Sights in Rough Weather

Celestial sights in rough weather are not easy. Take more sights than you would in calm water, so the errors will tend to average out. At twilight in rough weather, get as many sights as you can. Because twilight sights are more difficult (since there is only a brief time when both the horizon and the stars are clearly visible), be sure you sight all the bright planets that are available—especially in rough weather.

### Waves and the Dip Correction

One of the worst problems for small-boat navigators is avoiding a false horizon. When the waves are high, it helps to have an assistant call out when the boat is on top of a wave, so the navigator can make the contact of the body with the real horizon, rather than a nearby wave. There is also the question of whether to adjust the dip correction to allow for the amount the boat is lifted by the waves. The recommended procedure is to take each sight when the boat is at its highest point, and use the regular dip correction, unchanged (because the observer and the horizon will both be on the wave tops).

### Sextant Care

Clean the sextant mirrors, telescope, and filters now and then with ethyl or methyl alcohol and a soft cloth or tissue. If the sextant gets splashed with salt water, wipe it with a rag dampened with fresh water, then dry it thoroughly before putting it away. If you oil the sextant, use a tiny amount, of the type recommended by the manufacturer.

### Special Sextant Features

There are two optional devices offered with some sextants. Some navigators like them and some don't, so try them out before buying.

**The Prism Level.** This accessory (sold under various brand names) can be bought with some new sextants, or as an add-on to existing ones. It splits the view of the horizon, so that if the sextant is tilted, one half of the horizon is seen below the other half. When the sextant is level, the horizon is seen as one straight line. This accomplishes the same thing as swinging the arc, but is easier and, some say, more accurate.

**The Whole-Horizon Mirror.** This type of horizon mirror is partially silvered over its entire surface, rather than being silvered on the right half and clear on the left. The regular half-and-half mirror reflects the body in the right half and the horizon in the left (although there is some overlap—especially when a telescope is used). The whole-horizon mirror shows both the body and the horizon in the entire field of view. There is a slight loss in brightness, but those who prefer the device believe this minor disadvantage is more than offset by the advantage of the full field.

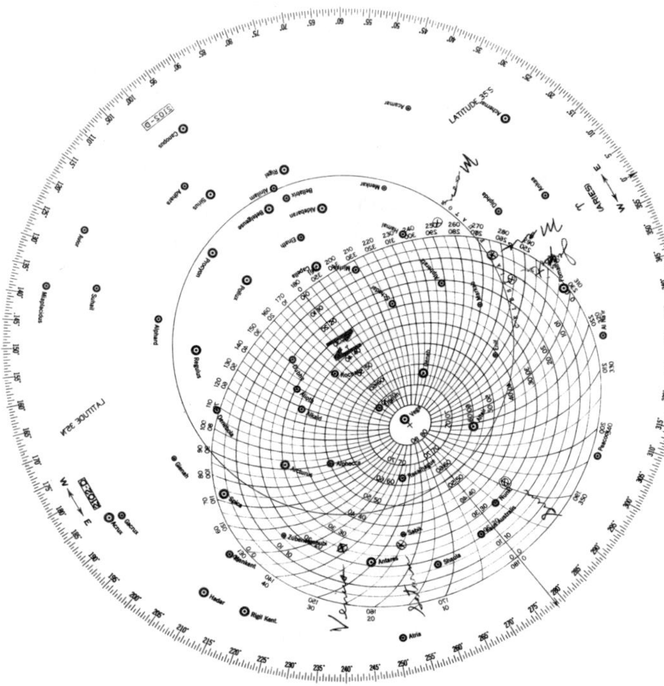

LATITUDE 35°S
LATITUDE 35°N
(ARIES)
2102-D

CHAPTER 10

# The Star Finder

CELESTIAL NAVIGATION CAN BE ACCOMPLISHED quite well without using a star finder. But the serious navigator should sooner or later start using Rude's Star Finder and Identifier, 2102-D, which is inexpensive and is sold in many nautical-supply stores.

Rude's is the only star finder widely used for navigation. It was once sold by the government as H. O. 2102-D, but is now made and sold commercially. In spite of the name, its main use is for finding and identifying planets. H. O. 249 Vol. 1 is better than the star finder for making up a twilight plan for stars, showing predicted altitudes and azimuths (as described in Chapter 3). But the star finder is the only good means, except precomputation, for adding planets to the twilight plan. (It can also be used for stars.)

## Parts of the Star Finder

The star finder is simple to use. It has a white plastic base on which the star locations are printed (for N latitudes on one side, S on the other), with a surface on which locations of planets (and, if desired, the sun and moon) can be pencilled in and later erased. (The solar-system bodies cannot be shown permanently because their positions change constantly.) The reference point is Aries. A scale around the outer edge shows RA (right ascension), used for marking the base; the same scale indicates LHA♈, used for orienting the blue overlay. There are nine transparent overlays, each with a blue grid that shows altitudes and azimuths. Another overlay, printed in red, is used to mark the positions of the planets, moon, and sun.

### Using the Star Finder

To demonstrate the use of the star finder, we will mark the positions of the planets, moon, and sun on the base, then use the star finder to add any available planets and the moon to the January 7, 1987, A.M. twilight plan from Chapter 3. The steps are not difficult.

**Marking Positions of the Planets, Moon, and Sun.**

1. Find the RA for each body, for the desired day.

RA = GHA♈ − GHA of the body (+ 360° if necessary)

For example, the RA of the sun on January 7, 1987, is:

$$287° - 358° + 360° = 289°$$

(We chose the arbitrary time of 1200 GMT for entering the almanac tables. The time is not critical.) The RAs for all the bodies on January 7, 1987, are:

| | |
|---|---|
| Venus | 239° |
| Mars | 0° |
| Jupiter | 350° |
| Saturn | 255° |
| Sun | 288° |
| Moon | 21° |

2. Find the declination for each body, also at 1200 GMT.

3. Put the red overlay, NORTH LAT. side up, on the N side of the base, and mark with a pencil the position of each body. Turn the disc until the red index (at 0°) is at the number, on the base, that equals the RA for the body. Put a pencil mark on the base, through the narrow opening, at the number that equals the declination of

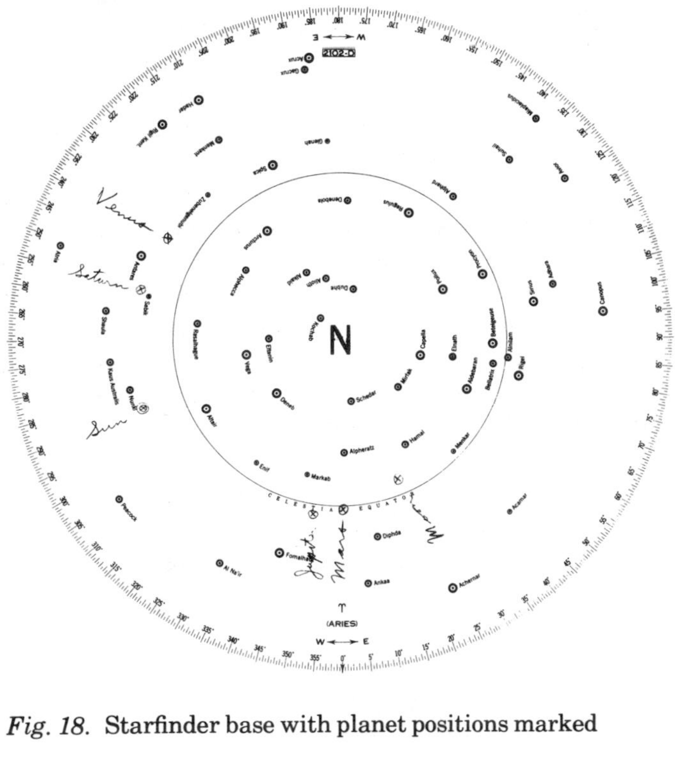


*Fig. 18.* Starfinder base with planet positions marked

the body, and label it. Note that in N latitude the upper declination scale is for N declination, the lower one for S declination; in S latitude, the upper one is for S declination, the lower one for N declination.

**Finding Predicted Hc and Zn.**

1. Now that the base is prepared (Fig. 18), replace the red overlay with the blue one for 35° latitude (the nearest one to our DR latitude of 31°), north side up.

2. Rotate the overlay until the blue arrow points to the LHA♈ for the time of A.M. civil twilight January 7, 1987, which we found in Chapter 3 was 205°.

3. Now we can read the predicted altitude and azimuth for each body that is visible at A.M. twilight (Fig. 19). Note that the altitude and azimuth shown by the star finder for each of the seven stars we included in the plan are close to what we found using H. O. 249 Vol. 1 (see Chapter 3). We can see also that on this day Venus and Saturn are visible at A.M. twilight, but Mars, Jupiter, and the moon are not. (They are outside the range of the blue scales when the overlay is rotated to show LHA♈ at the time of A.M. twilight.) We read the estimated altitude and azimuth for the three bodies, and add them to the A.M. twilight plan:

| | | *Predicted* | |
|---|---|---|---|
| *Mag.* | *Body* | *Alt.* | *Az.* |
| −4.5 | Venus | 32° | 141° |
| 0.5 | Saturn | 19° | 131° |

Note that we included both Saturn and Venus in the plan, although we might sight only one of them, since they are so close together.

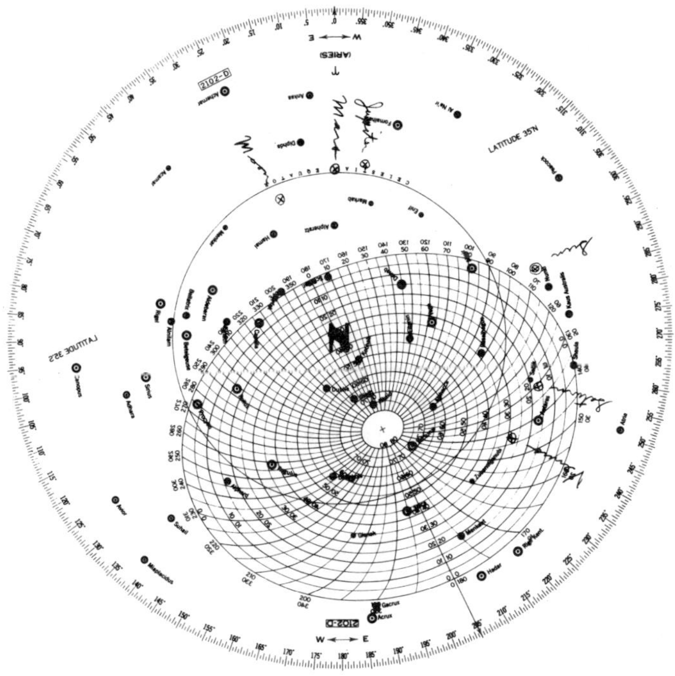

*Fig. 19.* Predicted altitude and azimuth

## Finding the Sun in Cloudy Weather

It's useful to have the sun's position marked on the star finder, too. Its mark should be close to 0° altitude, in the east, when the star finder is set for A.M. twilight, and close to 0° in the west at P.M. twilight. This gives a check on the way you set up the star finder. Also, it can help in sighting the sun (or moon) in cloudy weather. You can turn the overlay to where the index points to the LHA♈ for the LMT at which you want to take a sight, preset the sextant to the predicted altitude, look toward the predicted azimuth, and wait for a break in the clouds. (Refer to "The Twilight Plan" in Chapter 3 for the best way to get LHA♈.) The same can be done for the moon.

### Plans for Other Days

The moon and planet positions already marked on the base for the A.M. twilight plan are close enough to be used also for the P.M. twilight plan the same day. For the next day, a new mark should be made for the moon, whose position changes rapidly, but the positions for the other bodies are still close enough. After several days, the positions for the sun and Venus begin to get stale.

### Accuracy

One source of a slight inaccuracy is taking the same LHA♈ for all the twilight sights. You *could* calculate one LHA♈ for the estimated beginning time of the sighting period and another one for the end, and interpolate in between, but it's hardly worth the trouble.

There is also a slight inaccuracy from using a blue overlay that is not drawn for your precise latitude. You can improve this if you slip the overlay center hole out of the peg (after rotating the overlay to the LHA♈) and move the hole to where the peg marks the exact latitude—but you may not want to bother.

### Planning for Cruises

If you use a star finder on a cruise, you should pencil in the locations of all the solar-system bodies for the first week, and change them every week. Put a separate mark on the base for each day for the moon and each three days for Venus, and mark the location of each of the other bodies for the middle of the week—labelling everything, of course. Then when you want to use the star finder, all you need to do is determine the LHA♈ for the sighting time (see "Finding the Sun in Cloudy Weather," above) and rotate the overlay to that figure.

### Moon and Venus

You can find the time when the moon is visible during the day, and in position for a sun-moon fix, by rotating the overlay until the altitudes and azimuths of the bodies are favorable. Then convert the indicated LHA♈ to GHA♈ (by adding the time equivalent of west longitude—found on p. i., the first yellow page—or, if east longitude, subtracting). Find the GMT for this GHA♈ by consulting the almanac daily page for the hour and the yellow pages for the minutes and seconds. The same procedure can be followed for planning Venus sights during the day.

### Summary

1. Find the RA and declination of each planet, the moon, and the sun for about the middle of the desired day.

2. For each body, rotate the red overlay to the RA and put a mark at the declination. Label each mark.

3. Replace the red overlay with the blue one nearest to your latitude. Rotate it until the arrow points to the LHA♈ for the desired sighting time.

4. Read the predicted altitude and azimuth for each body.

# Glossary

♈ — Aries. The point on the celestial sphere from which the hour angle (SHA) of a star is measured. This is the point at which SHA = 0°.

altitude — The angle, at the observer, from the horizon up to a celestial body. (See hs, Ho, and Hc.)

AP — Assumed position. Chosen at a whole degree of latitude, and with a longitude that will make the LHA a whole degree.

*d* corr. — Increment added to or subtracted from the whole-hour value of the declination to allow for minutes and seconds of time (in the *Nautical Almanac*).

d corr. — Increment added to or subtracted from the tabulated altitude to allow for minutes of declination (in H. O. 249 and other tabular methods).

Dec. or d — Declination. Same as latitude, but applied to celestial bodies.

Dip corr. — Correction to hs for the observer's height of eye. Always minus. Inside the front cover of the *Nautical Almanac*.

DR — Dead reckoning. Determination of position from an earlier known position and distance (from speed and time) and direction of movement.

| | |
|---|---|
| GHA | Greenwich hour angle. Measured from the meridian of Greenwich to a celestial body. Similar to longitude, but measured westward, from 0° to 360° (rather than eastward or westward, from 0° to 180°). GHA of a star = GHA♈ + SHA of the star. |
| GMT | Greenwich mean time. The LMT (and LZT) at 0° longitude (the meridian of Greenwich). |
| Hc | Computed altitude of a celestial body, at a particular time, at the AP selected. Listed in H. O. 249 and other tabular methods. |
| HE | Height of eye of an observer above sea level. Used to find dip correction. |
| Ho | Observed altitude. The result of applying altitude corrections to hs. |
| HP | Horizontal parallax (of the moon). The parallax (the error resulting from observing the body from the surface, rather than the center, of the eon. |
| Ho | Observed altitude. The result of applying altitude corrections to hs. |
| HP | Horizontal parallax (of the moon). The tions are applied to get Ho. |
| IC | Index correction (of the sextant). The small error resulting from the lack of precise calibration of the sextant, so that the scale does not read zero when the horizon is aligned in both halves of the telescope field. |
| Intercept | The difference between Ho and Hc, in minutes, stated in nautical miles. Remember "computed greater away"—that is, if Hc is greater than Ho, the LOP is plotted away |

from the azimuth, a distance equal to the intercept. If Ho is greater than Hc, the LOP is plotted toward the azimuth.

LHA — Local hour angle. Measured from the observer's meridian, westward (0° to 360°) to a celestial body. GHA − west longitude (or + east longitude) = LHA.

LL — Lower limb (of the sun or moon). The lower edge. *Nautical Almanac* corrections for LL observations are the total of refraction, parallax, and semidiameter corrections.

LMT — Local mean time. Equal to GMT minus (for west longitude) or plus (for east longitude) the time equivalent of longitude.

LOP — Line of position. A line on which the observer is presumed to be located.

LZT — Local zone time. Differs from GMT by one hour for each 15° of longitude. LZT is similar to LMT, but LZT changes in one-hour steps, and LMT changes continuously, as the longitude changes.

RA — Right ascension. Used to mark the base of the star finder.

$$\text{RA} = \text{GHA}♈ - \text{GHA of the body, or}$$

$$\text{RA} = 360° - \text{SHA of the body}$$

R corr. — Refraction correction, for the error caused by the bending of the light rays (from a celestial body) by the atmosphere. Always minus.

SD — Semidiameter. The radius (of the sun or moon). The SD correction is plus for LL observations, minus for UL observations.

SHA — Sidereal hour angle. Measured from Aries, westward, to a star or (sometimes) another body (0° to 360°). Listed in the *Nautical Almanac* for all navigational stars on the left-hand daily page, and for the planets at the lower right of that page.

UL — Upper limb (of the sun or moon). The upper edge. *Nautical Almanac* corrections for UL observations are the total of refraction, parallax, and semidiameter corrections.

*v* corr. — The correction added to (or, sometimes, for Venus, subtracted from) GHA for minutes and seconds of time. For planets and the moon only. This is in addition to the minutes-and-seconds *increment* added to GHA. Both figures are found in the almanac yellow pages.

Z — Aximuth angle. Measured from north to south, toward east or west (0° to 180°). Must be converted to Zn, using the rules at the top (for N lat.) or bottom (for S lat.) of each page of H. O. 249 Vol. 2 or 3.

Zn — Azimuth. Measured from the north toward east (0° to 360°). Given directly in H. O. 249 Vol. 1.

# Reading List

Bayless, Allan E. *Compact Sight Reduction Table (Modified H. O. 211, Ageton's Table).* Centreville, Md.: Cornell Maritime Press, 1980.

Bowditch, Nathaniel. *American Practical Navigator,* Vols. I and II. Defense Mapping Agency.

Davies, Thomas D. *Concise Tables for Sight Reduction.* Centreville, Md.: Cornell Maritime Press, 1984.

Gray, Leonard. *Celestial Navigation Planning.* Centreville, Md.: Cornell Maritime Press, 1984.

Howell, Susan P. *Practical Celestial Navigation.* Hebron, Conn.: Susan P. Howell, 1979.

Letcher, John S., Jr. *Self-Contained Celestial Navigation with H. O. 208.* Camden Me.: International Marine Publishing Co., 1977.

Noer, H. Rolf. *Navigator's Pocket Calculator Handbook.* Centreville, Md.: Cornell Maritime Press, 1983.

Turner, Merle. *Celestial for the Cruising Navigator.* Centreville, Md.: Cornell Maritime Press, 1986.

## Sources of Government Publications

### Nautical Almanac and Air Almanac

U. S. Government Printing Office
Washington, D. C. 20402

**Sight Reduction Tables for Air Navigation, Pub. No. 249**

Vol. 1—Selected Stars
Vol. 2—Latitudes 0°–40°, Declinations 0°–29°
Vol. 3—Latitudes 40°–89°, Declinations 0°–29°
Defense Mapping Agency
Hydrographic/Topographic Center
Washington, D. C. 20315
or U. S. Government Printing Office
(address above)

**Sight Reduction Tables for Marine Navigation, Pub. No. 229**

Vol. 1—Latitudes 0°–15°
Vol. 2—Latitudes 15°–30°
Vol. 3—Latitudes 30°–45°
Vol. 4—Latitudes 45°–60°
Vol. 5—Latitudes 60°–75°
Vol. 6—Latitudes 75°–90°
Defense Mapping Agency or U. S. Government Printing Office (addresses above)

# Excerpts from the *Nautical Almanac* and H. O. 249 Vols. 1 and 2

## A2 ALTITUDE CORRECTION TABLES 10°-90°—SUN, STARS, PLANETS

### SUN

| OCT.—MAR. App. Alt. | Lower Limb | Upper Limb | APR.—SEPT. App. Alt. | Lower Limb | Upper Limb |
|---|---|---|---|---|---|
| ° ′ | ′ | ′ | ° ′ | ′ | ′ |
| 9 34 | | | 9 39 | | |
| | +10·8 | −21·5 | | +10·6 | −21·2 |
| 9 45 | | | 9 51 | | |
| | +10·9 | −21·4 | | +10·7 | −21·1 |
| 9 56 | | | 10 03 | | |
| | +11·0 | −21·3 | | +10·8 | −21·0 |
| 10 08 | | | 10 15 | | |
| | +11·1 | −21·2 | | +10·9 | −20·9 |
| 10 21 | | | 10 27 | | |
| | +11·2 | −21·1 | | +11·0 | −20·8 |
| 10 34 | | | 10 40 | | |
| | +11·3 | −21·0 | | +11·1 | −20·7 |
| 10 47 | | | 10 54 | | |
| | +11·4 | −20·9 | | +11·2 | −20·6 |
| 11 01 | | | 11 08 | | |
| | +11·5 | −20·8 | | +11·3 | −20·5 |
| 11 15 | | | 11 23 | | |
| | +11·6 | −20·7 | | +11·4 | −20·4 |
| 11 30 | | | 11 38 | | |
| | +11·7 | −20·6 | | +11·5 | −20·3 |
| 11 46 | | | 11 54 | | |
| | +11·8 | −20·5 | | +11·6 | −20·2 |
| 12 02 | | | 12 10 | | |
| | +11·9 | −20·4 | | +11·7 | −20·1 |
| 12 19 | | | 12 28 | | |
| | +12·0 | −20·3 | | +11·8 | −20·0 |
| 12 37 | | | 12 46 | | |
| | +12·1 | −20·2 | | +11·9 | −19·9 |
| 12 55 | | | 13 05 | | |
| | +12·2 | −20·1 | | +12·0 | −19·8 |
| 13 14 | | | 13 24 | | |
| | +12·3 | −20·0 | | +12·1 | −19·7 |
| 13 35 | | | 13 45 | | |
| | +12·4 | −19·9 | | +12·2 | −19·6 |
| 13 56 | | | 14 07 | | |
| | +12·5 | −19·8 | | +12·3 | −19·5 |
| 14 18 | | | 14 30 | | |
| | +12·6 | −19·7 | | +12·4 | −19·4 |
| 14 42 | | | 14 54 | | |
| | +12·7 | −19·6 | | +12·5 | −19·3 |
| 15 06 | | | 15 19 | | |
| | +12·8 | −19·5 | | +12·6 | −19·2 |
| 15 32 | | | 15 46 | | |
| | +12·9 | −19·4 | | +12·7 | −19·1 |
| 15 59 | | | 16 14 | | |
| | +13·0 | −19·3 | | +12·8 | −19·0 |
| 16 28 | | | 16 44 | | |
| | +13·1 | −19·2 | | +12·9 | −18·9 |
| 16 59 | | | 17 15 | | |
| | +13·2 | −19·1 | | +13·0 | −18·8 |
| 17 32 | | | 17 48 | | |
| | +13·3 | −19·0 | | +13·1 | −18·7 |
| 18 06 | | | 18 24 | | |
| | +13·4 | −18·9 | | +13·2 | −18·6 |
| 18 42 | | | 19 01 | | |
| | +13·5 | −18·8 | | +13·3 | −18·5 |
| 19 21 | | | 19 42 | | |
| | +13·6 | −18·7 | | +13·4 | −18·4 |
| 20 03 | | | 20 25 | | |
| | +13·7 | −18·6 | | +13·5 | −18·3 |
| 20 48 | | | 21 11 | | |
| | +13·8 | −18·5 | | +13·6 | −18·2 |
| 21 35 | | | 22 00 | | |
| | +13·9 | −18·4 | | +13·7 | −18·1 |
| 22 26 | | | 22 54 | | |
| | +14·0 | −18·3 | | +13·8 | −18·0 |
| 23 22 | | | 23 51 | | |
| | +14·1 | −18·2 | | +13·9 | −17·9 |
| 24 21 | | | 24 53 | | |
| | +14·2 | −18·1 | | +14·0 | −17·8 |
| 25 26 | | | 26 00 | | |
| | +14·3 | −18·0 | | +14·1 | −17·7 |
| 26 36 | | | 27 13 | | |
| | +14·4 | −17·9 | | +14·2 | −17·6 |
| 27 52 | | | 28 33 | | |
| | +14·5 | −17·8 | | +14·3 | −17·5 |
| 29 15 | | | 30 00 | | |
| | +14·6 | −17·7 | | +14·4 | −17·4 |
| 30 46 | | | 31 35 | | |
| | +14·7 | −17·6 | | +14·5 | −17·3 |
| 32 26 | | | 33 20 | | |
| | +14·8 | −17·5 | | +14·6 | −17·2 |
| 34 17 | | | 35 17 | | |
| | +14·9 | −17·4 | | +14·7 | −17·1 |
| 36 20 | | | 37 26 | | |
| | +15·0 | −17·3 | | +14·8 | −17·0 |
| 38 36 | | | 39 50 | | |
| | +15·1 | −17·2 | | +14·9 | −16·9 |
| 41 08 | | | 42 31 | | |
| | +15·2 | −17·1 | | +15·0 | −16·8 |
| 43 59 | | | 45 31 | | |
| | +15·3 | −17·0 | | +15·1 | −16·7 |
| 47 10 | | | 48 55 | | |
| | +15·4 | −16·9 | | +15·2 | −16·6 |
| 50 46 | | | 52 44 | | |
| | +15·5 | −16·8 | | +15·3 | −16·5 |
| 54 49 | | | 57 02 | | |
| | +15·6 | −16·7 | | +15·4 | −16·4 |
| 59 23 | | | 61 51 | | |
| | +15·7 | −16·6 | | +15·5 | −16·3 |
| 64 30 | | | 67 17 | | |
| | +15·8 | −16·5 | | +15·6 | −16·2 |
| 70 12 | | | 73 16 | | |
| | +15·9 | −16·4 | | +15·7 | −16·1 |
| 76 26 | | | 79 43 | | |
| | +16·0 | −16·3 | | +15·8 | −16·0 |
| 83 05 | | | 86 32 | | |
| | +16·1 | −16·2 | | +15·9 | −15·9 |
| 90 00 | | | 90 00 | | |

### STARS AND PLANETS

| App. Alt. | Corr^n |
|---|---|
| ° ′ | ′ |
| 9 56 | |
| | −5·3 |
| 10 08 | |
| | −5·2 |
| 10 20 | |
| | −5·1 |
| 10 33 | |
| | −5·0 |
| 10 46 | |
| | −4·9 |
| 11 00 | |
| | −4·8 |
| 11 14 | |
| | −4·7 |
| 11 29 | |
| | −4·6 |
| 11 45 | |
| | −4·5 |
| 12 01 | |
| | −4·4 |
| 12 18 | |
| | −4·3 |
| 12 35 | |
| | −4·2 |
| 12 54 | |
| | −4·1 |
| 13 13 | |
| | −4·0 |
| 13 33 | |
| | −3·9 |
| 13 54 | |
| | −3·8 |
| 14 16 | |
| | −3·7 |
| 14 40 | |
| | −3·6 |
| 15 04 | |
| | −3·5 |
| 15 30 | |
| | −3·4 |
| 15 57 | |
| | −3·3 |
| 16 26 | |
| | −3·2 |
| 16 56 | |
| | −3·1 |
| 17 28 | |
| | −3·0 |
| 18 02 | |
| | −2·9 |
| 18 38 | |
| | −2·8 |
| 19 17 | |
| | −2·7 |
| 19 58 | |
| | −2·6 |
| 20 42 | |
| | −2·5 |
| 21 28 | |
| | −2·4 |
| 22 19 | |
| | −2·3 |
| 23 13 | |
| | −2·2 |
| 24 11 | |
| | −2·1 |
| 25 14 | |
| | −2·0 |
| 26 22 | |
| | −1·9 |
| 27 36 | |
| | −1·8 |
| 28 56 | |
| | −1·7 |
| 30 24 | |
| | −1·6 |
| 32 00 | |
| | −1·5 |
| 33 45 | |
| | −1·4 |
| 35 40 | |
| | −1·3 |
| 37 48 | |
| | −1·2 |
| 40 08 | |
| | −1·1 |
| 42 44 | |
| | −1·0 |
| 45 36 | |
| | −0·9 |
| 48 47 | |
| | −0·8 |
| 52 18 | |
| | −0·7 |
| 56 11 | |
| | −0·6 |
| 60 28 | |
| | −0·5 |
| 65 08 | |
| | −0·4 |
| 70 11 | |
| | −0·3 |
| 75 34 | |
| | −0·2 |
| 81 13 | |
| | −0·1 |
| 87 03 | |
| | 0·0 |
| 90 00 | |

| App. Alt. | Additional Corr^n |
|---|---|
| **1987** | |
| **VENUS** | |
| Jan. 1-Jan. 4 | |
| ° | ′ |
| 0 | |
| | + 0·3 |
| 34 | |
| | + 0·2 |
| 60 | |
| | + 0·1 |
| 80 | |
| Jan. 5-Feb. 25 | |
| ° | ′ |
| 0 | |
| | + 0·2 |
| 41 | |
| | + 0·1 |
| 76 | |
| Feb. 26-Dec. 31 | |
| ° | ′ |
| 0 | |
| | + 0·1 |
| 60 | |
| **MARS** | |
| Jan. 1-Dec. 31 | |
| ° | ′ |
| 0 | |
| | + 0·1 |
| 60 | |

### DIP

| Ht. of Eye | Corr^n | Ht. of Eye |
|---|---|---|
| m | ′ | ft. |
| 2·4 | | 8·0 |
| | −2·8 | |
| 2·6 | | 8·6 |
| | −2·9 | |
| 2·8 | | 9·2 |
| | −3·0 | |
| 3·0 | | 9·8 |
| | −3·1 | |
| 3·2 | | 10·5 |
| | −3·2 | |
| 3·4 | | 11·2 |
| | −3·3 | |
| 3·6 | | 11·9 |
| | −3·4 | |
| 3·8 | | 12·6 |
| | −3·5 | |
| 4·0 | | 13·3 |
| | −3·6 | |
| 4·3 | | 14·1 |
| | −3·7 | |
| 4·5 | | 14·9 |
| | −3·8 | |
| 4·7 | | 15·7 |
| | −3·9 | |
| 5·0 | | 16·5 |
| | −4·0 | |
| 5·2 | | 17·4 |
| | −4·1 | |
| 5·5 | | 18·3 |
| | −4·2 | |
| 5·8 | | 19·1 |
| | −4·3 | |
| 6·1 | | 20·1 |
| | −4·4 | |
| 6·3 | | 21·0 |
| | −4·5 | |
| 6·6 | | 22·0 |
| | −4·6 | |
| 6·9 | | 22·9 |
| | −4·7 | |
| 7·2 | | 23·9 |
| | −4·8 | |
| 7·5 | | 24·9 |
| | −4·9 | |
| 7·9 | | 26·0 |
| | −5·0 | |
| 8·2 | | 27·1 |
| | −5·1 | |
| 8·5 | | 28·1 |
| | −5·2 | |
| 8·8 | | 29·2 |
| | −5·3 | |
| 9·2 | | 30·4 |
| | −5·4 | |
| 9·5 | | 31·5 |
| | −5·5 | |
| 9·9 | | 32·7 |
| | −5·6 | |
| 10·3 | | 33·9 |
| | −5·7 | |
| 10·6 | | 35·1 |
| | −5·8 | |
| 11·0 | | 36·3 |
| | −5·9 | |
| 11·4 | | 37·6 |
| | −6·0 | |
| 11·8 | | 38·9 |
| | −6·1 | |
| 12·2 | | 40·1 |
| | −6·2 | |
| 12·6 | | 41·5 |
| | −6·3 | |
| 13·0 | | 42·8 |
| | −6·4 | |
| 13·4 | | 44·2 |
| | −6·5 | |
| 13·8 | | 45·5 |
| | −6·6 | |
| 14·2 | | 46·9 |
| | −6·7 | |
| 14·7 | | 48·4 |
| | −6·8 | |
| 15·1 | | 49·8 |
| | −6·9 | |
| 15·5 | | 51·3 |
| | −7·0 | |
| 16·0 | | 52·8 |
| | −7·1 | |
| 16·5 | | 54·3 |
| | −7·2 | |
| 16·9 | | 55·8 |
| | −7·3 | |
| 17·4 | | 57·4 |
| | −7·4 | |
| 17·9 | | 58·9 |
| | −7·5 | |
| 18·4 | | 60·5 |
| | −7·6 | |
| 18·8 | | 62·1 |
| | −7·7 | |
| 19·3 | | 63·8 |
| | −7·8 | |
| 19·8 | | 65·4 |
| | −7·9 | |
| 20·4 | | 67·1 |
| | −8·0 | |
| 20·9 | | 68·8 |
| | −8·1 | |
| 21·4 | | 70·5 |

| Ht. of Eye | Corr^n |
|---|---|
| m | ′ |
| 1·0 | − 1·8 |
| 1·5 | − 2·2 |
| 2·0 | − 2·5 |
| 2·5 | − 2·8 |
| 3·0 | − 3·0 |
| See table ← | |
| m | ′ |
| 20 | − 7·9 |
| 22 | − 8·3 |
| 24 | − 8·6 |
| 26 | − 9·0 |
| 28 | − 9·3 |
| 30 | − 9·6 |
| 32 | −10·0 |
| 34 | −10·3 |
| 36 | −10·6 |
| 38 | −10·8 |
| 40 | −11·1 |
| 42 | −11·4 |
| 44 | −11·7 |
| 46 | −11·9 |
| 48 | −12·2 |
| ft. | ′ |
| 2 | − 1·4 |
| 4 | − 1·9 |
| 6 | − 2·4 |
| 8 | − 2·7 |
| 10 | − 3·1 |
| See table ← | |
| ft. | ′ |
| 70 | − 8·1 |
| 75 | − 8·4 |
| 80 | − 8·7 |
| 85 | − 8·9 |
| 90 | − 9·2 |
| 95 | − 9·5 |
| 100 | − 9·7 |
| 105 | − 9·9 |
| 110 | −10·2 |
| 115 | −10·4 |
| 120 | −10·6 |
| 125 | −10·8 |
| 130 | −11·1 |
| 135 | −11·3 |
| 140 | −11·5 |
| 145 | −11·7 |
| 150 | −11·9 |
| 155 | −12·1 |

App. Alt. = Apparent altitude = Sextant altitude corrected for index error and dip.

## ALTITUDE CORRECTION TABLES 0°–10°—SUN, STARS, PLANETS A3

| App. Alt. | OCT.–MAR. SUN Lower Limb | OCT.–MAR. SUN Upper Limb | APR.–SEPT. SUN Lower Limb | APR.–SEPT. SUN Upper Limb | STARS PLANETS |
|---|---|---|---|---|---|
| ° ′ | ′ | ′ | ′ | ′ | ′ |
| 0 00 | −18·2 | −50·5 | −18·4 | −50·2 | −34·5 |
| 03 | 17·5 | 49·8 | 17·8 | 49·6 | 33·8 |
| 06 | 16·9 | 49·2 | 17·1 | 48·9 | 33·2 |
| 09 | 16·3 | 48·6 | 16·5 | 48·3 | 32·6 |
| 12 | 15·7 | 48·0 | 15·9 | 47·7 | 32·0 |
| 15 | 15·1 | 47·4 | 15·3 | 47·1 | 31·4 |
| 0 18 | −14·5 | −46·8 | −14·8 | −46·6 | −30·8 |
| 21 | 14·0 | 46·3 | 14·2 | 46·0 | 30·3 |
| 24 | 13·5 | 45·8 | 13·7 | 45·5 | 29·8 |
| 27 | 12·9 | 45·2 | 13·2 | 45·0 | 29·2 |
| 30 | 12·4 | 44·7 | 12·7 | 44·5 | 28·7 |
| 33 | 11·9 | 44·2 | 12·2 | 44·0 | 28·2 |
| 0 36 | −11·5 | −43·8 | −11·7 | −43·5 | −27·8 |
| 39 | 11·0 | 43·3 | 11·2 | 43·0 | 27·3 |
| 42 | 10·5 | 42·8 | 10·8 | 42·6 | 26·8 |
| 45 | 10·1 | 42·4 | 10·3 | 42·1 | 26·4 |
| 48 | 9·6 | 41·9 | 9·9 | 41·7 | 25·9 |
| 51 | 9·2 | 41·5 | 9·5 | 41·3 | 25·5 |
| 0 54 | −8·8 | −41·1 | −9·1 | −40·9 | −25·1 |
| 0 57 | 8·4 | 40·7 | 8·7 | 40·5 | 24·7 |
| 1 00 | 8·0 | 40·3 | 8·3 | 40·1 | 24·3 |
| 03 | 7·7 | 40·0 | 7·9 | 39·7 | 24·0 |
| 06 | 7·3 | 39·6 | 7·5 | 39·3 | 23·6 |
| 09 | 6·9 | 39·2 | 7·2 | 39·0 | 23·2 |
| 1 12 | −6·6 | −38·9 | −6·8 | −38·6 | −22·9 |
| 15 | 6·2 | 38·5 | 6·5 | 38·3 | 22·5 |
| 18 | 5·9 | 38·2 | 6·2 | 38·0 | 22·2 |
| 21 | 5·6 | 37·9 | 5·8 | 37·6 | 21·9 |
| 24 | 5·3 | 37·6 | 5·5 | 37·3 | 21·6 |
| 27 | 4·9 | 37·2 | 5·2 | 37·0 | 21·2 |
| 1 30 | −4·6 | −36·9 | −4·9 | −36·7 | −20·9 |
| 35 | 4·2 | 36·5 | 4·4 | 36·2 | 20·5 |
| 40 | 3·7 | 36·0 | 4·0 | 35·8 | 20·0 |
| 45 | 3·2 | 35·5 | 3·5 | 35·3 | 19·5 |
| 50 | 2·8 | 35·1 | 3·1 | 34·9 | 19·1 |
| 1 55 | 2·4 | 34·7 | 2·6 | 34·4 | 18·7 |
| 2 00 | −2·0 | −34·3 | −2·2 | −34·0 | −18·3 |
| 05 | 1·6 | 33·9 | 1·8 | 33·6 | 17·9 |
| 10 | 1·2 | 33·5 | 1·5 | 33·3 | 17·5 |
| 15 | 0·9 | 33·2 | 1·1 | 32·9 | 17·2 |
| 20 | 0·5 | 32·8 | 0·8 | 32·6 | 16·8 |
| 25 | −0·2 | 32·5 | 0·4 | 32·2 | 16·5 |
| 2 30 | +0·2 | −32·1 | −0·1 | −31·9 | −16·1 |
| 35 | 0·5 | 31·8 | +0·2 | 31·6 | 15·8 |
| 40 | 0·8 | 31·5 | 0·5 | 31·3 | 15·5 |
| 45 | 1·1 | 31·2 | 0·8 | 31·0 | 15·2 |
| 50 | 1·4 | 30·9 | 1·1 | 30·7 | 14·9 |
| 2 55 | 1·6 | 30·7 | 1·4 | 30·4 | 14·7 |
| 3 00 | +1·9 | −30·4 | +1·7 | −30·1 | −14·4 |
| 05 | 2·2 | 30·1 | 1·9 | 29·9 | 14·1 |
| 10 | 2·4 | 29·9 | 2·1 | 29·7 | 13·9 |
| 15 | 2·6 | 29·7 | 2·4 | 29·4 | 13·7 |
| 20 | 2·9 | 29·4 | 2·6 | 29·2 | 13·4 |
| 25 | 3·1 | 29·2 | 2·9 | 28·9 | 13·2 |
| 3 30 | +3·3 | −29·0 | +3·1 | −28·7 | −13·0 |

| App. Alt. | OCT.–MAR. SUN Lower Limb | OCT.–MAR. SUN Upper Limb | APR.–SEPT. SUN Lower Limb | APR.–SEPT. SUN Upper Limb | STARS PLANETS |
|---|---|---|---|---|---|
| ° ′ | ′ | ′ | ′ | ′ | ′ |
| 3 30 | +3·3 | −29·0 | +3·1 | −28·7 | −13·0 |
| 35 | 3·6 | 28·7 | 3·3 | 28·5 | 12·7 |
| 40 | 3·8 | 28·5 | 3·5 | 28·3 | 12·5 |
| 45 | 4·0 | 28·3 | 3·7 | 28·1 | 12·3 |
| 50 | 4·2 | 28·1 | 3·9 | 27·9 | 12·1 |
| 3 55 | 4·4 | 27·9 | 4·1 | 27·7 | 11·9 |
| 4 00 | +4·5 | −27·8 | +4·3 | −27·5 | −11·8 |
| 05 | 4·7 | 27·6 | 4·5 | 27·3 | 11·6 |
| 10 | 4·9 | 27·4 | 4·6 | 27·2 | 11·4 |
| 15 | 5·1 | 27·2 | 4·8 | 27·0 | 11·2 |
| 20 | 5·2 | 27·1 | 5·0 | 26·8 | 11·1 |
| 25 | 5·4 | 26·9 | 5·1 | 26·7 | 10·9 |
| 4 30 | +5·6 | −26·7 | +5·3 | −26·5 | −10·7 |
| 35 | 5·7 | 26·6 | 5·5 | 26·3 | 10·6 |
| 40 | 5·9 | 26·4 | 5·6 | 26·2 | 10·4 |
| 45 | 6·0 | 26·3 | 5·8 | 26·0 | 10·3 |
| 50 | 6·2 | 26·1 | 5·9 | 25·9 | 10·1 |
| 4 55 | 6·3 | 26·0 | 6·0 | 25·8 | 10·0 |
| 5 00 | +6·4 | −25·9 | +6·2 | −25·6 | −9·9 |
| 05 | 6·6 | 25·7 | 6·3 | 25·5 | 9·7 |
| 10 | 6·7 | 25·6 | 6·4 | 25·4 | 9·6 |
| 15 | 6·8 | 25·5 | 6·6 | 25·2 | 9·5 |
| 20 | 6·9 | 25·4 | 6·7 | 25·1 | 9·4 |
| 25 | 7·1 | 25·2 | 6·8 | 25·0 | 9·2 |
| 5 30 | +7·2 | −25·1 | +6·9 | −24·9 | −9·1 |
| 35 | 7·3 | 25·0 | 7·0 | 24·8 | 9·0 |
| 40 | 7·4 | 24·9 | 7·2 | 24·6 | 8·9 |
| 45 | 7·5 | 24·8 | 7·3 | 24·5 | 8·8 |
| 50 | 7·6 | 24·7 | 7·4 | 24·4 | 8·7 |
| 5 55 | 7·7 | 24·6 | 7·5 | 24·3 | 8·6 |
| 6 00 | +7·8 | −24·5 | +7·6 | −24·2 | −8·5 |
| 10 | 8·0 | 24·3 | 7·8 | 24·0 | 8·3 |
| 20 | 8·2 | 24·1 | 8·0 | 23·8 | 8·1 |
| 30 | 8·4 | 23·9 | 8·1 | 23·7 | 7·9 |
| 40 | 8·6 | 23·7 | 8·3 | 23·5 | 7·7 |
| 6 50 | 8·7 | 23·6 | 8·5 | 23·3 | 7·6 |
| 7 00 | +8·9 | −23·4 | +8·6 | −23·2 | −7·4 |
| 10 | 9·1 | 23·2 | 8·8 | 23·0 | 7·2 |
| 20 | 9·2 | 23·1 | 9·0 | 22·8 | 7·1 |
| 30 | 9·3 | 23·0 | 9·1 | 22·7 | 7·0 |
| 40 | 9·5 | 22·8 | 9·2 | 22·6 | 6·8 |
| 7 50 | 9·6 | 22·7 | 9·4 | 22·4 | 6·7 |
| 8 00 | +9·7 | −22·6 | +9·5 | −22·3 | −6·6 |
| 10 | 9·9 | 22·4 | 9·6 | 22·2 | 6·4 |
| 20 | 10·0 | 22·3 | 9·7 | 22·1 | 6·3 |
| 30 | 10·1 | 22·2 | 9·8 | 22·0 | 6·2 |
| 40 | 10·2 | 22·1 | 10·0 | 21·8 | 6·1 |
| 8 50 | 10·3 | 22·0 | 10·1 | 21·7 | 6·0 |
| 9 00 | +10·4 | −21·9 | +10·2 | −21·6 | −5·9 |
| 10 | 10·5 | 21·8 | 10·3 | 21·5 | 5·8 |
| 20 | 10·6 | 21·7 | 10·4 | 21·4 | 5·7 |
| 30 | 10·7 | 21·6 | 10·5 | 21·3 | 5·6 |
| 40 | 10·8 | 21·5 | 10·6 | 21·2 | 5·5 |
| 9 50 | 10·9 | 21·4 | 10·6 | 21·2 | 5·4 |
| 10 00 | +11·0 | −21·3 | +10·7 | −21·1 | −5·3 |

Additional corrections for temperature and pressure are given on the following page.

For bubble sextant observations ignore dip and use the star corrections for Sun, planets, and stars.

## A4 ALTITUDE CORRECTION TABLES—ADDITIONAL CORRECTIONS

### ADDITIONAL REFRACTION CORRECTIONS FOR NON-STANDARD CONDITIONS

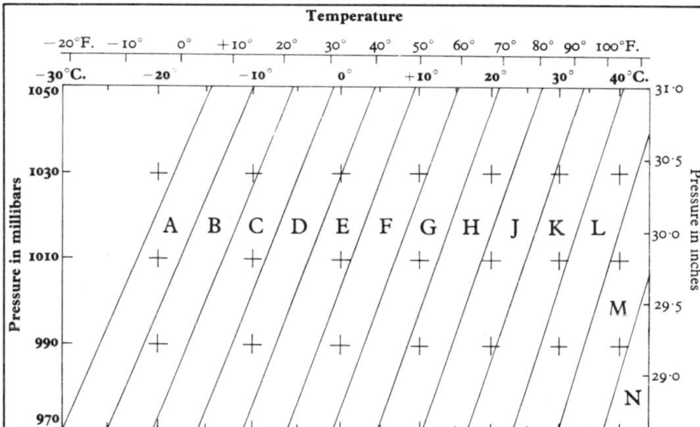


| App. Alt. | A | B | C | D | E | F | G | H | J | K | L | M | N | App. Alt. |
|---|---|---|---|---|---|---|---|---|---|---|---|---|---|---|
| ° ′ | ′ | ′ | ′ | ′ | ′ | ′ | ′ | ′ | ′ | ′ | ′ | ′ | ′ | ° ′ |
| 0 00 | −6·9 | −5·7 | −4·6 | −3·4 | −2·3 | −1·1 | 0·0 | +1·1 | +2·3 | +3·4 | +4·6 | +5·7 | +6·9 | 0 00 |
| 0 30 | 5·2 | 4·4 | 3·5 | 2·6 | 1·7 | 0·9 | 0·0 | 0·9 | 1·7 | 2·6 | 3·5 | 4·4 | 5·2 | 0 30 |
| 1 00 | 4·3 | 3·5 | 2·8 | 2·1 | 1·4 | 0·7 | 0·0 | 0·7 | 1·4 | 2·1 | 2·8 | 3·5 | 4·3 | 1 00 |
| 1 30 | 3·5 | 2·9 | 2·4 | 1·8 | 1·2 | 0·6 | 0·0 | 0·6 | 1·2 | 1·8 | 2·4 | 2·9 | 3·5 | 1 30 |
| 2 00 | 3·0 | 2·5 | 2·0 | 1·5 | 1·0 | 0·5 | 0·0 | 0·5 | 1·0 | 1·5 | 2·0 | 2·5 | 3·0 | 2 00 |
| 2 30 | −2·5 | −2·1 | −1·6 | −1·2 | −0·8 | −0·4 | 0·0 | +0·4 | +0·8 | +1·2 | +1·6 | +2·1 | +2·5 | 2 30 |
| 3 00 | 2·2 | 1·8 | 1·5 | 1·1 | 0·7 | 0·4 | 0·0 | 0·4 | 0·7 | 1·1 | 1·5 | 1·8 | 2·2 | 3 00 |
| 3 30 | 2·0 | 1·6 | 1·3 | 1·0 | 0·7 | 0·3 | 0·0 | 0·3 | 0·7 | 1·0 | 1·3 | 1·6 | 2·0 | 3 30 |
| 4 00 | 1·8 | 1·5 | 1·2 | 0·9 | 0·6 | 0·3 | 0·0 | 0·3 | 0·6 | 0·9 | 1·2 | 1·5 | 1·8 | 4 00 |
| 4 30 | 1·6 | 1·4 | 1·1 | 0·8 | 0·5 | 0·3 | 0·0 | 0·3 | 0·5 | 0·8 | 1·1 | 1·4 | 1·6 | 4 30 |
| 5 00 | −1·5 | −1·3 | −1·0 | −0·8 | −0·5 | −0·2 | 0·0 | +0·2 | +0·5 | +0·8 | +1·0 | +1·3 | +1·5 | 5 00 |
| 6 | 1·3 | 1·1 | 0·9 | 0·6 | 0·4 | 0·2 | 0·0 | 0·2 | 0·4 | 0·6 | 0·9 | 1·1 | 1·3 | 6 |
| 7 | 1·1 | 0·9 | 0·7 | 0·6 | 0·4 | 0·2 | 0·0 | 0·2 | 0·4 | 0·6 | 0·7 | 0·9 | 1·1 | 7 |
| 8 | 1·0 | 0·8 | 0·7 | 0·5 | 0·3 | 0·2 | 0·0 | 0·2 | 0·3 | 0·5 | 0·7 | 0·8 | 1·0 | 8 |
| 9 | 0·9 | 0·7 | 0·6 | 0·4 | 0·3 | 0·1 | 0·0 | 0·1 | 0·3 | 0·4 | 0·6 | 0·7 | 0·9 | 9 |
| 10 00 | −0·8 | −0·7 | −0·5 | −0·4 | −0·3 | −0·1 | 0·0 | +0·1 | +0·3 | +0·4 | +0·5 | +0·7 | +0·8 | 10 00 |
| 12 | 0·7 | 0·6 | 0·5 | 0·3 | 0·2 | 0·1 | 0·0 | 0·1 | 0·2 | 0·3 | 0·5 | 0·6 | 0·7 | 12 |
| 14 | 0·6 | 0·5 | 0·4 | 0·3 | 0·2 | 0·1 | 0·0 | 0·1 | 0·2 | 0·3 | 0·4 | 0·5 | 0·6 | 14 |
| 16 | 0·5 | 0·4 | 0·3 | 0·3 | 0·2 | 0·1 | 0·0 | 0·1 | 0·2 | 0·3 | 0·3 | 0·4 | 0·5 | 16 |
| 18 | 0·4 | 0·4 | 0·3 | 0·2 | 0·2 | 0·1 | 0·0 | 0·1 | 0·2 | 0·2 | 0·3 | 0·4 | 0·4 | 18 |
| 20 00 | −0·4 | −0·3 | −0·3 | −0·2 | −0·1 | −0·1 | 0·0 | +0·1 | +0·1 | +0·2 | +0·3 | +0·3 | +0·4 | 20 00 |
| 25 | 0·3 | 0·3 | 0·2 | 0·2 | 0·1 | −0·1 | 0·0 | +0·1 | 0·1 | 0·2 | 0·2 | 0·3 | 0·3 | 25 |
| 30 | 0·3 | 0·2 | 0·2 | 0·1 | 0·1 | 0·0 | 0·0 | 0·0 | 0·1 | 0·1 | 0·2 | 0·2 | 0·3 | 30 |
| 35 | 0·2 | 0·2 | 0·1 | 0·1 | 0·1 | 0·0 | 0·0 | 0·0 | 0·1 | 0·1 | 0·1 | 0·2 | 0·2 | 35 |
| 40 | 0·2 | 0·1 | 0·1 | 0·1 | −0·1 | 0·0 | 0·0 | 0·0 | +0·1 | 0·1 | 0·1 | 0·1 | 0·2 | 40 |
| 50 00 | −0·1 | −0·1 | −0·1 | −0·1 | 0·0 | 0·0 | 0·0 | 0·0 | 0·0 | +0·1 | +0·1 | +0·1 | +0·1 | 50 00 |

The graph is entered with arguments temperature and pressure to find a zone letter; using as arguments this zone letter and apparent altitude (sextant altitude corrected for dip), a correction is taken from the table. This correction is to be applied to the sextant altitude in addition to the corrections for standard conditions (for the Sun, stars and planets from page A2 and for the Moon from pages xxxiv and xxxv).

# PLANET NOTES, 1987

## VISIBILITY OF PLANETS

VENUS is a brilliant object in the morning sky from the beginning of the year until mid-July (when it becomes too close to the Sun for observation), and in the evening sky from the end of September until the end of the year. Venus is in conjunction with Saturn on January 24 and November 20, with Jupiter on May 4, and with Mercury on July 12 and October 20.

MARS can only be seen in the evening sky for the first six months of the year, as it moves through Pisces, Aries, Taurus (passing 6°N. of *Aldebaran* on April 21), Gemini (passing 6°S. of *Pollux* on June 27) and into Cancer in early July. It soon becomes too close to the Sun for observation until shortly before mid-October when it reappears in the morning sky in Virgo. It passes 3°N. of *Spica* on November 12 and moves into Libra in early December, where it remains for the rest of the year.

JUPITER can only be seen in the evening sky at the beginning of the year in Aquarius, and it moves into Pisces in early February. In mid-March it becomes too close to the Sun for observation until shortly before mid-April when it reappears in the morning sky in Pisces, in which constellation it remains for the rest of the year. Its westward elongation gradually increases until it is at opposition on October 18 when it is visible throughout the night. Its eastward elongation then gradually decreases during the remainder of the year. Jupiter is in conjunction with Mercury on April 19 and with Venus on May 4.

SATURN rises shortly before sunrise at the beginning of the year in Ophiuchus, in which constellation it remains throughout the year, and can only be seen in the morning sky until early March. Its westward elongation gradually increases until it is at opposition on June 9, when it can be seen throughout the night. Its eastward elongation then gradually decreases, and from early September until late November it can only be seen in the evening sky. In late November it becomes too close to the Sun for observation for the remainder of the year. Saturn is in conjunction with Venus on January 24 and November 20.

MERCURY can be seen low in the east before sunrise, or low in the west after sunset (about the time of beginning or end of civil twilight). It is visible in the mornings between the following approximate dates: March 6 (+1·9) to April 29 (−1·1); July 12 (+2·2) to August 12 (−1·4); November 3 (+1·3) to December 6 (−0·6); the planet is brighter at the end of each period. It is visible in the evenings between the following approximate dates: January 26 (−1·0) to February 21 (+1·3); May 15 (−1·4) to June 26 (+2·3); August 30 (−0·8) to October 22 (+1·5); the planet is brighter at the beginning of each period. The figures in parentheses are the magnitudes.

## PLANET DIAGRAM

*General Description.* The diagram on the opposite page shows, in graphical form for any date during the year, the local mean time of meridian passage of the Sun, of the five planets Mercury, Venus, Mars, Jupiter, and Saturn, and of each 30° of S.H.A.; intermediate lines, corresponding to particular stars, may be drawn in by the user if he so desires. It is intended to provide a general picture of the availability of planets and stars for observation.

On each side of the line marking the time of meridian passage of the Sun a band, $45^m$ wide, is shaded to indicate that planets and most stars crossing the meridian within $45^m$ of the Sun are too close to the Sun for observation.

*Method of use and interpretation.* For any date the diagram provides immediately the local mean times of meridian passage of the Sun, planets and stars, and thus the following information:

(a) whether a planet or star is too close to the Sun for observation;

(b) some indication of its position in the sky, especially during twilight;

(c) the proximity of other planets.

When the meridian passage of an outer planet occurs at midnight the body is in opposition to the Sun and is visible all night; a planet may then be observable during both morning and evening twilights. As the time of meridian passage decreases, the body eventually ceases to be observable in the morning, but its altitude above the eastern horizon at sunset gradually increases; this continues until the body is on the meridian during evening twilight. From then onwards the body is observable above the western horizon and its altitude at sunset gradually decreases; eventually the body becomes too close to the Sun for observation. When the body again becomes visible it is seen low in the east during morning twilight; its altitude at sunrise increases until meridian passage occurs during morning twilight. Then, as the time of meridian passage decreases to $0^h$, the body is observable in the west during morning twilight with a gradually decreasing altitude, until it once again reaches opposition.

DO NOT CONFUSE

Venus with Saturn in late January and again for a few days after mid-November, with Jupiter in early May, and with Mercury for a few days before mid-July and again for a few days after mid-October; on all occasions Venus is the brighter object.

Mercury with Jupiter for a few days after mid-April when Jupiter is the brighter object.

Mercury with Mars in the first three weeks of June when Mercury is the brighter object. The reddish tint of Mars should assist in its identification.

## PLANETS, 1987

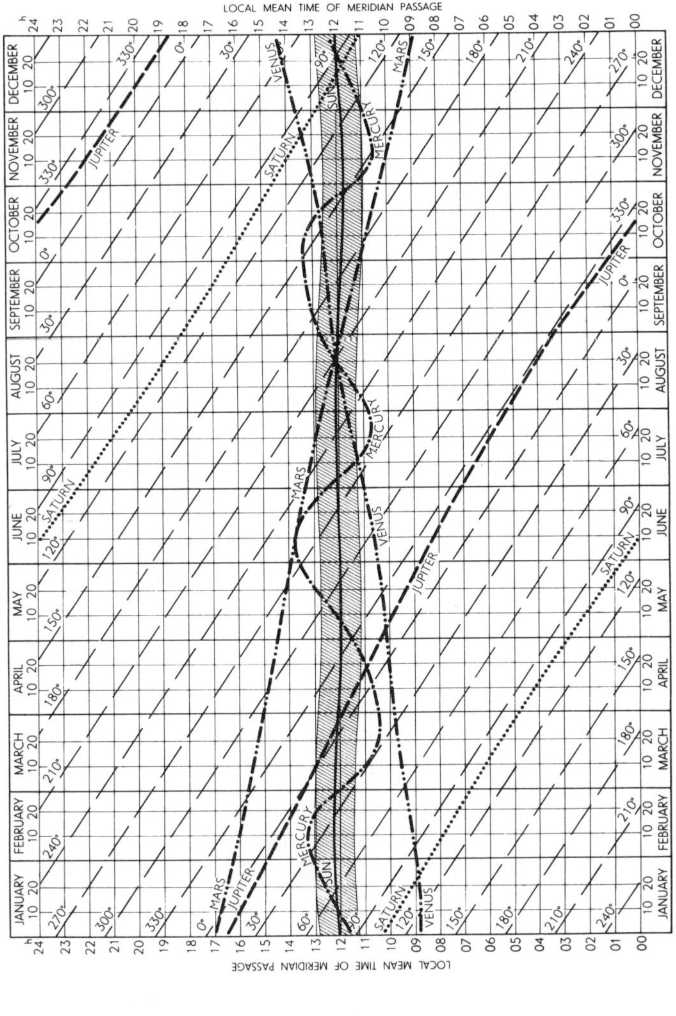

14

## 1987 JANUARY 7, 8, 9 (WED., THURS., FRI.)

| G.M.T. (UT) | ARIES | VENUS −4.5 | | MARS +0.7 | | JUPITER −2.2 | | SATURN +0.5 | | STARS | | |
|---|---|---|---|---|---|---|---|---|---|---|---|---|
| d h | G.H.A. ° ′ | G.H.A. ° ′ | Dec. ° ′ | G.H.A. ° ′ | Dec. ° ′ | G.H.A. ° ′ | Dec. ° ′ | G.H.A. ° ′ | Dec. ° ′ | Name | S.H.A. ° ′ | Dec. ° ′ |
| 7 00 | 106 01.6 | 227 48.1 | S16 26.0 | 106 51.8 | S 0 43.9 | 116 08.4 | S 5 38.7 | 211 01.2 | S21 14.1 | Acamar | 315 33.2 | S40 21.5 |
| 01 | 121 04.1 | 242 48.2 | 26.5 | 121 52.7 | 43.1 | 131 10.4 | 38.5 | 226 03.4 | 14.1 | Achernar | 335 41.3 | S57 18.4 |
| 02 | 136 06.5 | 257 48.2 | 27.0 | 136 53.6 | 42.4 | 146 12.5 | 38.3 | 241 05.6 | 14.1 | Acrux | 173 32.1 | S63 01.3 |
| 03 | 151 09.0 | 272 48.3 | · · 27.5 | 151 54.4 | · · 41.7 | 161 14.6 | · · 38.1 | 256 07.8 | · · 14.1 | Adhara | 255 27.9 | S28 57.1 |
| 04 | 166 11.5 | 287 48.3 | 28.0 | 166 55.3 | 40.9 | 176 16.6 | 38.0 | 271 09.9 | 14.2 | Aldebaran | 291 12.2 | N16 29.2 |
| 05 | 181 13.9 | 302 48.4 | 28.5 | 181 56.2 | 40.2 | 191 18.7 | 37.8 | 286 12.1 | 14.2 | | | |
| 06 | 196 16.4 | 317 48.4 | S16 29.0 | 196 57.1 | S 0 39.4 | 206 20.8 | S 5 37.6 | 301 14.3 | S21 14.2 | Alioth | 166 37.9 | N56 01.5 |
| W 07 | 211 18.9 | 332 48.5 | 29.5 | 211 58.0 | 38.7 | 221 22.9 | 37.4 | 316 16.5 | 14.3 | Alkaid | 153 14.5 | N49 22.3 |
| E 08 | 226 21.3 | 347 48.5 | 30.0 | 226 58.9 | 37.9 | 236 24.9 | 37.3 | 331 13.6 | 14.3 | Al Na'ir | 28 09.0 | S47 01.8 |
| D 09 | 241 23.8 | 2 48.6 | · · 30.5 | 241 59.7 | · · 37.2 | 251 27.0 | · · 37.1 | 346 20.8 | · · 14.3 | Alnilam | 276 06.4 | S 1 12.5 |
| N 10 | 256 26.3 | 17 48.6 | 31.0 | 257 00.6 | 36.5 | 266 29.1 | 36.9 | 1 23.0 | 14.3 | Alphard | 218 15.5 | S 8 36.0 |
| E 11 | 271 28.7 | 32 48.7 | 31.6 | 272 01.5 | 35.7 | 281 31.1 | 36.7 | 16 25.2 | 14.4 | | | |
| S 12 | 286 31.2 | 47 48.7 | S16 32.1 | 287 02.4 | S 0 35.0 | 296 33.2 | S 5 36.6 | 31 27.4 | S21 14.4 | Alphecca | 126 28.2 | N26 45.2 |
| D 13 | 301 33.6 | 62 48.7 | 32.6 | 302 03.3 | 34.2 | 311 35.3 | 36.4 | 46 29.5 | 14.4 | Alpheratz | 358 04.5 | N29 01.2 |
| A 14 | 316 36.1 | 77 48.8 | 33.1 | 317 04.1 | 33.5 | 326 37.4 | 36.2 | 61 31.7 | 14.4 | Altair | 62 28.2 | N 8 49.8 |
| Y 15 | 331 38.6 | 92 48.8 | · · 33.6 | 332 05.0 | · · 32.7 | 341 39.4 | · · 36.0 | 76 33.9 | · · 14.5 | Ankaa | 353 35.3 | S42 22.9 |
| 16 | 346 41.0 | 107 48.9 | 34.1 | 347 05.9 | 32.0 | 356 41.5 | 35.9 | 91 36.1 | 14.5 | Antares | 112 51.2 | S26 24.3 |
| 17 | 1 43.5 | 122 48.9 | 34.6 | 2 06.8 | 31.3 | 11 43.6 | 35.7 | 106 38.2 | 14.5 | | | |
| 18 | 16 46.0 | 137 48.9 | S16 35.1 | 17 07.7 | S 0 30.5 | 26 45.6 | S 5 35.5 | 121 40.4 | S21 14.6 | Arcturus | 146 14.1 | N19 14.8 |
| 19 | 31 48.4 | 152 49.0 | 35.6 | 32 08.5 | 29.8 | 41 47.7 | 35.4 | 136 42.6 | 14.6 | Atria | 108 11.8 | S69 00.3 |
| 20 | 46 50.9 | 167 49.0 | 36.1 | 47 09.4 | 29.0 | 56 49.8 | 35.2 | 151 44.8 | 14.6 | Avior | 234 25.8 | S59 27.8 |
| 21 | 61 53.4 | 182 49.1 | · · 36.6 | 62 10.3 | · · 28.3 | 71 51.9 | · · 35.0 | 166 46.9 | · · 14.6 | Bellatrix | 278 53.2 | N 6 20.4 |
| 22 | 76 55.8 | 197 49.1 | 37.1 | 77 11.2 | 27.5 | 86 53.9 | 34.8 | 181 49.1 | 14.7 | Betelgeuse | 271 22.7 | N 7 24.4 |
| 23 | 91 58.3 | 212 49.1 | 37.6 | 92 12.1 | 26.8 | 101 56.0 | 34.7 | 196 51.3 | 14.7 | | | |
| 8 00 | 107 00.8 | 227 49.1 | S16 38.1 | 107 13.0 | S 0 26.1 | 116 58.1 | S 5 34.5 | 211 53.5 | S21 14.7 | Canopus | 264 04.5 | S52 41.2 |
| 01 | 122 03.2 | 242 49.2 | 38.6 | 122 13.8 | 25.3 | 132 00.1 | 34.3 | 226 55.7 | 14.7 | Capella | 281 03.7 | N45 59.4 |
| 02 | 137 05.7 | 257 49.2 | 39.1 | 137 14.7 | 24.6 | 147 02.2 | 34.1 | 241 57.8 | 14.8 | Deneb | 49 45.7 | N45 14.0 |
| 03 | 152 08.1 | 272 49.2 | · · 39.6 | 152 15.6 | · · 23.8 | 162 04.3 | · · 34.0 | 257 00.0 | · · 14.8 | Denebola | 182 53.9 | N14 38.6 |
| 04 | 167 10.6 | 287 49.3 | 40.1 | 167 16.5 | 23.1 | 177 06.3 | 33.8 | 272 02.2 | 14.8 | Diphda | 349 16.0 | S18 03.6 |
| 05 | 182 13.1 | 302 49.3 | 40.6 | 182 17.4 | 22.4 | 192 08.4 | 33.6 | 287 04.4 | 14.8 | | | |
| 06 | 197 15.5 | 317 49.3 | S16 41.1 | 197 18.2 | S 0 21.6 | 207 10.5 | S 5 33.4 | 302 06.6 | S21 14.9 | Dubhe | 194 15.4 | N61 49.1 |
| 07 | 212 18.0 | 332 49.3 | 41.6 | 212 19.1 | 20.9 | 222 12.5 | 33.3 | 317 08.7 | 14.9 | Elnath | 278 37.7 | N28 36.0 |
| T 08 | 227 20.5 | 347 49.4 | 42.1 | 227 20.0 | 20.1 | 237 14.6 | 33.1 | 332 10.9 | 14.9 | Eltanin | 90 56.0 | N51 29.2 |
| H 09 | 242 22.9 | 2 49.4 | · · 42.6 | 242 20.9 | · · 19.4 | 252 16.7 | · · 32.9 | 347 13.1 | · · 15.0 | Enif | 34 07.1 | N 9 48.8 |
| U 10 | 257 25.4 | 17 49.4 | 43.0 | 257 21.8 | 18.6 | 267 18.7 | 32.7 | 2 15.3 | 15.0 | Fomalhaut | 15 46.2 | S29 41.7 |
| R 11 | 272 27.9 | 32 49.4 | 43.5 | 272 22.6 | 17.9 | 282 20.8 | 32.5 | 17 17.4 | 15.0 | | | |
| S 12 | 287 30.3 | 47 49.4 | S16 44.0 | 287 23.5 | S 0 17.2 | 297 22.9 | S 5 32.4 | 32 19.6 | S21 15.0 | Gacrux | 172 23.6 | S57 02.2 |
| D 13 | 302 32.8 | 62 49.4 | 44.5 | 302 24.4 | 16.4 | 312 24.9 | 32.2 | 47 21.8 | 15.1 | Gienah | 176 13.0 | S17 28.1 |
| A 14 | 317 35.3 | 77 49.5 | 45.0 | 317 25.3 | 15.7 | 327 27.0 | 32.0 | 62 24.0 | 15.1 | Hadar | 149 17.0 | S60 18.4 |
| Y 15 | 332 37.7 | 92 49.5 | · · 45.5 | 332 26.2 | · · 14.9 | 342 29.1 | · · 31.8 | 77 26.2 | · · 15.1 | Hamal | 328 23.4 | N23 24.2 |
| 16 | 347 40.2 | 107 49.5 | 46.0 | 347 27.0 | 14.2 | 357 31.1 | 31.7 | 92 28.3 | 15.1 | Kaus Aust. | 84 10.8 | S34 23.6 |
| 17 | 2 42.6 | 122 49.5 | 46.5 | 2 27.9 | 13.4 | 12 33.2 | 31.5 | 107 30.5 | 15.2 | | | |
| 18 | 17 45.1 | 137 49.5 | S16 47.0 | 17 28.8 | S 0 12.7 | 27 35.3 | S 5 31.3 | 122 32.7 | S21 15.2 | Kochab | 137 19.2 | N74 12.1 |
| 19 | 32 47.6 | 152 49.5 | 47.5 | 32 29.7 | 12.0 | 42 37.3 | 31.1 | 137 34.9 | 15.2 | Markab | 13 58.6 | N15 08.1 |
| 20 | 47 50.0 | 167 49.5 | 48.0 | 47 30.6 | 11.2 | 57 39.4 | 31.0 | 152 37.1 | 15.2 | Menkar | 314 35.9 | N 4 02.4 |
| 21 | 62 52.5 | 182 49.5 | · · 48.5 | 62 31.5 | · · 10.5 | 72 41.5 | · · 30.8 | 167 39.2 | · · 15.3 | Menkent | 148 31.5 | S36 18.3 |
| 22 | 77 55.0 | 197 49.5 | 49.0 | 77 32.3 | 09.7 | 87 43.5 | 30.6 | 182 41.4 | 15.3 | Miaplacidus | 221 43.5 | S69 39.6 |
| 23 | 92 57.4 | 212 49.6 | 49.5 | 92 33.2 | 09.0 | 102 45.6 | 30.4 | 197 43.6 | 15.3 | | | |
| 9 00 | 107 59.9 | 227 49.6 | S16 50.0 | 107 34.1 | S 0 08.3 | 117 47.7 | S 5 30.3 | 212 45.8 | S21 15.3 | Mirfak | 309 09.0 | N49 49.2 |
| 01 | 123 02.4 | 242 49.6 | 50.5 | 122 35.0 | 07.5 | 132 49.7 | 30.1 | 227 48.0 | 15.4 | Nunki | 76 23.5 | S26 19.0 |
| 02 | 138 04.8 | 257 49.6 | 51.0 | 137 35.9 | 06.8 | 147 51.8 | 29.9 | 242 50.1 | 15.4 | Peacock | 53 51.1 | S56 46.9 |
| 03 | 153 07.3 | 272 49.6 | · · 51.5 | 152 36.7 | · · 06.0 | 162 53.9 | · · 29.7 | 257 52.3 | · · 15.4 | Pollux | 243 51.8 | N28 03.6 |
| 04 | 168 09.7 | 287 49.6 | 52.0 | 167 37.6 | 05.3 | 177 55.9 | 29.5 | 272 54.5 | 15.5 | Procyon | 245 20.4 | N 5 15.6 |
| 05 | 183 12.2 | 302 49.6 | 52.5 | 182 38.5 | 04.5 | 192 58.0 | 29.4 | 287 56.7 | 15.5 | | | |
| 06 | 198 14.7 | 317 49.6 | S16 53.0 | 197 39.4 | S 0 03.8 | 208 00.0 | S 5 29.2 | 302 58.8 | S21 15.5 | Rasalhague | 96 25.4 | N12 33.9 |
| 07 | 213 17.1 | 332 49.6 | 53.5 | 212 40.3 | 03.1 | 223 02.1 | 29.0 | 318 01.0 | 15.5 | Regulus | 208 04.6 | N12 01.9 |
| 08 | 228 19.6 | 347 49.6 | 54.0 | 227 41.1 | 02.3 | 238 04.2 | 28.8 | 333 03.2 | 15.6 | Rigel | 281 31.0 | S 8 12.9 |
| F 09 | 243 22.1 | 2 49.5 | · · 54.5 | 242 42.0 | · · 01.6 | 253 06.2 | · · 28.7 | 348 05.4 | · · 15.6 | Rigil Kent. | 140 19.7 | S60 46.7 |
| R 10 | 258 24.5 | 17 49.5 | 55.0 | 257 42.9 | 00.8 | 268 08.3 | 28.5 | 3 07.6 | 15.6 | Sabik | 102 35.9 | S15 42.7 |
| I 11 | 273 27.0 | 32 49.5 | 55.5 | 272 43.8 | S 0 00.1 | 283 10.4 | 28.3 | 18 09.8 | 15.6 | | | |
| D 12 | 288 29.5 | 47 49.5 | S16 56.0 | 287 44.7 | N 0 00.6 | 298 12.4 | S 5 28.1 | 33 11.9 | S21 15.7 | Schedar | 350 03.9 | N56 28.2 |
| A 13 | 303 31.9 | 62 49.5 | 56.5 | 302 45.5 | 01.4 | 313 14.5 | 28.0 | 48 14.1 | 15.7 | Shaula | 96 49.6 | S37 05.8 |
| Y 14 | 318 34.4 | 77 49.5 | 57.0 | 317 46.4 | 02.1 | 328 16.6 | 27.8 | 63 16.3 | 15.7 | Sirius | 258 51.1 | S16 41.8 |
| 15 | 333 36.9 | 92 49.5 | · · 57.5 | 332 47.3 | · · 02.9 | 343 18.6 | · · 27.6 | 78 18.5 | · · 15.7 | Spica | 158 52.5 | S11 05.6 |
| 16 | 348 39.3 | 107 49.5 | 58.0 | 347 48.2 | 03.6 | 358 20.7 | 27.4 | 93 20.7 | 15.8 | Suhail | 223 07.0 | S43 22.6 |
| 17 | 3 41.8 | 122 49.5 | 58.5 | 2 49.1 | 04.4 | 13 22.7 | 27.2 | 108 22.8 | 15.8 | | | |
| 18 | 18 44.2 | 137 49.5 | S16 58.9 | 17 50.0 | N 0 05.1 | 28 24.8 | S 5 27.1 | 123 25.0 | S21 15.8 | Vega | 80 53.0 | N38 46.1 |
| 19 | 33 46.7 | 152 49.4 | 59.4 | 32 50.8 | 05.8 | 43 26.9 | 26.9 | 138 27.2 | 15.8 | Zuben'ubi | 137 27.9 | S15 59.3 |
| 20 | 48 49.2 | 167 49.4 | 16 59.9 | 47 51.7 | 06.6 | 58 28.9 | 26.7 | 153 29.4 | 15.9 | | S.H.A. ° ′ | Mer. Pass. h m |
| 21 | 63 51.6 | 182 49.4 | 17 00.4 | 62 52.6 | · · 07.3 | 73 31.0 | · · 26.5 | 168 31.6 | · · 15.9 | | | |
| 22 | 78 54.1 | 197 49.4 | 00.9 | 77 53.5 | 08.1 | 88 33.0 | 26.3 | 183 33.7 | 15.9 | Venus | 120 48.4 | 8 49 |
| 23 | 93 56.6 | 212 49.4 | 01.4 | 92 54.4 | 08.8 | 103 35.1 | 26.2 | 198 35.9 | 15.9 | Mars | 0 12.2 | 16 50 |
| Mer. Pass. | h m 16 49.2 | v 0.0 | d 0.5 | v 0.9 | d 0.7 | v 2.1 | d 0.2 | v 2.2 | d 0.0 | Jupiter | 9 57.3 | 16 10 |
| | | | | | | | | | | Saturn | 104 52.7 | 9 51 |

## 1987 JANUARY 7, 8, 9 (WED., THURS., FRI.)



| | G.M.T. (UT) d h | SUN G.H.A. ° ′ | SUN Dec. ° ′ | MOON G.H.A. ° ′ | v ′ | MOON Dec. ° ′ | d ′ | H.P. ′ |
|---|---|---|---|---|---|---|---|---|
| | 7 00 | 178 31.2 | S22 28.1 | 90 31.9 | 15.0 | N 6 39.5 | 14.7 | 56.3 |
| | 01 | 193 30.9 | 27.8 | 105 05.9 | 15.0 | 6 54.2 | 14.7 | 56.3 |
| | 02 | 208 30.7 | 27.4 | 119 39.9 | 15.0 | 7 08.9 | 14.7 | 56.3 |
| | 03 | 223 30.4 | . . 27.1 | 134 13.9 | 15.0 | 7 23.6 | 14.6 | 56.2 |
| | 04 | 238 30.1 | 26.8 | 148 47.9 | 15.0 | 7 38.2 | 14.5 | 56.2 |
| | 05 | 253 29.9 | 26.5 | 163 21.9 | 15.1 | 7 52.7 | 14.5 | 56.2 |
| | 06 | 268 29.6 | S22 26.2 | 177 56.0 | 15.0 | N 8 07.2 | 14.5 | 56.1 |
| W | 07 | 283 29.3 | 25.9 | 192 30.0 | 15.0 | 8 21.7 | 14.4 | 56.1 |
| E | 08 | 298 29.0 | 25.6 | 207 04.0 | 15.0 | 8 36.1 | 14.4 | 56.1 |
| D | 09 | 313 28.8 | . . 25.3 | 221 38.0 | 15.0 | 8 50.5 | 14.3 | 56.0 |
| N | 10 | 328 28.5 | 25.0 | 236 12.0 | 15.0 | 9 04.8 | 14.2 | 56.0 |
| E | 11 | 343 28.2 | 24.7 | 250 46.0 | 15.0 | 9 19.0 | 14.2 | 56.0 |
| S | 12 | 358 28.0 | S22 24.3 | 265 20.0 | 14.9 | N 9 33.2 | 14.2 | 55.9 |
| D | 13 | 13 27.7 | 24.0 | 279 53.9 | 15.0 | 9 47.4 | 14.1 | 55.9 |
| A | 14 | 28 27.4 | 23.7 | 294 27.9 | 15.0 | 10 01.5 | 14.0 | 55.9 |
| Y | 15 | 43 27.1 | . . 23.4 | 309 01.9 | 14.9 | 10 15.5 | 14.0 | 55.9 |
| | 16 | 58 26.9 | 23.1 | 323 35.8 | 14.9 | 10 29.5 | 13.9 | 55.8 |
| | 17 | 73 26.6 | 22.8 | 338 09.7 | 14.9 | 10 43.4 | 13.9 | 55.8 |
| | 18 | 88 26.3 | S22 22.4 | 352 43.6 | 14.9 | N10 57.3 | 13.8 | 55.8 |
| | 19 | 103 26.1 | 22.1 | 7 17.5 | 14.9 | 11 11.1 | 13.7 | 55.7 |
| | 20 | 118 25.8 | 21.8 | 21 51.4 | 14.9 | 11 24.8 | 13.7 | 55.7 |
| | 21 | 133 25.5 | . . 21.5 | 36 25.3 | 14.9 | 11 38.5 | 13.6 | 55.7 |
| | 22 | 148 25.3 | 21.2 | 50 59.2 | 14.8 | 11 52.1 | 13.6 | 55.6 |
| | 23 | 163 25.0 | 20.8 | 65 33.0 | 14.8 | 12 05.7 | 13.5 | 55.6 |
| | 8 00 | 178 24.7 | S22 20.5 | 80 06.8 | 14.8 | N12 19.2 | 13.4 | 55.6 |
| | 01 | 193 24.5 | 20.2 | 94 40.6 | 14.8 | 12 32.6 | 13.4 | 55.6 |
| | 02 | 208 24.2 | 19.9 | 109 14.4 | 14.7 | 12 46.0 | 13.3 | 55.5 |
| | 03 | 223 23.9 | . . 19.5 | 123 48.1 | 14.7 | 12 59.3 | 13.3 | 55.5 |
| | 04 | 238 23.7 | 19.2 | 138 21.8 | 14.7 | 13 12.6 | 13.1 | 55.5 |
| | 05 | 253 23.4 | 18.9 | 152 55.5 | 14.7 | 13 25.7 | 13.1 | 55.5 |
| | 06 | 268 23.1 | S22 18.6 | 167 29.2 | 14.6 | N13 38.8 | 13.1 | 55.4 |
| | 07 | 283 22.8 | 18.2 | 182 02.8 | 14.6 | 13 51.9 | 13.0 | 55.4 |
| T | 08 | 298 22.6 | 17.9 | 196 36.4 | 14.6 | 14 04.9 | 12.9 | 55.4 |
| H | 09 | 313 22.3 | . . 17.6 | 211 10.0 | 14.6 | 14 17.8 | 12.8 | 55.3 |
| U | 10 | 328 22.1 | 17.3 | 225 43.6 | 14.5 | 14 30.6 | 12.8 | 55.3 |
| R | 11 | 343 21.8 | 16.9 | 240 17.1 | 14.5 | 14 43.4 | 12.7 | 55.3 |
| S | 12 | 358 21.5 | S22 16.6 | 254 50.6 | 14.5 | N14 56.1 | 12.6 | 55.3 |
| D | 13 | 13 21.3 | 16.3 | 269 24.1 | 14.4 | 15 08.7 | 12.5 | 55.2 |
| A | 14 | 28 21.0 | 15.9 | 283 57.5 | 14.4 | 15 21.2 | 12.5 | 55.2 |
| Y | 15 | 43 20.7 | . . 15.6 | 298 30.9 | 14.4 | 15 33.7 | 12.4 | 55.2 |
| | 16 | 58 20.5 | 15.3 | 313 04.3 | 14.3 | 15 46.1 | 12.4 | 55.2 |
| | 17 | 73 20.2 | 14.9 | 327 37.6 | 14.3 | 15 58.5 | 12.2 | 55.1 |
| | 18 | 88 19.9 | S22 14.6 | 342 10.9 | 14.2 | N16 10.7 | 12.2 | 55.1 |
| | 19 | 103 19.7 | 14.2 | 356 44.1 | 14.2 | 16 22.9 | 12.1 | 55.1 |
| | 20 | 118 19.4 | 13.9 | 11 17.3 | 14.2 | 16 35.0 | 12.0 | 55.1 |
| | 21 | 133 19.1 | . . 13.6 | 25 50.5 | 14.1 | 16 47.0 | 12.0 | 55.1 |
| | 22 | 148 18.9 | 13.2 | 40 23.6 | 14.1 | 16 59.0 | 11.8 | 55.0 |
| | 23 | 163 18.6 | 12.9 | 54 56.7 | 14.1 | 17 10.8 | 11.8 | 55.0 |
| | 9 00 | 178 18.4 | S22 12.5 | 69 29.8 | 14.0 | N17 22.6 | 11.7 | 55.0 |
| | 01 | 193 18.1 | 12.2 | 84 02.8 | 14.0 | 17 34.3 | 11.6 | 55.0 |
| | 02 | 208 17.8 | 11.9 | 98 35.8 | 13.9 | 17 45.9 | 11.6 | 54.9 |
| | 03 | 223 17.6 | . . 11.5 | 113 08.7 | 13.9 | 17 57.5 | 11.4 | 54.9 |
| | 04 | 238 17.3 | 11.2 | 127 41.6 | 13.8 | 18 08.9 | 11.4 | 54.9 |
| | 05 | 253 17.0 | 10.8 | 142 14.4 | 13.8 | 18 20.3 | 11.3 | 54.9 |
| | 06 | 268 16.8 | S22 10.5 | 156 47.2 | 13.8 | N18 31.6 | 11.2 | 54.9 |
| | 07 | 283 16.5 | 10.1 | 171 20.0 | 13.7 | 18 42.8 | 11.1 | 54.8 |
| | 08 | 298 16.3 | 09.8 | 185 52.7 | 13.7 | 18 53.9 | 11.1 | 54.8 |
| F | 09 | 313 16.0 | . . 09.4 | 200 25.4 | 13.6 | 19 05.0 | 10.9 | 54.8 |
| R | 10 | 328 15.7 | 09.1 | 214 58.0 | 13.5 | 19 15.9 | 10.9 | 54.8 |
| I | 11 | 343 15.5 | 08.7 | 229 30.5 | 13.5 | 19 26.8 | 10.7 | 54.8 |
| D | 12 | 358 15.2 | S22 08.4 | 244 03.0 | 13.5 | N19 37.5 | 10.7 | 54.7 |
| A | 13 | 13 15.0 | 08.0 | 258 35.5 | 13.4 | 19 48.2 | 10.6 | 54.7 |
| Y | 14 | 28 14.7 | 07.7 | 273 07.9 | 13.4 | 19 58.8 | 10.5 | 54.7 |
| | 15 | 43 14.4 | . . 07.3 | 287 40.3 | 13.3 | 20 09.3 | 10.4 | 54.7 |
| | 16 | 58 14.2 | 07.0 | 302 12.6 | 13.3 | 20 19.7 | 10.3 | 54.7 |
| | 17 | 73 13.9 | 06.6 | 316 44.9 | 13.2 | 20 30.0 | 10.3 | 54.6 |
| | 18 | 88 13.7 | S22 06.3 | 331 17.1 | 13.2 | N20 40.3 | 10.1 | 54.6 |
| | 19 | 103 13.4 | 05.9 | 345 49.3 | 13.1 | 20 50.4 | 10.0 | 54.6 |
| | 20 | 118 13.1 | 05.6 | 0 21.4 | 13.1 | 21 00.4 | 10.0 | 54.6 |
| | 21 | 133 12.9 | . . 05.2 | 14 53.5 | 13.0 | 21 10.4 | 9.8 | 54.6 |
| | 22 | 148 12.6 | 04.9 | 29 25.5 | 13.0 | 21 20.2 | 9.7 | 54.6 |
| | 23 | 163 12.4 | 04.5 | 43 57.5 | 12.9 | 21 29.9 | 9.7 | 54.5 |
| | | S.D. 16.3 | *d* 0.3 | S.D. 15.2 | | 15.1 | | 14.9 |

| Lat. | Twilight Naut. | Twilight Civil | Sunrise | Moonrise 7 | Moonrise 8 | Moonrise 9 | Moonrise 10 |
|---|---|---|---|---|---|---|---|
| ° | h m | h m | h m | h m | h m | h m | h m |
| N 72 | 08 16 | 10 21 | ■ | 10 19 | 09 30 | ▭ | ▭ |
| N 70 | 07 59 | 09 37 | ■ | 10 32 | 09 58 | 08 55 | ▭ |
| 68 | 07 45 | 09 08 | 11 12 | 10 43 | 10 19 | 09 43 | ▭ |
| 66 | 07 33 | 08 47 | 10 14 | 10 52 | 10 36 | 10 15 | 09 34 |
| 64 | 07 23 | 08 29 | 09 41 | 10 59 | 10 50 | 10 38 | 10 21 |
| 62 | 07 15 | 08 15 | 09 17 | 11 06 | 11 01 | 10 57 | 10 52 |
| 60 | 07 07 | 08 02 | 08 57 | 11 12 | 11 12 | 11 12 | 11 15 |
| N 58 | 07 00 | 07 52 | 08 42 | 11 17 | 11 20 | 11 25 | 11 34 |
| 56 | 06 54 | 07 42 | 08 28 | 11 22 | 11 28 | 11 37 | 11 49 |
| 54 | 06 48 | 07 34 | 08 17 | 11 26 | 11 35 | 11 47 | 12 03 |
| 52 | 06 43 | 07 26 | 08 06 | 11 29 | 11 41 | 11 56 | 12 15 |
| 50 | 06 38 | 07 19 | 07 57 | 11 33 | 11 47 | 12 04 | 12 25 |
| 45 | 06 28 | 07 04 | 07 38 | 11 40 | 11 59 | 12 21 | 12 47 |
| N 40 | 06 18 | 06 52 | 07 22 | 11 47 | 12 10 | 12 35 | 13 05 |
| 35 | 06 09 | 06 41 | 07 09 | 11 52 | 12 18 | 12 47 | 13 20 |
| 30 | 06 01 | 06 31 | 06 57 | 11 57 | 12 26 | 12 58 | 13 34 |
| 20 | 05 46 | 06 13 | 06 37 | 12 05 | 12 40 | 13 16 | 13 56 |
| N 10 | 05 31 | 05 57 | 06 19 | 12 13 | 12 52 | 13 32 | 14 16 |
| 0 | 05 14 | 05 40 | 06 03 | 12 20 | 13 03 | 13 47 | 14 34 |
| S 10 | 04 56 | 05 23 | 05 46 | 12 27 | 13 14 | 14 03 | 14 53 |
| 20 | 04 35 | 05 04 | 05 28 | 12 34 | 13 26 | 14 19 | 15 13 |
| 30 | 04 07 | 04 40 | 05 07 | 12 43 | 13 40 | 14 38 | 15 36 |
| 35 | 03 50 | 04 26 | 04 55 | 12 48 | 13 49 | 14 49 | 15 49 |
| 40 | 03 28 | 04 09 | 04 41 | 12 54 | 13 58 | 15 02 | 16 05 |
| 45 | 02 59 | 03 47 | 04 24 | 13 01 | 14 09 | 15 17 | 16 24 |
| S 50 | 02 18 | 03 20 | 04 03 | 13 09 | 14 22 | 15 35 | 16 48 |
| 52 | 01 54 | 03 06 | 03 53 | 13 13 | 14 29 | 15 44 | 16 59 |
| 54 | 01 21 | 02 49 | 03 41 | 13 17 | 14 36 | 15 54 | 17 12 |
| 56 | //// | 02 30 | 03 28 | 13 22 | 14 43 | 16 06 | 17 27 |
| 58 | //// | 02 04 | 03 13 | 13 27 | 14 52 | 16 19 | 17 45 |
| S 60 | //// | 01 28 | 02 55 | 13 33 | 15 02 | 16 34 | 18 07 |

| Lat. | Sunset | Twilight Civil | Twilight Naut. | Moonset 7 | Moonset 8 | Moonset 9 | Moonset 10 |
|---|---|---|---|---|---|---|---|
| ° | h m | h m | h m | h m | h m | h m | h m |
| N 72 | ■ | 13 53 | 15 58 | 01 28 | 03 48 | ▭ | ▭ |
| N 70 | ■ | 14 36 | 16 15 | 01 17 | 03 22 | 05 58 | ▭ |
| 68 | 13 01 | 15 05 | 16 29 | 01 09 | 03 03 | 05 11 | ▭ |
| 66 | 14 00 | 15 27 | 16 41 | 01 02 | 02 47 | 04 40 | 06 57 |
| 64 | 14 33 | 15 44 | 16 50 | 00 56 | 02 35 | 04 18 | 06 11 |
| 62 | 14 57 | 15 59 | 16 59 | 00 51 | 02 24 | 04 00 | 05 41 |
| 60 | 15 16 | 16 11 | 17 07 | 00 46 | 02 15 | 03 46 | 05 18 |
| N 58 | 15 32 | 16 22 | 17 13 | 00 42 | 02 08 | 03 33 | 05 00 |
| 56 | 15 45 | 16 31 | 17 19 | 00 39 | 02 01 | 03 23 | 04 45 |
| 54 | 15 57 | 16 40 | 17 25 | 00 36 | 01 55 | 03 13 | 04 32 |
| 52 | 16 07 | 16 47 | 17 30 | 00 33 | 01 49 | 03 05 | 04 20 |
| 50 | 16 16 | 16 54 | 17 35 | 00 31 | 01 44 | 02 57 | 04 10 |
| 45 | 16 36 | 17 09 | 17 46 | 00 25 | 01 34 | 02 42 | 03 49 |
| N 40 | 16 51 | 17 21 | 17 55 | 00 21 | 01 25 | 02 29 | 03 32 |
| 35 | 17 05 | 17 32 | 18 04 | 00 17 | 01 17 | 02 18 | 03 18 |
| 30 | 17 16 | 17 42 | 18 12 | 00 13 | 01 11 | 02 08 | 03 06 |
| 20 | 17 36 | 18 00 | 18 27 | 00 07 | 00 59 | 01 52 | 02 45 |
| N 10 | 17 54 | 18 16 | 18 43 | 00 02 | 00 50 | 01 37 | 02 27 |
| 0 | 18 10 | 18 33 | 18 59 | 24 40 | 00 40 | 01 24 | 02 10 |
| S 10 | 18 27 | 18 50 | 19 17 | 24 31 | 00 31 | 01 11 | 01 53 |
| 20 | 18 45 | 19 09 | 19 38 | 24 21 | 00 21 | 00 57 | 01 35 |
| 30 | 19 06 | 19 33 | 20 05 | 24 10 | 00 10 | 00 41 | 01 14 |
| 35 | 19 18 | 19 47 | 20 23 | 24 04 | 00 04 | 00 31 | 01 02 |
| 40 | 19 32 | 20 04 | 20 45 | 23 57 | 24 21 | 00 21 | 00 49 |
| 45 | 19 49 | 20 25 | 21 13 | 23 48 | 24 09 | 00 09 | 00 32 |
| S 50 | 20 10 | 20 53 | 21 54 | 23 38 | 23 54 | 24 13 | 00 13 |
| 52 | 20 20 | 21 06 | 22 17 | 23 34 | 23 47 | 24 03 | 00 03 |
| 54 | 20 31 | 21 23 | 22 50 | 23 29 | 23 39 | 23 53 | 24 12 |
| 56 | 20 44 | 21 42 | //// | 23 23 | 23 30 | 23 41 | 23 56 |
| 58 | 20 59 | 22 07 | //// | 23 17 | 23 21 | 23 27 | 23 38 |
| S 60 | 21 17 | 22 43 | //// | 23 10 | 23 10 | 23 11 | 23 15 |

| Day | SUN Eqn. of Time 00ʰ | SUN Eqn. of Time 12ʰ | SUN Mer. Pass. | MOON Mer. Pass. Upper | MOON Mer. Pass. Lower | MOON Age | MOON Phase |
|---|---|---|---|---|---|---|---|
| | m s | m s | h m | h m | h m | d | |
| 7 | 05 55 | 06 08 | 12 06 | 18 30 | 06 09 | 07 | |
| 8 | 06 21 | 06 33 | 12 07 | 19 13 | 06 52 | 08 | ◐ |
| 9 | 06 46 | 06 59 | 12 07 | 19 59 | 07 36 | 09 | |

## CONVERSION OF ARC TO TIME

| 0°–59° | | 60°–119° | | 120°–179° | | 180°–239° | | 240°–299° | | 300°–359° | | | 0′·00 | 0′·25 | 0′·50 | 0′·75 |
|---|---|---|---|---|---|---|---|---|---|---|---|---|---|---|---|---|
| ° | h m | ° | h m | ° | h m | ° | h m | ° | h m | ° | h m | ′ | m s | m s | m s | m s |
| 0 | 0 00 | 60 | 4 00 | 120 | 8 00 | 180 | 12 00 | 240 | 16 00 | 300 | 20 00 | 0 | 0 00 | 0 01 | 0 02 | 0 03 |
| 1 | 0 04 | 61 | 4 04 | 121 | 8 04 | 181 | 12 04 | 241 | 16 04 | 301 | 20 04 | 1 | 0 04 | 0 05 | 0 06 | 0 07 |
| 2 | 0 08 | 62 | 4 08 | 122 | 8 08 | 182 | 12 08 | 242 | 16 08 | 302 | 20 08 | 2 | 0 08 | 0 09 | 0 10 | 0 11 |
| 3 | 0 12 | 63 | 4 12 | 123 | 8 12 | 183 | 12 12 | 243 | 16 12 | 303 | 20 12 | 3 | 0 12 | 0 13 | 0 14 | 0 15 |
| 4 | 0 16 | 64 | 4 16 | 124 | 8 16 | 184 | 12 16 | 244 | 16 16 | 304 | 20 16 | 4 | 0 16 | 0 17 | 0 18 | 0 19 |
| 5 | 0 20 | 65 | 4 20 | 125 | 8 20 | 185 | 12 20 | 245 | 16 20 | 305 | 20 20 | 5 | 0 20 | 0 21 | 0 22 | 0 23 |
| 6 | 0 24 | 66 | 4 24 | 126 | 8 24 | 186 | 12 24 | 246 | 16 24 | 306 | 20 24 | 6 | 0 24 | 0 25 | 0 26 | 0 27 |
| 7 | 0 28 | 67 | 4 28 | 127 | 8 28 | 187 | 12 28 | 247 | 16 28 | 307 | 20 28 | 7 | 0 28 | 0 29 | 0 30 | 0 31 |
| 8 | 0 32 | 68 | 4 32 | 128 | 8 32 | 188 | 12 32 | 248 | 16 32 | 308 | 20 32 | 8 | 0 32 | 0 33 | 0 34 | 0 35 |
| 9 | 0 36 | 69 | 4 36 | 129 | 8 36 | 189 | 12 36 | 249 | 16 36 | 309 | 20 36 | 9 | 0 36 | 0 37 | 0 38 | 0 39 |
| 10 | 0 40 | 70 | 4 40 | 130 | 8 40 | 190 | 12 40 | 250 | 16 40 | 310 | 20 40 | 10 | 0 40 | 0 41 | 0 42 | 0 43 |
| 11 | 0 44 | 71 | 4 44 | 131 | 8 44 | 191 | 12 44 | 251 | 16 44 | 311 | 20 44 | 11 | 0 44 | 0 45 | 0 46 | 0 47 |
| 12 | 0 48 | 72 | 4 48 | 132 | 8 48 | 192 | 12 48 | 252 | 16 48 | 312 | 20 48 | 12 | 0 48 | 0 49 | 0 50 | 0 51 |
| 13 | 0 52 | 73 | 4 52 | 133 | 8 52 | 193 | 12 52 | 253 | 16 52 | 313 | 20 52 | 13 | 0 52 | 0 53 | 0 54 | 0 55 |
| 14 | 0 56 | 74 | 4 56 | 134 | 8 56 | 194 | 12 56 | 254 | 16 56 | 314 | 20 56 | 14 | 0 56 | 0 57 | 0 58 | 0 59 |
| 15 | 1 00 | 75 | 5 00 | 135 | 9 00 | 195 | 13 00 | 255 | 17 00 | 315 | 21 00 | 15 | 1 00 | 1 01 | 1 02 | 1 03 |
| 16 | 1 04 | 76 | 5 04 | 136 | 9 04 | 196 | 13 04 | 256 | 17 04 | 316 | 21 04 | 16 | 1 04 | 1 05 | 1 06 | 1 07 |
| 17 | 1 08 | 77 | 5 08 | 137 | 9 08 | 197 | 13 08 | 257 | 17 08 | 317 | 21 08 | 17 | 1 08 | 1 09 | 1 10 | 1 11 |
| 18 | 1 12 | 78 | 5 12 | 138 | 9 12 | 198 | 13 12 | 258 | 17 12 | 318 | 21 12 | 18 | 1 12 | 1 13 | 1 14 | 1 15 |
| 19 | 1 16 | 79 | 5 16 | 139 | 9 16 | 199 | 13 16 | 259 | 17 16 | 319 | 21 16 | 19 | 1 16 | 1 17 | 1 18 | 1 19 |
| 20 | 1 20 | 80 | 5 20 | 140 | 9 20 | 200 | 13 20 | 260 | 17 20 | 320 | 21 20 | 20 | 1 20 | 1 21 | 1 22 | 1 23 |
| 21 | 1 24 | 81 | 5 24 | 141 | 9 24 | 201 | 13 24 | 261 | 17 24 | 321 | 21 24 | 21 | 1 24 | 1 25 | 1 26 | 1 27 |
| 22 | 1 28 | 82 | 5 28 | 142 | 9 28 | 202 | 13 28 | 262 | 17 28 | 322 | 21 28 | 22 | 1 28 | 1 29 | 1 30 | 1 31 |
| 23 | 1 32 | 83 | 5 32 | 143 | 9 32 | 203 | 13 32 | 263 | 17 32 | 323 | 21 32 | 23 | 1 32 | 1 33 | 1 34 | 1 35 |
| 24 | 1 36 | 84 | 5 36 | 144 | 9 36 | 204 | 13 36 | 264 | 17 36 | 324 | 21 36 | 24 | 1 36 | 1 37 | 1 38 | 1 39 |
| 25 | 1 40 | 85 | 5 40 | 145 | 9 40 | 205 | 13 40 | 265 | 17 40 | 325 | 21 40 | 25 | 1 40 | 1 41 | 1 42 | 1 43 |
| 26 | 1 44 | 86 | 5 44 | 146 | 9 44 | 206 | 13 44 | 266 | 17 44 | 326 | 21 44 | 26 | 1 44 | 1 45 | 1 46 | 1 47 |
| 27 | 1 48 | 87 | 5 48 | 147 | 9 48 | 207 | 13 48 | 267 | 17 48 | 327 | 21 48 | 27 | 1 48 | 1 49 | 1 50 | 1 51 |
| 28 | 1 52 | 88 | 5 52 | 148 | 9 52 | 208 | 13 52 | 268 | 17 52 | 328 | 21 52 | 28 | 1 52 | 1 53 | 1 54 | 1 55 |
| 29 | 1 56 | 89 | 5 56 | 149 | 9 56 | 209 | 13 56 | 269 | 17 56 | 329 | 21 56 | 29 | 1 56 | 1 57 | 1 58 | 1 59 |
| 30 | 2 00 | 90 | 6 00 | 150 | 10 00 | 210 | 14 00 | 270 | 18 00 | 330 | 22 00 | 30 | 2 00 | 2 01 | 2 02 | 2 03 |
| 31 | 2 04 | 91 | 6 04 | 151 | 10 04 | 211 | 14 04 | 271 | 18 04 | 331 | 22 04 | 31 | 2 04 | 2 05 | 2 06 | 2 07 |
| 32 | 2 08 | 92 | 6 08 | 152 | 10 08 | 212 | 14 08 | 272 | 18 08 | 332 | 22 08 | 32 | 2 08 | 2 09 | 2 10 | 2 11 |
| 33 | 2 12 | 93 | 6 12 | 153 | 10 12 | 213 | 14 12 | 273 | 18 12 | 333 | 22 12 | 33 | 2 12 | 2 13 | 2 14 | 2 15 |
| 34 | 2 16 | 94 | 6 16 | 154 | 10 16 | 214 | 14 16 | 274 | 18 16 | 334 | 22 16 | 34 | 2 16 | 2 17 | 2 18 | 2 19 |
| 35 | 2 20 | 95 | 6 20 | 155 | 10 20 | 215 | 14 20 | 275 | 18 20 | 335 | 22 20 | 35 | 2 20 | 2 21 | 2 22 | 2 23 |
| 36 | 2 24 | 96 | 6 24 | 156 | 10 24 | 216 | 14 24 | 276 | 18 24 | 336 | 22 24 | 36 | 2 24 | 2 25 | 2 26 | 2 27 |
| 37 | 2 28 | 97 | 6 28 | 157 | 10 28 | 217 | 14 28 | 277 | 18 28 | 337 | 22 28 | 37 | 2 28 | 2 29 | 2 30 | 2 31 |
| 38 | 2 32 | 98 | 6 32 | 158 | 10 32 | 218 | 14 32 | 278 | 18 32 | 338 | 22 32 | 38 | 2 32 | 2 33 | 2 34 | 2 35 |
| 39 | 2 36 | 99 | 6 36 | 159 | 10 36 | 219 | 14 36 | 279 | 18 36 | 339 | 22 36 | 39 | 2 36 | 2 37 | 2 38 | 2 39 |
| 40 | 2 40 | 100 | 6 40 | 160 | 10 40 | 220 | 14 40 | 280 | 18 40 | 340 | 22 40 | 40 | 2 40 | 2 41 | 2 42 | 2 43 |
| 41 | 2 44 | 101 | 6 44 | 161 | 10 44 | 221 | 14 44 | 281 | 18 44 | 341 | 22 44 | 41 | 2 44 | 2 45 | 2 46 | 2 47 |
| 42 | 2 48 | 102 | 6 48 | 162 | 10 48 | 222 | 14 48 | 282 | 18 48 | 342 | 22 48 | 42 | 2 48 | 2 49 | 2 50 | 2 51 |
| 43 | 2 52 | 103 | 6 52 | 163 | 10 52 | 223 | 14 52 | 283 | 18 52 | 343 | 22 52 | 43 | 2 52 | 2 53 | 2 54 | 2 55 |
| 44 | 2 56 | 104 | 6 56 | 164 | 10 56 | 224 | 14 56 | 284 | 18 56 | 344 | 22 56 | 44 | 2 56 | 2 57 | 2 58 | 2 59 |
| 45 | 3 00 | 105 | 7 00 | 165 | 11 00 | 225 | 15 00 | 285 | 19 00 | 345 | 23 00 | 45 | 3 00 | 3 01 | 3 02 | 3 03 |
| 46 | 3 04 | 106 | 7 04 | 166 | 11 04 | 226 | 15 04 | 286 | 19 04 | 346 | 23 04 | 46 | 3 04 | 3 05 | 3 06 | 3 07 |
| 47 | 3 08 | 107 | 7 08 | 167 | 11 08 | 227 | 15 08 | 287 | 19 08 | 347 | 23 08 | 47 | 3 08 | 3 09 | 3 10 | 3 11 |
| 48 | 3 12 | 108 | 7 12 | 168 | 11 12 | 228 | 15 12 | 288 | 19 12 | 348 | 23 12 | 48 | 3 12 | 3 13 | 3 14 | 3 15 |
| 49 | 3 16 | 109 | 7 16 | 169 | 11 16 | 229 | 15 16 | 289 | 19 16 | 349 | 23 16 | 49 | 3 16 | 3 17 | 3 18 | 3 19 |
| 50 | 3 20 | 110 | 7 20 | 170 | 11 20 | 230 | 15 20 | 290 | 19 20 | 350 | 23 20 | 50 | 3 20 | 3 21 | 3 22 | 3 23 |
| 51 | 3 24 | 111 | 7 24 | 171 | 11 24 | 231 | 15 24 | 291 | 19 24 | 351 | 23 24 | 51 | 3 24 | 3 25 | 3 26 | 3 27 |
| 52 | 3 28 | 112 | 7 28 | 172 | 11 28 | 232 | 15 28 | 292 | 19 28 | 352 | 23 28 | 52 | 3 28 | 3 29 | 3 30 | 3 31 |
| 53 | 3 32 | 113 | 7 32 | 173 | 11 32 | 233 | 15 32 | 293 | 19 32 | 353 | 23 32 | 53 | 3 32 | 3 33 | 3 34 | 3 35 |
| 54 | 3 36 | 114 | 7 36 | 174 | 11 36 | 234 | 15 36 | 294 | 19 36 | 354 | 23 36 | 54 | 3 36 | 3 37 | 3 38 | 3 39 |
| 55 | 3 40 | 115 | 7 40 | 175 | 11 40 | 235 | 15 40 | 295 | 19 40 | 355 | 23 40 | 55 | 3 40 | 3 41 | 3 42 | 3 43 |
| 56 | 3 44 | 116 | 7 44 | 176 | 11 44 | 236 | 15 44 | 296 | 19 44 | 356 | 23 44 | 56 | 3 44 | 3 45 | 3 46 | 3 47 |
| 57 | 3 48 | 117 | 7 48 | 177 | 11 48 | 237 | 15 48 | 297 | 19 48 | 357 | 23 48 | 57 | 3 48 | 3 49 | 3 50 | 3 51 |
| 58 | 3 52 | 118 | 7 52 | 178 | 11 52 | 238 | 15 52 | 298 | 19 52 | 358 | 23 52 | 58 | 3 52 | 3 53 | 3 54 | 3 55 |
| 59 | 3 56 | 119 | 7 56 | 179 | 11 56 | 239 | 15 56 | 299 | 19 56 | 359 | 23 56 | 59 | 3 56 | 3 57 | 3 58 | 3 59 |

The above table is for converting expressions in arc to their equivalent in time ; its main use in this Almanac is for the conversion of longitude for application to L.M.T. (*added* if *west*, *subtracted* if *east*) to give G.M.T. or vice versa, particularly in the case of sunrise, sunset, etc.

## 0ᵐ INCREMENTS AND CORRECTIONS Iᵐ

| 0ᵐ | SUN PLANETS | ARIES | MOON | v or d | Corrⁿ | v or d | Corrⁿ | v or d | Corrⁿ |
|---|---|---|---|---|---|---|---|---|---|
| s | ° ′ | ° ′ | ° ′ | ′ | ′ | ′ | ′ | ′ | ′ |
| 00 | 0 00·0 | 0 00·0 | 0 00·0 | 0·0 | 0·0 | 6·0 | 0·1 | 12·0 | 0·1 |
| 01 | 0 00·3 | 0 00·3 | 0 00·2 | 0·1 | 0·0 | 6·1 | 0·1 | 12·1 | 0·1 |
| 02 | 0 00·5 | 0 00·5 | 0 00·5 | 0·2 | 0·0 | 6·2 | 0·1 | 12·2 | 0·1 |
| 03 | 0 00·8 | 0 00·8 | 0 00·7 | 0·3 | 0·0 | 6·3 | 0·1 | 12·3 | 0·1 |
| 04 | 0 01·0 | 0 01·0 | 0 01·0 | 0·4 | 0·0 | 6·4 | 0·1 | 12·4 | 0·1 |
| 05 | 0 01·3 | 0 01·3 | 0 01·2 | 0·5 | 0·0 | 6·5 | 0·1 | 12·5 | 0·1 |
| 06 | 0 01·5 | 0 01·5 | 0 01·4 | 0·6 | 0·0 | 6·6 | 0·1 | 12·6 | 0·1 |
| 07 | 0 01·8 | 0 01·8 | 0 01·7 | 0·7 | 0·0 | 6·7 | 0·1 | 12·7 | 0·1 |
| 08 | 0 02·0 | 0 02·0 | 0 01·9 | 0·8 | 0·0 | 6·8 | 0·1 | 12·8 | 0·1 |
| 09 | 0 02·3 | 0 02·3 | 0 02·1 | 0·9 | 0·0 | 6·9 | 0·1 | 12·9 | 0·1 |
| 10 | 0 02·5 | 0 02·5 | 0 02·4 | 1·0 | 0·0 | 7·0 | 0·1 | 13·0 | 0·1 |
| 11 | 0 02·8 | 0 02·8 | 0 02·6 | 1·1 | 0·0 | 7·1 | 0·1 | 13·1 | 0·1 |
| 12 | 0 03·0 | 0 03·0 | 0 02·9 | 1·2 | 0·0 | 7·2 | 0·1 | 13·2 | 0·1 |
| 13 | 0 03·3 | 0 03·3 | 0 03·1 | 1·3 | 0·0 | 7·3 | 0·1 | 13·3 | 0·1 |
| 14 | 0 03·5 | 0 03·5 | 0 03·3 | 1·4 | 0·0 | 7·4 | 0·1 | 13·4 | 0·1 |
| 15 | 0 03·8 | 0 03·8 | 0 03·6 | 1·5 | 0·0 | 7·5 | 0·1 | 13·5 | 0·1 |
| 16 | 0 04·0 | 0 04·0 | 0 03·8 | 1·6 | 0·0 | 7·6 | 0·1 | 13·6 | 0·1 |
| 17 | 0 04·3 | 0 04·3 | 0 04·1 | 1·7 | 0·0 | 7·7 | 0·1 | 13·7 | 0·1 |
| 18 | 0 04·5 | 0 04·5 | 0 04·3 | 1·8 | 0·0 | 7·8 | 0·1 | 13·8 | 0·1 |
| 19 | 0 04·8 | 0 04·8 | 0 04·5 | 1·9 | 0·0 | 7·9 | 0·1 | 13·9 | 0·1 |
| 20 | 0 05·0 | 0 05·0 | 0 04·8 | 2·0 | 0·0 | 8·0 | 0·1 | 14·0 | 0·1 |
| 21 | 0 05·3 | 0 05·3 | 0 05·0 | 2·1 | 0·0 | 8·1 | 0·1 | 14·1 | 0·1 |
| 22 | 0 05·5 | 0 05·5 | 0 05·2 | 2·2 | 0·0 | 8·2 | 0·1 | 14·2 | 0·1 |
| 23 | 0 05·8 | 0 05·8 | 0 05·5 | 2·3 | 0·0 | 8·3 | 0·1 | 14·3 | 0·1 |
| 24 | 0 06·0 | 0 06·0 | 0 05·7 | 2·4 | 0·0 | 8·4 | 0·1 | 14·4 | 0·1 |
| 25 | 0 06·3 | 0 06·3 | 0 06·0 | 2·5 | 0·0 | 8·5 | 0·1 | 14·5 | 0·1 |
| 26 | 0 06·5 | 0 06·5 | 0 06·2 | 2·6 | 0·0 | 8·6 | 0·1 | 14·6 | 0·1 |
| 27 | 0 06·8 | 0 06·8 | 0 06·4 | 2·7 | 0·0 | 8·7 | 0·1 | 14·7 | 0·1 |
| 28 | 0 07·0 | 0 07·0 | 0 06·7 | 2·8 | 0·0 | 8·8 | 0·1 | 14·8 | 0·1 |
| 29 | 0 07·3 | 0 07·3 | 0 06·9 | 2·9 | 0·0 | 8·9 | 0·1 | 14·9 | 0·1 |
| 30 | 0 07·5 | 0 07·5 | 0 07·2 | 3·0 | 0·0 | 9·0 | 0·1 | 15·0 | 0·1 |
| 31 | 0 07·8 | 0 07·8 | 0 07·4 | 3·1 | 0·0 | 9·1 | 0·1 | 15·1 | 0·1 |
| 32 | 0 08·0 | 0 08·0 | 0 07·6 | 3·2 | 0·0 | 9·2 | 0·1 | 15·2 | 0·1 |
| 33 | 0 08·3 | 0 08·3 | 0 07·9 | 3·3 | 0·0 | 9·3 | 0·1 | 15·3 | 0·1 |
| 34 | 0 08·5 | 0 08·5 | 0 08·1 | 3·4 | 0·0 | 9·4 | 0·1 | 15·4 | 0·1 |
| 35 | 0 08·8 | 0 08·8 | 0 08·4 | 3·5 | 0·0 | 9·5 | 0·1 | 15·5 | 0·1 |
| 36 | 0 09·0 | 0 09·0 | 0 08·6 | 3·6 | 0·0 | 9·6 | 0·1 | 15·6 | 0·1 |
| 37 | 0 09·3 | 0 09·3 | 0 08·8 | 3·7 | 0·0 | 9·7 | 0·1 | 15·7 | 0·1 |
| 38 | 0 09·5 | 0 09·5 | 0 09·1 | 3·8 | 0·0 | 9·8 | 0·1 | 15·8 | 0·1 |
| 39 | 0 09·8 | 0 09·8 | 0 09·3 | 3·9 | 0·0 | 9·9 | 0·1 | 15·9 | 0·1 |
| 40 | 0 10·0 | 0 10·0 | 0 09·5 | 4·0 | 0·0 | 10·0 | 0·1 | 16·0 | 0·1 |
| 41 | 0 10·3 | 0 10·3 | 0 09·8 | 4·1 | 0·0 | 10·1 | 0·1 | 16·1 | 0·1 |
| 42 | 0 10·5 | 0 10·5 | 0 10·0 | 4·2 | 0·0 | 10·2 | 0·1 | 16·2 | 0·1 |
| 43 | 0 10·8 | 0 10·8 | 0 10·3 | 4·3 | 0·0 | 10·3 | 0·1 | 16·3 | 0·1 |
| 44 | 0 11·0 | 0 11·0 | 0 10·5 | 4·4 | 0·0 | 10·4 | 0·1 | 16·4 | 0·1 |
| 45 | 0 11·3 | 0 11·3 | 0 10·7 | 4·5 | 0·0 | 10·5 | 0·1 | 16·5 | 0·1 |
| 46 | 0 11·5 | 0 11·5 | 0 11·0 | 4·6 | 0·0 | 10·6 | 0·1 | 16·6 | 0·1 |
| 47 | 0 11·8 | 0 11·8 | 0 11·2 | 4·7 | 0·0 | 10·7 | 0·1 | 16·7 | 0·1 |
| 48 | 0 12·0 | 0 12·0 | 0 11·5 | 4·8 | 0·0 | 10·8 | 0·1 | 16·8 | 0·1 |
| 49 | 0 12·3 | 0 12·3 | 0 11·7 | 4·9 | 0·0 | 10·9 | 0·1 | 16·9 | 0·1 |
| 50 | 0 12·5 | 0 12·5 | 0 11·9 | 5·0 | 0·0 | 11·0 | 0·1 | 17·0 | 0·1 |
| 51 | 0 12·8 | 0 12·8 | 0 12·2 | 5·1 | 0·0 | 11·1 | 0·1 | 17·1 | 0·1 |
| 52 | 0 13·0 | 0 13·0 | 0 12·4 | 5·2 | 0·0 | 11·2 | 0·1 | 17·2 | 0·1 |
| 53 | 0 13·3 | 0 13·3 | 0 12·6 | 5·3 | 0·0 | 11·3 | 0·1 | 17·3 | 0·1 |
| 54 | 0 13·5 | 0 13·5 | 0 12·9 | 5·4 | 0·0 | 11·4 | 0·1 | 17·4 | 0·1 |
| 55 | 0 13·8 | 0 13·8 | 0 13·1 | 5·5 | 0·0 | 11·5 | 0·1 | 17·5 | 0·1 |
| 56 | 0 14·0 | 0 14·0 | 0 13·4 | 5·6 | 0·0 | 11·6 | 0·1 | 17·6 | 0·1 |
| 57 | 0 14·3 | 0 14·3 | 0 13·6 | 5·7 | 0·0 | 11·7 | 0·1 | 17·7 | 0·1 |
| 58 | 0 14·5 | 0 14·5 | 0 13·8 | 5·8 | 0·0 | 11·8 | 0·1 | 17·8 | 0·1 |
| 59 | 0 14·8 | 0 14·8 | 0 14·1 | 5·9 | 0·0 | 11·9 | 0·1 | 17·9 | 0·1 |
| 60 | 0 15·0 | 0 15·0 | 0 14·3 | 6·0 | 0·1 | 12·0 | 0·1 | 18·0 | 0·2 |

| 1ᵐ | SUN PLANETS | ARIES | MOON | v or d | Corrⁿ | v or d | Corrⁿ | v or d | Corrⁿ |
|---|---|---|---|---|---|---|---|---|---|
| s | ° ′ | ° ′ | ° ′ | ′ | ′ | ′ | ′ | ′ | ′ |
| 00 | 0 15·0 | 0 15·0 | 0 14·3 | 0·0 | 0·0 | 6·0 | 0·2 | 12·0 | 0·3 |
| 01 | 0 15·3 | 0 15·3 | 0 14·6 | 0·1 | 0·0 | 6·1 | 0·2 | 12·1 | 0·3 |
| 02 | 0 15·5 | 0 15·5 | 0 14·8 | 0·2 | 0·0 | 6·2 | 0·2 | 12·2 | 0·3 |
| 03 | 0 15·8 | 0 15·8 | 0 15·0 | 0·3 | 0·0 | 6·3 | 0·2 | 12·3 | 0·3 |
| 04 | 0 16·0 | 0 16·0 | 0 15·3 | 0·4 | 0·0 | 6·4 | 0·2 | 12·4 | 0·3 |
| 05 | 0 16·3 | 0 16·3 | 0 15·5 | 0·5 | 0·0 | 6·5 | 0·2 | 12·5 | 0·3 |
| 06 | 0 16·5 | 0 16·5 | 0 15·7 | 0·6 | 0·0 | 6·6 | 0·2 | 12·6 | 0·3 |
| 07 | 0 16·8 | 0 16·8 | 0 16·0 | 0·7 | 0·0 | 6·7 | 0·2 | 12·7 | 0·3 |
| 08 | 0 17·0 | 0 17·0 | 0 16·2 | 0·8 | 0·0 | 6·8 | 0·2 | 12·8 | 0·3 |
| 09 | 0 17·3 | 0 17·3 | 0 16·5 | 0·9 | 0·0 | 6·9 | 0·2 | 12·9 | 0·3 |
| 10 | 0 17·5 | 0 17·5 | 0 16·7 | 1·0 | 0·0 | 7·0 | 0·2 | 13·0 | 0·3 |
| 11 | 0 17·8 | 0 17·8 | 0 16·9 | 1·1 | 0·0 | 7·1 | 0·2 | 13·1 | 0·3 |
| 12 | 0 18·0 | 0 18·0 | 0 17·2 | 1·2 | 0·0 | 7·2 | 0·2 | 13·2 | 0·3 |
| 13 | 0 18·3 | 0 18·3 | 0 17·4 | 1·3 | 0·0 | 7·3 | 0·2 | 13·3 | 0·3 |
| 14 | 0 18·5 | 0 18·6 | 0 17·7 | 1·4 | 0·0 | 7·4 | 0·2 | 13·4 | 0·3 |
| 15 | 0 18·8 | 0 18·8 | 0 17·9 | 1·5 | 0·0 | 7·5 | 0·2 | 13·5 | 0·3 |
| 16 | 0 19·0 | 0 19·1 | 0 18·1 | 1·6 | 0·0 | 7·6 | 0·2 | 13·6 | 0·3 |
| 17 | 0 19·3 | 0 19·3 | 0 18·4 | 1·7 | 0·0 | 7·7 | 0·2 | 13·7 | 0·3 |
| 18 | 0 19·5 | 0 19·6 | 0 18·6 | 1·8 | 0·0 | 7·8 | 0·2 | 13·8 | 0·3 |
| 19 | 0 19·8 | 0 19·8 | 0 18·9 | 1·9 | 0·0 | 7·9 | 0·2 | 13·9 | 0·3 |
| 20 | 0 20·0 | 0 20·1 | 0 19·1 | 2·0 | 0·1 | 8·0 | 0·2 | 14·0 | 0·4 |
| 21 | 0 20·3 | 0 20·3 | 0 19·3 | 2·1 | 0·1 | 8·1 | 0·2 | 14·1 | 0·4 |
| 22 | 0 20·5 | 0 20·6 | 0 19·6 | 2·2 | 0·1 | 8·2 | 0·2 | 14·2 | 0·4 |
| 23 | 0 20·8 | 0 20·8 | 0 19·8 | 2·3 | 0·1 | 8·3 | 0·2 | 14·3 | 0·4 |
| 24 | 0 21·0 | 0 21·1 | 0 20·0 | 2·4 | 0·1 | 8·4 | 0·2 | 14·4 | 0·4 |
| 25 | 0 21·3 | 0 21·3 | 0 20·3 | 2·5 | 0·1 | 8·5 | 0·2 | 14·5 | 0·4 |
| 26 | 0 21·5 | 0 21·6 | 0 20·5 | 2·6 | 0·1 | 8·6 | 0·2 | 14·6 | 0·4 |
| 27 | 0 21·8 | 0 21·8 | 0 20·8 | 2·7 | 0·1 | 8·7 | 0·2 | 14·7 | 0·4 |
| 28 | 0 22·0 | 0 22·1 | 0 21·0 | 2·8 | 0·1 | 8·8 | 0·2 | 14·8 | 0·4 |
| 29 | 0 22·3 | 0 22·3 | 0 21·2 | 2·9 | 0·1 | 8·9 | 0·2 | 14·9 | 0·4 |
| 30 | 0 22·5 | 0 22·6 | 0 21·5 | 3·0 | 0·1 | 9·0 | 0·2 | 15·0 | 0·4 |
| 31 | 0 22·8 | 0 22·8 | 0 21·7 | 3·1 | 0·1 | 9·1 | 0·2 | 15·1 | 0·4 |
| 32 | 0 23·0 | 0 23·1 | 0 22·0 | 3·2 | 0·1 | 9·2 | 0·2 | 15·2 | 0·4 |
| 33 | 0 23·3 | 0 23·3 | 0 22·2 | 3·3 | 0·1 | 9·3 | 0·2 | 15·3 | 0·4 |
| 34 | 0 23·5 | 0 23·6 | 0 22·4 | 3·4 | 0·1 | 9·4 | 0·2 | 15·4 | 0·4 |
| 35 | 0 23·8 | 0 23·8 | 0 22·7 | 3·5 | 0·1 | 9·5 | 0·2 | 15·5 | 0·4 |
| 36 | 0 24·0 | 0 24·1 | 0 22·9 | 3·6 | 0·1 | 9·6 | 0·2 | 15·6 | 0·4 |
| 37 | 0 24·3 | 0 24·3 | 0 23·1 | 3·7 | 0·1 | 9·7 | 0·2 | 15·7 | 0·4 |
| 38 | 0 24·5 | 0 24·6 | 0 23·4 | 3·8 | 0·1 | 9·8 | 0·2 | 15·8 | 0·4 |
| 39 | 0 24·8 | 0 24·8 | 0 23·6 | 3·9 | 0·1 | 9·9 | 0·2 | 15·9 | 0·4 |
| 40 | 0 25·0 | 0 25·1 | 0 23·9 | 4·0 | 0·1 | 10·0 | 0·3 | 16·0 | 0·4 |
| 41 | 0 25·3 | 0 25·3 | 0 24·1 | 4·1 | 0·1 | 10·1 | 0·3 | 16·1 | 0·4 |
| 42 | 0 25·5 | 0 25·6 | 0 24·3 | 4·2 | 0·1 | 10·2 | 0·3 | 16·2 | 0·4 |
| 43 | 0 25·8 | 0 25·8 | 0 24·6 | 4·3 | 0·1 | 10·3 | 0·3 | 16·3 | 0·4 |
| 44 | 0 26·0 | 0 26·1 | 0 24·8 | 4·4 | 0·1 | 10·4 | 0·3 | 16·4 | 0·4 |
| 45 | 0 26·3 | 0 26·3 | 0 25·1 | 4·5 | 0·1 | 10·5 | 0·3 | 16·5 | 0·4 |
| 46 | 0 26·5 | 0 26·6 | 0 25·3 | 4·6 | 0·1 | 10·6 | 0·3 | 16·6 | 0·4 |
| 47 | 0 26·8 | 0 26·8 | 0 25·5 | 4·7 | 0·1 | 10·7 | 0·3 | 16·7 | 0·4 |
| 48 | 0 27·0 | 0 27·1 | 0 25·8 | 4·8 | 0·1 | 10·8 | 0·3 | 16·8 | 0·4 |
| 49 | 0 27·3 | 0 27·3 | 0 26·0 | 4·9 | 0·1 | 10·9 | 0·3 | 16·9 | 0·4 |
| 50 | 0 27·5 | 0 27·6 | 0 26·2 | 5·0 | 0·1 | 11·0 | 0·3 | 17·0 | 0·4 |
| 51 | 0 27·8 | 0 27·8 | 0 26·5 | 5·1 | 0·1 | 11·1 | 0·3 | 17·1 | 0·4 |
| 52 | 0 28·0 | 0 28·1 | 0 26·7 | 5·2 | 0·1 | 11·2 | 0·3 | 17·2 | 0·4 |
| 53 | 0 28·3 | 0 28·3 | 0 27·0 | 5·3 | 0·1 | 11·3 | 0·3 | 17·3 | 0·4 |
| 54 | 0 28·5 | 0 28·6 | 0 27·2 | 5·4 | 0·1 | 11·4 | 0·3 | 17·4 | 0·4 |
| 55 | 0 28·8 | 0 28·8 | 0 27·4 | 5·5 | 0·1 | 11·5 | 0·3 | 17·5 | 0·4 |
| 56 | 0 29·0 | 0 29·1 | 0 27·7 | 5·6 | 0·1 | 11·6 | 0·3 | 17·6 | 0·4 |
| 57 | 0 29·3 | 0 29·3 | 0 27·9 | 5·7 | 0·1 | 11·7 | 0·3 | 17·7 | 0·4 |
| 58 | 0 29·5 | 0 29·6 | 0 28·2 | 5·8 | 0·1 | 11·8 | 0·3 | 17·8 | 0·4 |
| 59 | 0 29·8 | 0 29·8 | 0 28·4 | 5·9 | 0·1 | 11·9 | 0·3 | 17·9 | 0·4 |
| 60 | 0 30·0 | 0 30·1 | 0 28·6 | 6·0 | 0·2 | 12·0 | 0·3 | 18·0 | 0·5 |

## INCREMENTS AND CORRECTIONS

**2m**

| 2m s | SUN PLANETS | ARIES | MOON | v or d | Corrn | v or d | Corrn | v or d | Corrn |
|---|---|---|---|---|---|---|---|---|---|
| | ° ′ | ° ′ | ° ′ | ′ | ′ | ′ | ′ | ′ | ′ |
| 00 | 0 30·0 | 0 30·1 | 0 28·6 | 0·0 | 0·0 | 6·0 | 0·3 | 12·0 | 0·5 |
| 01 | 0 30·3 | 0 30·3 | 0 28·9 | 0·1 | 0·0 | 6·1 | 0·3 | 12·1 | 0·5 |
| 02 | 0 30·5 | 0 30·6 | 0 29·1 | 0·2 | 0·0 | 6·2 | 0·3 | 12·2 | 0·5 |
| 03 | 0 30·8 | 0 30·8 | 0 29·3 | 0·3 | 0·0 | 6·3 | 0·3 | 12·3 | 0·5 |
| 04 | 0 31·0 | 0 31·1 | 0 29·6 | 0·4 | 0·0 | 6·4 | 0·3 | 12·4 | 0·5 |
| 05 | 0 31·3 | 0 31·3 | 0 29·8 | 0·5 | 0·0 | 6·5 | 0·3 | 12·5 | 0·5 |
| 06 | 0 31·5 | 0 31·6 | 0 30·1 | 0·6 | 0·0 | 6·6 | 0·3 | 12·6 | 0·5 |
| 07 | 0 31·8 | 0 31·8 | 0 30·3 | 0·7 | 0·0 | 6·7 | 0·3 | 12·7 | 0·5 |
| 08 | 0 32·0 | 0 32·1 | 0 30·5 | 0·8 | 0·0 | 6·8 | 0·3 | 12·8 | 0·5 |
| 09 | 0 32·3 | 0 32·3 | 0 30·8 | 0·9 | 0·0 | 6·9 | 0·3 | 12·9 | 0·5 |
| 10 | 0 32·5 | 0 32·6 | 0 31·0 | 1·0 | 0·0 | 7·0 | 0·3 | 13·0 | 0·5 |
| 11 | 0 32·8 | 0 32·8 | 0 31·3 | 1·1 | 0·0 | 7·1 | 0·3 | 13·1 | 0·5 |
| 12 | 0 33·0 | 0 33·1 | 0 31·5 | 1·2 | 0·1 | 7·2 | 0·3 | 13·2 | 0·6 |
| 13 | 0 33·3 | 0 33·3 | 0 31·7 | 1·3 | 0·1 | 7·3 | 0·3 | 13·3 | 0·6 |
| 14 | 0 33·5 | 0 33·6 | 0 32·0 | 1·4 | 0·1 | 7·4 | 0·3 | 13·4 | 0·6 |
| 15 | 0 33·8 | 0 33·8 | 0 32·2 | 1·5 | 0·1 | 7·5 | 0·3 | 13·5 | 0·6 |
| 16 | 0 34·0 | 0 34·1 | 0 32·5 | 1·6 | 0·1 | 7·6 | 0·3 | 13·6 | 0·6 |
| 17 | 0 34·3 | 0 34·3 | 0 32·7 | 1·7 | 0·1 | 7·7 | 0·3 | 13·7 | 0·6 |
| 18 | 0 34·5 | 0 34·6 | 0 32·9 | 1·8 | 0·1 | 7·8 | 0·3 | 13·8 | 0·6 |
| 19 | 0 34·8 | 0 34·8 | 0 33·2 | 1·9 | 0·1 | 7·9 | 0·3 | 13·9 | 0·6 |
| 20 | 0 35·0 | 0 35·1 | 0 33·4 | 2·0 | 0·1 | 8·0 | 0·3 | 14·0 | 0·6 |
| 21 | 0 35·3 | 0 35·3 | 0 33·6 | 2·1 | 0·1 | 8·1 | 0·3 | 14·1 | 0·6 |
| 22 | 0 35·5 | 0 35·6 | 0 33·9 | 2·2 | 0·1 | 8·2 | 0·3 | 14·2 | 0·6 |
| 23 | 0 35·8 | 0 35·8 | 0 34·1 | 2·3 | 0·1 | 8·3 | 0·3 | 14·3 | 0·6 |
| 24 | 0 36·0 | 0 36·1 | 0 34·4 | 2·4 | 0·1 | 8·4 | 0·4 | 14·4 | 0·6 |
| 25 | 0 36·3 | 0 36·3 | 0 34·6 | 2·5 | 0·1 | 8·5 | 0·4 | 14·5 | 0·6 |
| 26 | 0 36·5 | 0 36·6 | 0 34·8 | 2·6 | 0·1 | 8·6 | 0·4 | 14·6 | 0·6 |
| 27 | 0 36·8 | 0 36·9 | 0 35·1 | 2·7 | 0·1 | 8·7 | 0·4 | 14·7 | 0·6 |
| 28 | 0 37·0 | 0 37·1 | 0 35·3 | 2·8 | 0·1 | 8·8 | 0·4 | 14·8 | 0·6 |
| 29 | 0 37·3 | 0 37·4 | 0 35·6 | 2·9 | 0·1 | 8·9 | 0·4 | 14·9 | 0·6 |
| 30 | 0 37·5 | 0 37·6 | 0 35·8 | 3·0 | 0·1 | 9·0 | 0·4 | 15·0 | 0·6 |
| 31 | 0 37·8 | 0 37·9 | 0 36·0 | 3·1 | 0·1 | 9·1 | 0·4 | 15·1 | 0·6 |
| 32 | 0 38·0 | 0 38·1 | 0 36·3 | 3·2 | 0·1 | 9·2 | 0·4 | 15·2 | 0·6 |
| 33 | 0 38·3 | 0 38·4 | 0 36·5 | 3·3 | 0·1 | 9·3 | 0·4 | 15·3 | 0·6 |
| 34 | 0 38·5 | 0 38·6 | 0 36·7 | 3·4 | 0·1 | 9·4 | 0·4 | 15·4 | 0·6 |
| 35 | 0 38·8 | 0 38·9 | 0 37·0 | 3·5 | 0·1 | 9·5 | 0·4 | 15·5 | 0·6 |
| 36 | 0 39·0 | 0 39·1 | 0 37·2 | 3·6 | 0·2 | 9·6 | 0·4 | 15·6 | 0·7 |
| 37 | 0 39·3 | 0 39·4 | 0 37·5 | 3·7 | 0·2 | 9·7 | 0·4 | 15·7 | 0·7 |
| 38 | 0 39·5 | 0 39·6 | 0 37·7 | 3·8 | 0·2 | 9·8 | 0·4 | 15·8 | 0·7 |
| 39 | 0 39·8 | 0 39·9 | 0 37·9 | 3·9 | 0·2 | 9·9 | 0·4 | 15·9 | 0·7 |
| 40 | 0 40·0 | 0 40·1 | 0 38·2 | 4·0 | 0·2 | 10·0 | 0·4 | 16·0 | 0·7 |
| 41 | 0 40·3 | 0 40·4 | 0 38·4 | 4·1 | 0·2 | 10·1 | 0·4 | 16·1 | 0·7 |
| 42 | 0 40·5 | 0 40·6 | 0 38·7 | 4·2 | 0·2 | 10·2 | 0·4 | 16·2 | 0·7 |
| 43 | 0 40·8 | 0 40·9 | 0 38·9 | 4·3 | 0·2 | 10·3 | 0·4 | 16·3 | 0·7 |
| 44 | 0 41·0 | 0 41·1 | 0 39·1 | 4·4 | 0·2 | 10·4 | 0·4 | 16·4 | 0·7 |
| 45 | 0 41·3 | 0 41·4 | 0 39·4 | 4·5 | 0·2 | 10·5 | 0·4 | 16·5 | 0·7 |
| 46 | 0 41·5 | 0 41·6 | 0 39·6 | 4·6 | 0·2 | 10·6 | 0·4 | 16·6 | 0·7 |
| 47 | 0 41·8 | 0 41·9 | 0 39·8 | 4·7 | 0·2 | 10·7 | 0·4 | 16·7 | 0·7 |
| 48 | 0 42·0 | 0 42·1 | 0 40·1 | 4·8 | 0·2 | 10·8 | 0·5 | 16·8 | 0·7 |
| 49 | 0 42·3 | 0 42·4 | 0 40·3 | 4·9 | 0·2 | 10·9 | 0·5 | 16·9 | 0·7 |
| 50 | 0 42·5 | 0 42·6 | 0 40·6 | 5·0 | 0·2 | 11·0 | 0·5 | 17·0 | 0·7 |
| 51 | 0 42·8 | 0 42·9 | 0 40·8 | 5·1 | 0·2 | 11·1 | 0·5 | 17·1 | 0·7 |
| 52 | 0 43·0 | 0 43·1 | 0 41·0 | 5·2 | 0·2 | 11·2 | 0·5 | 17·2 | 0·7 |
| 53 | 0 43·3 | 0 43·4 | 0 41·3 | 5·3 | 0·2 | 11·3 | 0·5 | 17·3 | 0·7 |
| 54 | 0 43·5 | 0 43·6 | 0 41·5 | 5·4 | 0·2 | 11·4 | 0·5 | 17·4 | 0·7 |
| 55 | 0 43·8 | 0 43·9 | 0 41·8 | 5·5 | 0·2 | 11·5 | 0·5 | 17·5 | 0·7 |
| 56 | 0 44·0 | 0 44·1 | 0 42·0 | 5·6 | 0·2 | 11·6 | 0·5 | 17·6 | 0·7 |
| 57 | 0 44·3 | 0 44·4 | 0 42·2 | 5·7 | 0·2 | 11·7 | 0·5 | 17·7 | 0·7 |
| 58 | 0 44·5 | 0 44·6 | 0 42·5 | 5·8 | 0·2 | 11·8 | 0·5 | 17·8 | 0·7 |
| 59 | 0 44·8 | 0 44·9 | 0 42·7 | 5·9 | 0·2 | 11·9 | 0·5 | 17·9 | 0·7 |
| 60 | 0 45·0 | 0 [illegible] | [illegible] 43·0 | 6·0 | 0·3 | [illegible] | [illegible] | 18·0 | 0·8 |

**3m**

| 3m s | SUN PLANETS | ARIES | MOON | v or d | Corrn | v or d | Corrn | v or d | Corrn |
|---|---|---|---|---|---|---|---|---|---|
| | ° ′ | ° ′ | ° ′ | ′ | ′ | ′ | ′ | ′ | ′ |
| 00 | 0 45·0 | 0 45·1 | 0 43·0 | 0·0 | 0·0 | 6·0 | 0·4 | 12·0 | 0·7 |
| 01 | 0 45·3 | 0 45·4 | 0 43·2 | 0·1 | 0·0 | 6·1 | 0·4 | 12·1 | 0·7 |
| 02 | 0 45·5 | 0 45·6 | 0 43·4 | 0·2 | 0·0 | 6·2 | 0·4 | 12·2 | 0·7 |
| 03 | 0 45·8 | 0 45·9 | 0 43·7 | 0·3 | 0·0 | 6·3 | 0·4 | 12·3 | 0·7 |
| 04 | 0 46·0 | 0 46·1 | 0 43·9 | 0·4 | 0·0 | 6·4 | 0·4 | 12·4 | 0·7 |
| 05 | 0 46·3 | 0 46·4 | 0 44·1 | 0·5 | 0·0 | 6·5 | 0·4 | 12·5 | 0·7 |
| 06 | 0 46·5 | 0 46·6 | 0 44·4 | 0·6 | 0·0 | 6·6 | 0·4 | 12·6 | 0·7 |
| 07 | 0 46·8 | 0 46·9 | 0 44·6 | 0·7 | 0·0 | 6·7 | 0·4 | 12·7 | 0·7 |
| 08 | 0 47·0 | 0 47·1 | 0 44·9 | 0·8 | 0·0 | 6·8 | 0·4 | 12·8 | 0·7 |
| 09 | 0 47·3 | 0 47·4 | 0 45·1 | 0·9 | 0·1 | 6·9 | 0·4 | 12·9 | 0·8 |
| 10 | 0 47·5 | 0 47·6 | 0 45·3 | 1·0 | 0·1 | 7·0 | 0·4 | 13·0 | 0·8 |
| 11 | 0 47·8 | 0 47·9 | 0 45·6 | 1·1 | 0·1 | 7·1 | 0·4 | 13·1 | 0·8 |
| 12 | 0 48·0 | 0 48·1 | 0 45·8 | 1·2 | 0·1 | 7·2 | 0·4 | 13·2 | 0·8 |
| 13 | 0 48·3 | 0 48·4 | 0 46·1 | 1·3 | 0·1 | 7·3 | 0·4 | 13·3 | 0·8 |
| 14 | 0 48·5 | 0 48·6 | 0 46·3 | 1·4 | 0·1 | 7·4 | 0·4 | 13·4 | 0·8 |
| 15 | 0 48·8 | 0 48·9 | 0 46·5 | 1·5 | 0·1 | 7·5 | 0·4 | 13·5 | 0·8 |
| 16 | 0 49·0 | 0 49·1 | 0 46·8 | 1·6 | 0·1 | 7·6 | 0·4 | 13·6 | 0·8 |
| 17 | 0 49·3 | 0 49·4 | 0 47·0 | 1·7 | 0·1 | 7·7 | 0·4 | 13·7 | 0·8 |
| 18 | 0 49·5 | 0 49·6 | 0 47·2 | 1·8 | 0·1 | 7·8 | 0·5 | 13·8 | 0·8 |
| 19 | 0 49·8 | 0 49·9 | 0 47·5 | 1·9 | 0·1 | 7·9 | 0·5 | 13·9 | 0·8 |
| 20 | 0 50·0 | 0 50·1 | 0 47·7 | 2·0 | 0·1 | 8·0 | 0·5 | 14·0 | 0·8 |
| 21 | 0 50·3 | 0 50·4 | 0 48·0 | 2·1 | 0·1 | 8·1 | 0·5 | 14·1 | 0·8 |
| 22 | 0 50·5 | 0 50·6 | 0 48·2 | 2·2 | 0·1 | 8·2 | 0·5 | 14·2 | 0·8 |
| 23 | 0 50·8 | 0 50·9 | 0 48·4 | 2·3 | 0·1 | 8·3 | 0·5 | 14·3 | 0·8 |
| 24 | 0 51·0 | 0 51·1 | 0 48·7 | 2·4 | 0·1 | 8·4 | 0·5 | 14·4 | 0·8 |
| 25 | 0 51·3 | 0 51·4 | 0 48·9 | 2·5 | 0·1 | 8·5 | 0·5 | 14·5 | 0·8 |
| 26 | 0 51·5 | 0 51·6 | 0 49·2 | 2·6 | 0·2 | 8·6 | 0·5 | 14·6 | 0·9 |
| 27 | 0 51·8 | 0 51·9 | 0 49·4 | 2·7 | 0·2 | 8·7 | 0·5 | 14·7 | 0·9 |
| 28 | 0 52·0 | 0 52·1 | 0 49·6 | 2·8 | 0·2 | 8·8 | 0·5 | 14·8 | 0·9 |
| 29 | 0 52·3 | 0 52·4 | 0 49·9 | 2·9 | 0·2 | 8·9 | 0·5 | 14·9 | 0·9 |
| 30 | 0 52·5 | 0 52·6 | 0 50·1 | 3·0 | 0·2 | 9·0 | 0·5 | 15·0 | 0·9 |
| 31 | 0 52·8 | 0 52·9 | 0 50·3 | 3·1 | 0·2 | 9·1 | 0·5 | 15·1 | 0·9 |
| 32 | 0 53·0 | 0 53·1 | 0 50·6 | 3·2 | 0·2 | 9·2 | 0·5 | 15·2 | 0·9 |
| 33 | 0 53·3 | 0 53·4 | 0 50·8 | 3·3 | 0·2 | 9·3 | 0·5 | 15·3 | 0·9 |
| 34 | 0 53·5 | 0 53·6 | 0 51·1 | 3·4 | 0·2 | 9·4 | 0·5 | 15·4 | 0·9 |
| 35 | 0 53·8 | 0 53·9 | 0 51·3 | 3·5 | 0·2 | 9·5 | 0·6 | 15·5 | 0·9 |
| 36 | 0 54·0 | 0 54·1 | 0 51·5 | 3·6 | 0·2 | 9·6 | 0·6 | 15·6 | 0·9 |
| 37 | 0 54·3 | 0 54·4 | 0 51·8 | 3·7 | 0·2 | 9·7 | 0·6 | 15·7 | 0·9 |
| 38 | 0 54·5 | 0 54·6 | 0 52·0 | 3·8 | 0·2 | 9·8 | 0·6 | 15·8 | 0·9 |
| 39 | 0 54·8 | 0 54·9 | 0 52·3 | 3·9 | 0·2 | 9·9 | 0·6 | 15·9 | 0·9 |
| 40 | 0 55·0 | 0 55·2 | 0 52·5 | 4·0 | 0·2 | 10·0 | 0·6 | 16·0 | 0·9 |
| 41 | 0 55·3 | 0 55·4 | 0 52·7 | 4·1 | 0·2 | 10·1 | 0·6 | 16·1 | 0·9 |
| 42 | 0 55·5 | 0 55·7 | 0 53·0 | 4·2 | 0·2 | 10·2 | 0·6 | 16·2 | 0·9 |
| 43 | 0 55·8 | 0 55·9 | 0 53·2 | 4·3 | 0·3 | 10·3 | 0·6 | 16·3 | 1·0 |
| 44 | 0 56·0 | 0 56·2 | 0 53·4 | 4·4 | 0·3 | 10·4 | 0·6 | 16·4 | 1·0 |
| 45 | 0 56·3 | 0 56·4 | 0 53·7 | 4·5 | 0·3 | 10·5 | 0·6 | 16·5 | 1·0 |
| 46 | 0 56·5 | 0 56·7 | 0 53·9 | 4·6 | 0·3 | 10·6 | 0·6 | 16·6 | 1·0 |
| 47 | 0 56·8 | 0 56·9 | 0 54·2 | 4·7 | 0·3 | 10·7 | 0·6 | 16·7 | 1·0 |
| 48 | 0 57·0 | 0 57·2 | 0 54·4 | 4·8 | 0·3 | 10·8 | 0·6 | 16·8 | 1·0 |
| 49 | 0 57·3 | 0 57·4 | 0 54·6 | 4·9 | 0·3 | 10·9 | 0·6 | 16·9 | 1·0 |
| 50 | 0 57·5 | 0 57·7 | 0 54·9 | 5·0 | 0·3 | 11·0 | 0·6 | 17·0 | 1·0 |
| 51 | 0 57·8 | 0 57·9 | 0 55·1 | 5·1 | 0·3 | 11·1 | 0·6 | 17·1 | 1·0 |
| 52 | 0 58·0 | 0 58·2 | 0 55·4 | 5·2 | 0·3 | 11·2 | 0·7 | 17·2 | 1·0 |
| 53 | 0 58·3 | 0 58·4 | 0 55·6 | 5·3 | 0·3 | 11·3 | 0·7 | 17·3 | 1·0 |
| 54 | 0 58·5 | 0 58·7 | 0 55·8 | 5·4 | 0·3 | 11·4 | 0·7 | 17·4 | 1·0 |
| 55 | 0 58·8 | 0 58·9 | 0 56·1 | 5·5 | 0·3 | 11·5 | 0·7 | 17·5 | 1·0 |
| 56 | 0 59·0 | 0 59·2 | 0 56·3 | 5·6 | 0·3 | 11·6 | 0·7 | 17·6 | 1·0 |
| 57 | 0 59·3 | 0 59·4 | 0 56·6 | 5·7 | 0·3 | 11·7 | 0·7 | 17·7 | 1·0 |
| 58 | 0 59·5 | 0 59·7 | 0 56·8 | 5·8 | 0·3 | 11·8 | 0·7 | 17·8 | 1·0 |
| 59 | 0 59·8 | 0 59·9 | 0 57·0 | 5·9 | 0·3 | 11·9 | 0·7 | 17·9 | 1·0 |
| [illegible] | 1 00·0 | 1 [illegible] | [illegible] 57·3 | 6·0 | [illegible] | [illegible] | 0·7 | 18·0 | [illegible] |

4m INCREMENTS AND CORRECTIONS 5m

| 4m | SUN PLANETS | ARIES | MOON | v or d | Corrn | v or d | Corrn | v or d | Corrn |
|---|---|---|---|---|---|---|---|---|---|
| s | ° ′ | ° ′ | ° ′ | ′ | ′ | ′ | ′ | ′ | ′ |
| 00 | 1 00·0 | 1 00·2 | 0 57·3 | 0·0 | 0·0 | 6·0 | 0·5 | 12·0 | 0·9 |
| 01 | 1 00·3 | 1 00·4 | 0 57·5 | 0·1 | 0·0 | 6·1 | 0·5 | 12·1 | 0·9 |
| 02 | 1 00·5 | 1 00·7 | 0 57·7 | 0·2 | 0·0 | 6·2 | 0·5 | 12·2 | 0·9 |
| 03 | 1 00·8 | 1 00·9 | 0 58·0 | 0·3 | 0·0 | 6·3 | 0·5 | 12·3 | 0·9 |
| 04 | 1 01·0 | 1 01·2 | 0 58·2 | 0·4 | 0·0 | 6·4 | 0·5 | 12·4 | 0·9 |
| 05 | 1 01·3 | 1 01·4 | 0 58·5 | 0·5 | 0·0 | 6·5 | 0·5 | 12·5 | 0·9 |
| 06 | 1 01·5 | 1 01·7 | 0 58·7 | 0·6 | 0·0 | 6·6 | 0·5 | 12·6 | 0·9 |
| 07 | 1 01·8 | 1 01·9 | 0 58·9 | 0·7 | 0·1 | 6·7 | 0·5 | 12·7 | 1·0 |
| 08 | 1 02·0 | 1 02·2 | 0 59·2 | 0·8 | 0·1 | 6·8 | 0·5 | 12·8 | 1·0 |
| 09 | 1 02·3 | 1 02·4 | 0 59·4 | 0·9 | 0·1 | 6·9 | 0·5 | 12·9 | 1·0 |
| 10 | 1 02·5 | 1 02·7 | 0 59·7 | 1·0 | 0·1 | 7·0 | 0·5 | 13·0 | 1·0 |
| 11 | 1 02·8 | 1 02·9 | 0 59·9 | 1·1 | 0·1 | 7·1 | 0·5 | 13·1 | 1·0 |
| 12 | 1 03·0 | 1 03·2 | 1 00·1 | 1·2 | 0·1 | 7·2 | 0·5 | 13·2 | 1·0 |
| 13 | 1 03·3 | 1 03·4 | 1 00·4 | 1·3 | 0·1 | 7·3 | 0·5 | 13·3 | 1·0 |
| 14 | 1 03·5 | 1 03·7 | 1 00·6 | 1·4 | 0·1 | 7·4 | 0·6 | 13·4 | 1·0 |
| 15 | 1 03·8 | 1 03·9 | 1 00·8 | 1·5 | 0·1 | 7·5 | 0·6 | 13·5 | 1·0 |
| 16 | 1 04·0 | 1 04·2 | 1 01·1 | 1·6 | 0·1 | 7·6 | 0·6 | 13·6 | 1·0 |
| 17 | 1 04·3 | 1 04·4 | 1 01·3 | 1·7 | 0·1 | 7·7 | 0·6 | 13·7 | 1·0 |
| 18 | 1 04·5 | 1 04·7 | 1 01·6 | 1·8 | 0·1 | 7·8 | 0·6 | 13·8 | 1·0 |
| 19 | 1 04·8 | 1 04·9 | 1 01·8 | 1·9 | 0·1 | 7·9 | 0·6 | 13·9 | 1·0 |
| 20 | 1 05·0 | 1 05·2 | 1 02·0 | 2·0 | 0·2 | 8·0 | 0·6 | 14·0 | 1·1 |
| 21 | 1 05·3 | 1 05·4 | 1 02·3 | 2·1 | 0·2 | 8·1 | 0·6 | 14·1 | 1·1 |
| 22 | 1 05·5 | 1 05·7 | 1 02·5 | 2·2 | 0·2 | 8·2 | 0·6 | 14·2 | 1·1 |
| 23 | 1 05·8 | 1 05·9 | 1 02·8 | 2·3 | 0·2 | 8·3 | 0·6 | 14·3 | 1·1 |
| 24 | 1 06·0 | 1 06·2 | 1 03·0 | 2·4 | 0·2 | 8·4 | 0·6 | 14·4 | 1·1 |
| 25 | 1 06·3 | [illegible] | 1 03·2 | 2·5 | 0·2 | [illegible] | 0·6 | 14·5 | 1·1 |
| [illegible]6 | 1 06·5 | [illegible] | 1 03·5 | 2·6 | [illegible] | [illegible] | [illegible] | 14·6 | [illegible] |
| [illegible] | 1 [illegible] | [illegible] | [illegible]·7 | [illegible] | [illegible] | [illegible] | [illegible] | 14·7 | [illegible] |

| 5m | SUN PLANETS | ARIES | MOON | v or d | Corrn | v or d | Corrn | v or d | Corrn |
|---|---|---|---|---|---|---|---|---|---|
| s | ° ′ | ° ′ | ° ′ | ′ | ′ | ′ | ′ | ′ | ′ |
| 00 | 1 15·0 | 1 15·2 | 1 11·6 | 0·0 | 0·0 | 6·0 | 0·6 | 12·0 | 1·1 |
| 01 | 1 15·3 | 1 15·5 | 1 11·8 | 0·1 | 0·0 | 6·1 | 0·6 | 12·1 | 1·1 |
| 02 | 1 15·5 | 1 15·7 | 1 12·1 | 0·2 | 0·0 | 6·2 | 0·6 | 12·2 | 1·1 |
| 03 | 1 15·8 | 1 16·0 | 1 12·3 | 0·3 | 0·0 | 6·3 | 0·6 | 12·3 | 1·1 |
| 04 | 1 16·0 | 1 16·2 | 1 12·5 | 0·4 | 0·0 | 6·4 | 0·6 | 12·4 | 1·1 |
| 05 | 1 16·3 | 1 16·5 | 1 12·8 | 0·5 | 0·0 | 6·5 | 0·6 | 12·5 | 1·1 |
| 06 | 1 16·5 | 1 16·7 | 1 13·0 | 0·6 | 0·1 | 6·6 | 0·6 | 12·6 | 1·2 |
| 07 | 1 16·8 | 1 17·0 | 1 13·3 | 0·7 | 0·1 | 6·7 | 0·6 | 12·7 | 1·2 |
| 08 | 1 17·0 | 1 17·2 | 1 13·5 | 0·8 | 0·1 | 6·8 | 0·6 | 12·8 | 1·2 |
| 09 | 1 17·3 | 1 17·5 | 1 13·7 | 0·9 | 0·1 | 6·9 | 0·6 | 12·9 | 1·2 |
| 10 | 1 17·5 | 1 17·7 | 1 14·0 | 1·0 | 0·1 | 7·0 | 0·6 | 13·0 | 1·2 |
| 11 | 1 17·8 | 1 18·0 | 1 14·2 | 1·1 | 0·1 | 7·1 | 0·7 | 13·1 | 1·2 |
| 12 | 1 18·0 | 1 18·2 | 1 14·4 | 1·2 | 0·1 | 7·2 | 0·7 | 13·2 | 1·2 |
| 13 | 1 18·3 | 1 18·5 | 1 14·7 | 1·3 | 0·1 | 7·3 | 0·7 | 13·3 | 1·2 |
| 14 | 1 18·5 | 1 18·7 | 1 14·9 | 1·4 | 0·1 | 7·4 | 0·7 | 13·4 | 1·2 |
| 15 | 1 18·8 | 1 19·0 | 1 15·2 | 1·5 | 0·1 | 7·5 | 0·7 | 13·5 | 1·2 |
| 16 | 1 19·0 | 1 19·2 | 1 15·4 | 1·6 | 0·1 | 7·6 | 0·7 | 13·6 | 1·2 |
| 17 | 1 19·3 | 1 19·5 | 1 15·6 | 1·7 | 0·2 | 7·7 | 0·7 | 13·7 | 1·3 |
| 18 | 1 19·5 | 1 19·7 | 1 15·9 | 1·8 | 0·2 | 7·8 | 0·7 | 13·8 | 1·3 |
| 19 | 1 19·8 | 1 20·0 | 1 16·1 | 1·9 | 0·2 | 7·9 | 0·7 | 13·9 | 1·3 |
| 20 | 1 20·0 | 1 20·2 | 1 16·4 | 2·0 | 0·2 | 8·0 | 0·7 | 14·0 | 1·3 |
| 21 | 1 20·3 | 1 20·5 | 1 16·6 | 2·1 | 0·2 | 8·1 | 0·7 | 14·1 | 1·3 |
| 22 | 1 20·5 | 1 20·7 | 1 16·8 | 2·2 | 0·2 | 8·2 | 0·8 | 14·2 | 1·3 |
| 23 | 1 20·8 | 1 21·0 | 1 17·1 | 2·3 | 0·2 | 8·3 | 0·8 | 14·3 | 1·3 |
| 24 | 1 21·0 | 1 21·2 | 1 17·3 | 2·4 | 0·2 | 8·4 | 0·8 | 14·4 | 1·3 |
| [illegible]5 | 1 21·3 | 1 21·[illegible] | 1 17·5 | 2·5 | 0·2 | [illegible] | 0·8 | 14·5 | 1·3 |
| [illegible] | 1 21·5 | 1 [illegible] | [illegible]7·8 | 2·6 | 0·[illegible] | [illegible] | [illegible]8 | 14·6 | 1·[illegible] |
| [illegible] | [illegible]1·8 | [illegible] | [illegible] | 2·7 | [illegible] | [illegible] | [illegible] | 14·7 | [illegible] |

6m INCREMENTS AND CORRECTIONS 7m

| 6m | SUN PLANETS | ARIES | MOON | v or d | Corrn | v or d | Corrn | v or d | Corrn |
|---|---|---|---|---|---|---|---|---|---|
| s | ° ′ | ° ′ | ° ′ | ′ | ′ | ′ | ′ | ′ | ′ |
| 00 | 1 30·0 | 1 30·2 | 1 25·9 | 0·0 | 0·0 | 6·0 | 0·7 | 12·0 | 1·3 |
| 01 | 1 30·3 | 1 30·5 | 1 26·1 | 0·1 | 0·0 | 6·1 | 0·7 | 12·1 | 1·3 |
| 02 | 1 30·5 | 1 30·7 | 1 26·4 | 0·2 | 0·0 | 6·2 | 0·7 | 12·2 | 1·3 |
| 03 | 1 30·8 | 1 31·0 | 1 26·6 | 0·3 | 0·0 | 6·3 | 0·7 | 12·3 | 1·3 |
| 04 | 1 31·0 | 1 31·2 | 1 26·9 | 0·4 | 0·0 | 6·4 | 0·7 | 12·4 | 1·3 |
| 05 | 1 31·3 | 1 31·5 | 1 27·1 | 0·5 | 0·1 | 6·5 | 0·7 | 12·5 | 1·4 |
| 06 | 1 31·5 | 1 31·8 | 1 27·3 | 0·6 | 0·1 | 6·6 | 0·7 | 12·6 | 1·4 |
| 07 | 1 31·8 | 1 32·0 | 1 27·6 | 0·7 | 0·1 | 6·7 | 0·7 | 12·7 | 1·4 |
| 08 | 1 32·0 | 1 32·3 | 1 27·8 | 0·8 | 0·1 | 6·8 | 0·7 | 12·8 | 1·4 |
| 09 | 1 32·3 | 1 32·5 | 1 28·0 | 0·9 | 0·1 | 6·9 | 0·7 | 12·9 | 1·4 |
| 10 | 1 32·5 | 1 32·8 | 1 28·3 | 1·0 | 0·1 | 7·0 | 0·8 | 13·0 | 1·4 |
| 11 | 1 32·8 | 1 33·0 | 1 28·5 | 1·1 | 0·1 | 7·1 | 0·8 | 13·1 | 1·4 |
| 12 | 1 33·0 | 1 33·3 | 1 28·8 | 1·2 | 0·1 | 7·2 | 0·8 | 13·2 | 1·4 |
| 13 | 1 33·3 | 1 33·5 | 1 29·0 | 1·3 | 0·1 | 7·3 | 0·8 | 13·3 | 1·4 |
| 14 | 1 33·5 | 1 33·8 | 1 29·2 | 1·4 | 0·2 | 7·4 | 0·8 | 13·4 | 1·5 |
| 15 | 1 33·8 | 1 34·0 | 1 29·5 | 1·5 | 0·2 | 7·5 | 0·8 | 13·5 | 1·5 |
| 16 | 1 34·0 | 1 34·3 | 1 29·7 | 1·6 | 0·2 | 7·6 | 0·8 | 13·6 | 1·5 |
| 17 | 1 34·3 | 1 34·5 | 1 30·0 | 1·7 | 0·2 | 7·7 | 0·8 | 13·7 | 1·5 |
| 18 | 1 34·5 | 1 34·8 | 1 30·2 | 1·8 | 0·2 | 7·8 | 0·8 | 13·8 | 1·5 |
| 19 | 1 34·8 | 1 35·0 | 1 30·4 | 1·9 | 0·2 | 7·9 | 0·9 | 13·9 | 1·5 |
| 20 | 1 35·0 | 1 35·3 | 1 30·7 | 2·0 | 0·2 | 8·0 | 0·9 | 14·0 | 1·5 |
| 21 | 1 35·3 | 1 35·5 | 1 30·9 | 2·1 | 0·2 | 8·1 | 0·9 | 14·1 | 1·5 |
| 22 | 1 35·5 | 1 35·8 | 1 31·1 | 2·2 | 0·2 | 8·2 | 0·9 | 14·2 | 1·5 |
| 23 | 1 35·8 | 1 36·0 | 1 31·4 | 2·3 | 0·2 | 8·3 | 0·9 | 14·3 | 1·5 |
| 24 | 1 36·0 | 1 36·3 | 1 31·6 | 2·4 | 0·3 | 8·4 | 0·9 | 14·4 | 1·6 |
| 25 | 1 36·3 | 1 3[illegible] | 1 31·9 | 2·5 | 0·3 | [illegible] | 0·9 | 14·5 | 1·6 |
| [illegible] | 1 36·5 | [illegible] | [illegible]2·1 | 2·6 | [illegible] | [illegible] | [illegible]9 | 14·6 | 1·[illegible] |
| [illegible] | 1 36·[illegible] | [illegible] | [illegible] | [illegible] | [illegible] | [illegible] | [illegible] | 14·[illegible] | [illegible] |

| 7m | SUN PLANETS | ARIES | MOON | v or d | Corrn | v or d | Corrn | v or d | Corrn |
|---|---|---|---|---|---|---|---|---|---|
| s | ° ′ | ° ′ | ° ′ | ′ | ′ | ′ | ′ | ′ | ′ |
| 00 | 1 45·0 | 1 45·3 | 1 40·2 | 0·0 | 0·0 | 6·0 | 0·8 | 12·0 | 1·5 |
| 01 | 1 45·3 | 1 45·5 | 1 40·5 | 0·1 | 0·0 | 6·1 | 0·8 | 12·1 | 1·5 |
| 02 | 1 45·5 | 1 45·8 | 1 40·7 | 0·2 | 0·0 | 6·2 | 0·8 | 12·2 | 1·5 |
| 03 | 1 45·8 | 1 46·0 | 1 40·9 | 0·3 | 0·0 | 6·3 | 0·8 | 12·3 | 1·5 |
| 04 | 1 46·0 | 1 46·3 | 1 41·2 | 0·4 | 0·1 | 6·4 | 0·8 | 12·4 | 1·6 |
| 05 | 1 46·3 | 1 46·5 | 1 41·4 | 0·5 | 0·1 | 6·5 | 0·8 | 12·5 | 1·6 |
| 06 | 1 46·5 | 1 46·8 | 1 41·6 | 0·6 | 0·1 | 6·6 | 0·8 | 12·6 | 1·6 |
| 07 | 1 46·8 | 1 47·0 | 1 41·9 | 0·7 | 0·1 | 6·7 | 0·8 | 12·7 | 1·6 |
| 08 | 1 47·0 | 1 47·3 | 1 42·1 | 0·8 | 0·1 | 6·8 | 0·9 | 12·8 | 1·6 |
| 09 | 1 47·3 | 1 47·5 | 1 42·4 | 0·9 | 0·1 | 6·9 | 0·9 | 12·9 | 1·6 |
| 10 | 1 47·5 | 1 47·8 | 1 42·6 | 1·0 | 0·1 | 7·0 | 0·9 | 13·0 | 1·6 |
| 11 | 1 47·8 | 1 48·0 | 1 42·8 | 1·1 | 0·1 | 7·1 | 0·9 | 13·1 | 1·6 |
| 12 | 1 48·0 | 1 48·3 | 1 43·1 | 1·2 | 0·2 | 7·2 | 0·9 | 13·2 | 1·7 |
| 13 | 1 48·3 | 1 48·5 | 1 43·3 | 1·3 | 0·2 | 7·3 | 0·9 | 13·3 | 1·7 |
| 14 | 1 48·5 | 1 48·8 | 1 43·6 | 1·4 | 0·2 | 7·4 | 0·9 | 13·4 | 1·7 |
| 15 | 1 48·8 | 1 49·0 | 1 43·8 | 1·5 | 0·2 | 7·5 | 0·9 | 13·5 | 1·7 |
| 16 | 1 49·0 | 1 49·3 | 1 44·0 | 1·6 | 0·2 | 7·6 | 1·0 | 13·6 | 1·7 |
| 17 | 1 49·3 | 1 49·5 | 1 44·3 | 1·7 | 0·2 | 7·7 | 1·0 | 13·7 | 1·7 |
| 18 | 1 49·5 | 1 49·8 | 1 44·5 | 1·8 | 0·2 | 7·8 | 1·0 | 13·8 | 1·7 |
| 19 | 1 49·8 | 1 50·1 | 1 44·8 | 1·9 | 0·2 | 7·9 | 1·0 | 13·9 | 1·7 |
| 20 | 1 50·0 | 1 50·3 | 1 45·0 | 2·0 | 0·3 | 8·0 | 1·0 | 14·0 | 1·8 |
| 21 | 1 50·3 | 1 50·6 | 1 45·2 | 2·1 | 0·3 | 8·1 | 1·0 | 14·1 | 1·8 |
| 22 | 1 50·5 | 1 50·8 | 1 45·5 | 2·2 | 0·3 | 8·2 | 1·0 | 14·2 | 1·8 |
| 23 | 1 50·8 | 1 51·1 | 1 45·7 | 2·3 | 0·3 | 8·3 | 1·0 | 14·3 | 1·8 |
| 24 | 1 51·0 | 1 51·3 | 1 45·9 | 2·4 | 0·3 | 8·4 | 1·1 | 14·4 | 1·8 |
| [illegible] | 1 51·3 | 1 51·[illegible] | [illegible]46·2 | 2·5 | 0·3 | [illegible] | 1·1 | 14·5 | 1·8 |
| [illegible] | 1 51·5 | 1 [illegible] | [illegible]4 | 2·6 | 0·[illegible] | [illegible] | [illegible] | 14·6 | 1·[illegible] |
| [illegible] | [illegible]1·8 | [illegible] | [illegible] | 2·7 | [illegible] | [illegible] | [illegible] | [illegible]4·7 | [illegible] |

## 8m INCREMENTS AND CORRECTIONS 9m

| 8m s | SUN PLANETS ° ′ | ARIES ° ′ | MOON ° ′ | v or d ′ | Corrⁿ ′ | v or d ′ | Corrⁿ ′ | v or d ′ | Corrⁿ ′ |
|---|---|---|---|---|---|---|---|---|---|
| 00 | 2 00·0 | 2 00·3 | 1 54·5 | 0·0 | 0·0 | 6·0 | 0·9 | 12·0 | 1·7 |
| 01 | 2 00·3 | 2 00·6 | 1 54·8 | 0·1 | 0·0 | 6·1 | 0·9 | 12·1 | 1·7 |
| 02 | 2 00·5 | 2 00·8 | 1 55·0 | 0·2 | 0·0 | 6·2 | 0·9 | 12·2 | 1·7 |
| 03 | 2 00·8 | 2 01·1 | 1 55·2 | 0·3 | 0·0 | 6·3 | 0·9 | 12·3 | 1·7 |
| 04 | 2 01·0 | 2 01·3 | 1 55·5 | 0·4 | 0·1 | 6·4 | 0·9 | 12·4 | 1·8 |
| 05 | 2 01·3 | 2 01·6 | 1 55·7 | 0·5 | 0·1 | 6·5 | 0·9 | 12·5 | 1·8 |
| 06 | 2 01·5 | 2 01·8 | 1 56·0 | 0·6 | 0·1 | 6·6 | 0·9 | 12·6 | 1·8 |
| 07 | 2 01·8 | 2 02·1 | 1 56·2 | 0·7 | 0·1 | 6·7 | 0·9 | 12·7 | 1·8 |
| 08 | 2 02·0 | 2 02·3 | 1 56·4 | 0·8 | 0·1 | 6·8 | 1·0 | 12·8 | 1·8 |
| 09 | 2 02·3 | 2 02·6 | 1 56·7 | 0·9 | 0·1 | 6·9 | 1·0 | 12·9 | 1·8 |
| 10 | 2 02·5 | 2 02·8 | 1 56·9 | 1·0 | 0·1 | 7·0 | 1·0 | 13·0 | 1·8 |
| 11 | 2 02·8 | 2 03·1 | 1 57·2 | 1·1 | 0·2 | 7·1 | 1·0 | 13·1 | 1·9 |
| 12 | 2 03·0 | 2 03·3 | 1 57·4 | 1·2 | 0·2 | 7·2 | 1·0 | 13·2 | 1·9 |
| 13 | 2 03·3 | 2 03·6 | 1 57·6 | 1·3 | 0·2 | 7·3 | 1·0 | 13·3 | 1·9 |
| 14 | 2 03·5 | 2 03·8 | 1 57·9 | 1·4 | 0·2 | 7·4 | 1·0 | 13·4 | 1·9 |
| 15 | 2 03·8 | 2 04·1 | 1 58·1 | 1·5 | 0·2 | 7·5 | 1·1 | 13·5 | 1·9 |
| 16 | 2 04·0 | 2 04·3 | 1 58·4 | 1·6 | 0·2 | 7·6 | 1·1 | 13·6 | 1·9 |
| 17 | 2 04·3 | 2 04·6 | 1 58·6 | 1·7 | 0·2 | 7·7 | 1·1 | 13·7 | 1·9 |
| 18 | 2 04·5 | 2 04·8 | 1 58·8 | 1·8 | 0·3 | 7·8 | 1·1 | 13·8 | 2·0 |
| 19 | 2 04·8 | 2 05·1 | 1 59·1 | 1·9 | 0·3 | 7·9 | 1·1 | 13·9 | 2·0 |
| 20 | 2 05·0 | 2 05·3 | 1 59·3 | 2·0 | 0·3 | 8·0 | 1·1 | 14·0 | 2·0 |
| 21 | 2 05·3 | 2 05·6 | 1 59·5 | 2·1 | 0·3 | 8·1 | 1·1 | 14·1 | 2·0 |
| 22 | 2 05·5 | 2 05·8 | 1 59·8 | 2·2 | 0·3 | 8·2 | 1·2 | 14·2 | 2·0 |
| 23 | 2 05·8 | 2 06·1 | 2 00·0 | 2·3 | 0·3 | 8·3 | 1·2 | 14·3 | 2·0 |
| 24 | 2 06·0 | 2 06·3 | 2 00·3 | 2·4 | 0·3 | 8·4 | 1·2 | 14·4 | 2·0 |
| 25 | 2 06·3 | 2 06·6 | [illegible]0·5 | 2·5 | 0·4 | 8·5 | 1·[illegible] | 14·5 | 2·1 |
| [illegible] | 2 06·5 | 2 [illegible] | | 2·6 | 0·4 | 8·[illegible] | | | 2·1 |
| | 2 06·8 | | | [illegible]7 | 0·4 | | | | [illegible] |

| 9m s | SUN PLANETS ° ′ | ARIES ° ′ | MOON ° ′ | v or d ′ | Corrⁿ ′ | v or d ′ | Corrⁿ ′ | v or d ′ | Corrⁿ ′ |
|---|---|---|---|---|---|---|---|---|---|
| 00 | 2 15·0 | 2 15·4 | 2 08·9 | 0·0 | 0·0 | 6·0 | 1·0 | 12·0 | 1·9 |
| 01 | 2 15·3 | 2 15·6 | 2 09·1 | 0·1 | 0·0 | 6·1 | 1·0 | 12·1 | 1·9 |
| 02 | 2 15·5 | 2 15·9 | 2 09·3 | 0·2 | 0·0 | 6·2 | 1·0 | 12·2 | 1·9 |
| 03 | 2 15·8 | 2 16·1 | 2 09·6 | 0·3 | 0·0 | 6·3 | 1·0 | 12·3 | 1·9 |
| 04 | 2 16·0 | 2 16·4 | 2 09·8 | 0·4 | 0·1 | 6·4 | 1·0 | 12·4 | 2·0 |
| 05 | 2 16·3 | 2 16·6 | 2 10·0 | 0·5 | 0·1 | 6·5 | 1·0 | 12·5 | 2·0 |
| 06 | 2 16·5 | 2 16·9 | 2 10·3 | 0·6 | 0·1 | 6·6 | 1·0 | 12·6 | 2·0 |
| 07 | 2 16·8 | 2 17·1 | 2 10·5 | 0·7 | 0·1 | 6·7 | 1·1 | 12·7 | 2·0 |
| 08 | 2 17·0 | 2 17·4 | 2 10·8 | 0·8 | 0·1 | 6·8 | 1·1 | 12·8 | 2·0 |
| 09 | 2 17·3 | 2 17·6 | 2 11·0 | 0·9 | 0·1 | 6·9 | 1·1 | 12·9 | 2·0 |
| 10 | 2 17·5 | 2 17·9 | 2 11·2 | 1·0 | 0·2 | 7·0 | 1·1 | 13·0 | 2·1 |
| 11 | 2 17·8 | 2 18·1 | 2 11·5 | 1·1 | 0·2 | 7·1 | 1·1 | 13·1 | 2·1 |
| 12 | 2 18·0 | 2 18·4 | 2 11·7 | 1·2 | 0·2 | 7·2 | 1·1 | 13·2 | 2·1 |
| 13 | 2 18·3 | 2 18·6 | 2 12·0 | 1·3 | 0·2 | 7·3 | 1·2 | 13·3 | 2·1 |
| 14 | 2 18·5 | 2 18·9 | 2 12·2 | 1·4 | 0·2 | 7·4 | 1·2 | 13·4 | 2·1 |
| 15 | 2 18·8 | 2 19·1 | 2 12·4 | 1·5 | 0·2 | 7·5 | 1·2 | 13·5 | 2·1 |
| 16 | 2 19·0 | 2 19·4 | 2 12·7 | 1·6 | 0·3 | 7·6 | 1·2 | 13·6 | 2·2 |
| 17 | 2 19·3 | 2 19·6 | 2 12·9 | 1·7 | 0·3 | 7·7 | 1·2 | 13·7 | 2·2 |
| 18 | 2 19·5 | 2 19·9 | 2 13·1 | 1·8 | 0·3 | 7·8 | 1·2 | 13·8 | 2·2 |
| 19 | 2 19·8 | 2 20·1 | 2 13·4 | 1·9 | 0·3 | 7·9 | 1·3 | 13·9 | 2·2 |
| 20 | 2 20·0 | 2 20·4 | 2 13·6 | 2·0 | 0·3 | 8·0 | 1·3 | 14·0 | 2·2 |
| 21 | 2 20·3 | 2 20·6 | 2 13·9 | 2·1 | 0·3 | 8·1 | 1·3 | 14·1 | 2·2 |
| 22 | 2 20·5 | 2 20·9 | 2 14·1 | 2·2 | 0·3 | 8·2 | 1·3 | 14·2 | 2·2 |
| 23 | 2 20·8 | 2 21·1 | 2 14·3 | 2·3 | 0·4 | 8·3 | 1·3 | 14·3 | 2·3 |
| 24 | 2 21·0 | 2 21·4 | 2 14·6 | 2·4 | 0·4 | 8·4 | 1·3 | 14·4 | 2·3 |
| 25 | [illegible]1·3 | 2 21·6 | 2 [illegible] | 2·5 | 0·4 | 8·5 | 1·3 | [illegible] | 2·3 |
| 26 | | 2 21·9 | | [illegible] | 0·4 | 8·6 | [illegible] | | [illegible]3 |
| | | [illegible] 22·[illegible] | | | [illegible]4 | [illegible] | | | |

## 10m INCREMENTS AND CORRECTIONS 11m

| 10m s | SUN PLANETS ° ′ | ARIES ° ′ | MOON ° ′ | v or d ′ | Corrⁿ ′ | v or d ′ | Corrⁿ ′ | v or d ′ | Corrⁿ ′ |
|---|---|---|---|---|---|---|---|---|---|
| 00 | 2 30·0 | 2 30·4 | 2 23·2 | 0·0 | 0·0 | 6·0 | 1·1 | 12·0 | 2·1 |
| 01 | 2 30·3 | 2 30·7 | 2 23·4 | 0·1 | 0·0 | 6·1 | 1·1 | 12·1 | 2·1 |
| 02 | 2 30·5 | 2 30·9 | 2 23·6 | 0·2 | 0·0 | 6·2 | 1·1 | 12·2 | 2·1 |
| 03 | 2 30·8 | 2 31·2 | 2 23·9 | 0·3 | 0·1 | 6·3 | 1·1 | 12·3 | 2·2 |
| 04 | 2 31·0 | 2 31·4 | 2 24·1 | 0·4 | 0·1 | 6·4 | 1·1 | 12·4 | 2·2 |
| 05 | 2 31·3 | 2 31·7 | 2 24·4 | 0·5 | 0·1 | 6·5 | 1·1 | 12·5 | 2·2 |
| 06 | 2 31·5 | 2 31·9 | 2 24·6 | 0·6 | 0·1 | 6·6 | 1·2 | 12·6 | 2·2 |
| 07 | 2 31·8 | 2 32·2 | 2 24·8 | 0·7 | 0·1 | 6·7 | 1·2 | 12·7 | 2·2 |
| 08 | 2 32·0 | 2 32·4 | 2 25·1 | 0·8 | 0·1 | 6·8 | 1·2 | 12·8 | 2·2 |
| 09 | 2 32·3 | 2 32·7 | 2 25·3 | 0·9 | 0·2 | 6·9 | 1·2 | 12·9 | 2·3 |
| 10 | 2 32·5 | 2 32·9 | 2 25·6 | 1·0 | 0·2 | 7·0 | 1·2 | 13·0 | 2·3 |
| 11 | 2 32·8 | 2 33·2 | 2 25·8 | 1·1 | 0·2 | 7·1 | 1·2 | 13·1 | 2·3 |
| 12 | 2 33·0 | 2 33·4 | 2 26·0 | 1·2 | 0·2 | 7·2 | 1·3 | 13·2 | 2·3 |
| 13 | 2 33·3 | 2 33·7 | 2 26·3 | 1·3 | 0·2 | 7·3 | 1·3 | 13·3 | 2·3 |
| 14 | 2 33·5 | 2 33·9 | 2 26·5 | 1·4 | 0·2 | 7·4 | 1·3 | 13·4 | 2·3 |
| 15 | 2 33·8 | 2 34·2 | 2 26·7 | 1·5 | 0·3 | 7·5 | 1·3 | 13·5 | 2·4 |
| 16 | 2 34·0 | 2 34·4 | 2 27·0 | 1·6 | 0·3 | 7·6 | 1·3 | 13·6 | 2·4 |
| 17 | 2 34·3 | 2 34·7 | 2 27·2 | 1·7 | 0·3 | 7·7 | 1·3 | 13·7 | 2·4 |
| 18 | 2 34·5 | 2 34·9 | 2 27·5 | 1·8 | 0·3 | 7·8 | 1·4 | 13·8 | 2·4 |
| 19 | 2 34·8 | 2 35·2 | 2 27·7 | 1·9 | 0·3 | 7·9 | 1·4 | 13·9 | 2·4 |
| 20 | 2 35·0 | 2 35·4 | 2 27·9 | 2·0 | 0·4 | 8·0 | 1·4 | 14·0 | 2·5 |
| 21 | 2 35·3 | 2 35·7 | 2 28·2 | 2·1 | 0·4 | 8·1 | 1·4 | 14·1 | 2·5 |
| 22 | 2 35·5 | 2 35·9 | 2 28·4 | 2·2 | 0·4 | 8·2 | 1·4 | 14·2 | 2·5 |
| 23 | 2 35·8 | 2 36·2 | 2 28·7 | 2·3 | 0·4 | 8·3 | 1·5 | 14·3 | 2·5 |
| 24 | 2 36·0 | 2 36·4 | 2 28·9 | 2·4 | 0·4 | 8·4 | 1·5 | 14·4 | 2·5 |
| 25 | 2 36·3 | 2 36[illegible] | [illegible]29·1 | 2·5 | 0·4 | 8·[illegible] | [illegible]5 | 14·5 | 2·5 |
| | 2 36·5 | 2 [illegible] | | 2·6 | 0·5 | | | 14·6 | 2·6 |
| | [illegible]36·8 | | | [illegible]7 | 0·[illegible] | | | [illegible]7 | 2[illegible] |

| 11m s | SUN PLANETS ° ′ | ARIES ° ′ | MOON ° ′ | v or d ′ | Corrⁿ ′ | v or d ′ | Corrⁿ ′ | v or d ′ | Corrⁿ ′ |
|---|---|---|---|---|---|---|---|---|---|
| 00 | 2 45·0 | 2 45·5 | 2 37·5 | 0·0 | 0·0 | 6·0 | 1·2 | 12·0 | 2·3 |
| 01 | 2 45·3 | 2 45·7 | 2 37·7 | 0·1 | 0·0 | 6·1 | 1·2 | 12·1 | 2·3 |
| 02 | 2 45·5 | 2 46·0 | 2 38·0 | 0·2 | 0·0 | 6·2 | 1·2 | 12·2 | 2·3 |
| 03 | 2 45·8 | 2 46·2 | 2 38·2 | 0·3 | 0·1 | 6·3 | 1·2 | 12·3 | 2·4 |
| 04 | 2 46·0 | 2 46·5 | 2 38·4 | 0·4 | 0·1 | 6·4 | 1·2 | 12·4 | 2·4 |
| 05 | 2 46·3 | 2 46·7 | 2 38·7 | 0·5 | 0·1 | 6·5 | 1·2 | 12·5 | 2·4 |
| 06 | 2 46·5 | 2 47·0 | 2 38·9 | 0·6 | 0·1 | 6·6 | 1·3 | 12·6 | 2·4 |
| 07 | 2 46·8 | 2 47·2 | 2 39·2 | 0·7 | 0·1 | 6·7 | 1·3 | 12·7 | 2·4 |
| 08 | 2 47·0 | 2 47·5 | 2 39·4 | 0·8 | 0·2 | 6·8 | 1·3 | 12·8 | 2·5 |
| 09 | 2 47·3 | 2 47·7 | 2 39·6 | 0·9 | 0·2 | 6·9 | 1·3 | 12·9 | 2·5 |
| 10 | 2 47·5 | 2 48·0 | 2 39·9 | 1·0 | 0·2 | 7·0 | 1·3 | 13·0 | 2·5 |
| 11 | 2 47·8 | 2 48·2 | 2 40·1 | 1·1 | 0·2 | 7·1 | 1·4 | 13·1 | 2·5 |
| 12 | 2 48·0 | 2 48·5 | 2 40·3 | 1·2 | 0·2 | 7·2 | 1·4 | 13·2 | 2·5 |
| 13 | 2 48·3 | 2 48·7 | 2 40·6 | 1·3 | 0·2 | 7·3 | 1·4 | 13·3 | 2·5 |
| 14 | 2 48·5 | 2 49·0 | 2 40·8 | 1·4 | 0·3 | 7·4 | 1·4 | 13·4 | 2·6 |
| 15 | 2 48·8 | 2 49·2 | 2 41·1 | 1·5 | 0·3 | 7·5 | 1·4 | 13·5 | 2·6 |
| 16 | 2 49·0 | 2 49·5 | 2 41·3 | 1·6 | 0·3 | 7·6 | 1·5 | 13·6 | 2·6 |
| 17 | 2 49·3 | 2 49·7 | 2 41·5 | 1·7 | 0·3 | 7·7 | 1·5 | 13·7 | 2·6 |
| 18 | 2 49·5 | 2 50·0 | 2 41·8 | 1·8 | 0·3 | 7·8 | 1·5 | 13·8 | 2·6 |
| 19 | 2 49·8 | 2 50·2 | 2 42·0 | 1·9 | 0·4 | 7·9 | 1·5 | 13·9 | 2·7 |
| 20 | 2 50·0 | 2 50·5 | 2 42·3 | 2·0 | 0·4 | 8·0 | 1·5 | 14·0 | 2·7 |
| 21 | 2 50·3 | 2 50·7 | 2 42·5 | 2·1 | 0·4 | 8·1 | 1·6 | 14·1 | 2·7 |
| 22 | 2 50·5 | 2 51·0 | 2 42·7 | 2·2 | 0·4 | 8·2 | 1·6 | 14·2 | 2·7 |
| 23 | 2 50·8 | 2 51·2 | 2 43·0 | 2·3 | 0·4 | 8·3 | 1·6 | 14·3 | 2·7 |
| 24 | 2 51·0 | 2 51·5 | 2 43·2 | 2·4 | 0·5 | 8·4 | 1·6 | 14·4 | 2·8 |
| [illegible] | 2 51·3 | 2 51·7 | [illegible]3·4 | 2·5 | 0·5 | [illegible] | 1·6 | 14·5 | 2·8 |
| | [illegible]1·5 | 2 5[illegible] | [illegible]7 | 2·6 | 0[illegible] | | [illegible]·6 | 14·6 | |
| | [illegible] | 2[illegible] | | 2·7 | | | | 1[illegible] | |

12^m INCREMENTS AND CORRECTIONS 13^m

| 12^m | SUN PLANETS | ARIES | MOON | v or d | Corr^n | v or d | Corr^n | v or d | Corr^n |
|---|---|---|---|---|---|---|---|---|---|
| s | ° ′ | ° ′ | ° ′ | ′ | ′ | ′ | ′ | ′ | ′ |
| 00 | 3 00·0 | 3 00·5 | 2 51·8 | 0·0 | 0·0 | 6·0 | 1·3 | 12·0 | 2·5 |
| 01 | 3 00·3 | 3 00·7 | 2 52·0 | 0·1 | 0·0 | 6·1 | 1·3 | 12·1 | 2·5 |
| 02 | 3 00·5 | 3 01·0 | 2 52·3 | 0·2 | 0·0 | 6·2 | 1·3 | 12·2 | 2·5 |
| 03 | 3 00·8 | 3 01·2 | 2 52·5 | 0·3 | 0·1 | 6·3 | 1·3 | 12·3 | 2·6 |
| 04 | 3 01·0 | 3 01·5 | 2 52·8 | 0·4 | 0·1 | 6·4 | 1·3 | 12·4 | 2·6 |
| 05 | 3 01·3 | 3 01·7 | 2 53·0 | 0·5 | 0·1 | 6·5 | 1·4 | 12·5 | 2·6 |
| 06 | 3 01·5 | 3 02·0 | 2 53·2 | 0·6 | 0·1 | 6·6 | 1·4 | 12·6 | 2·6 |
| 07 | 3 01·8 | 3 02·2 | 2 53·5 | 0·7 | 0·1 | 6·7 | 1·4 | 12·7 | 2·6 |
| 08 | 3 02·0 | 3 02·5 | 2 53·7 | 0·8 | 0·2 | 6·8 | 1·4 | 12·8 | 2·7 |
| 09 | 3 02·3 | 3 02·7 | 2 53·9 | 0·9 | 0·2 | 6·9 | 1·4 | 12·9 | 2·7 |
| 10 | 3 02·5 | 3 03·0 | 2 54·2 | 1·0 | 0·2 | 7·0 | 1·5 | 13·0 | 2·7 |
| 11 | 3 02·8 | 3 03·3 | 2 54·4 | 1·1 | 0·2 | 7·1 | 1·5 | 13·1 | 2·7 |
| 12 | 3 03·0 | 3 03·5 | 2 54·7 | 1·2 | 0·3 | 7·2 | 1·5 | 13·2 | 2·8 |
| 13 | 3 03·3 | 3 03·8 | 2 54·9 | 1·3 | 0·3 | 7·3 | 1·5 | 13·3 | 2·8 |
| 14 | 3 03·5 | 3 04·0 | 2 55·1 | 1·4 | 0·3 | 7·4 | 1·5 | 13·4 | 2·8 |
| 15 | 3 03·8 | 3 04·3 | 2 55·4 | 1·5 | 0·3 | 7·5 | 1·6 | 13·5 | 2·8 |
| 16 | 3 04·0 | 3 04·5 | 2 55·6 | 1·6 | 0·3 | 7·6 | 1·6 | 13·6 | 2·8 |
| 17 | 3 04·3 | 3 04·8 | 2 55·9 | 1·7 | 0·4 | 7·7 | 1·6 | 13·7 | 2·9 |
| 18 | 3 04·5 | 3 05·0 | 2 56·1 | 1·8 | 0·4 | 7·8 | 1·6 | 13·8 | 2·9 |
| 19 | 3 04·8 | 3 05·3 | 2 56·3 | 1·9 | 0·4 | 7·9 | 1·6 | 13·9 | 2·9 |
| 20 | 3 05·0 | 3 05·5 | 2 56·6 | 2·0 | 0·4 | 8·0 | 1·7 | 14·0 | 2·9 |
| 21 | 3 05·3 | 3 05·8 | 2 56·8 | 2·1 | 0·4 | 8·1 | 1·7 | 14·1 | 2·9 |
| 22 | 3 05·5 | 3 06·0 | 2 57·0 | 2·2 | 0·5 | 8·2 | 1·7 | 14·2 | 3·0 |
| 23 | 3 05·8 | 3 06·3 | 2 57·3 | 2·3 | 0·5 | 8·3 | 1·7 | 14·3 | 3·0 |
| 24 | 3 06·0 | 3 06·5 | 2 57·5 | 2·4 | 0·5 | 8·4 | 1·8 | 14·4 | 3·0 |
| 25 | 3 06·3 | 3 06·8 | 57·8 | 2·5 | 0·5 | 8·5 | [illegible] | 14·5 | 3·0 |
| [illegible] | 3 06·5 | 3 0[illegible] | [illegible] | 2·6 | 0·5 | [illegible] | [illegible] | [illegible] | 3·0 |
| [illegible] | 06·8 | | | [illegible]7 | 0·[illegible] | | | | [illegible]1 |

| 13^m | SUN PLANETS | ARIES | MOON | v or d | Corr^n | v or d | Corr^n | v or d | Corr^n |
|---|---|---|---|---|---|---|---|---|---|
| s | ° ′ | ° ′ | ° ′ | ′ | ′ | ′ | ′ | ′ | ′ |
| 00 | 3 15·0 | 3 15·5 | 3 06·1 | 0·0 | 0·0 | 6·0 | 1·4 | 12·0 | 2·7 |
| 01 | 3 15·3 | 3 15·8 | 3 06·4 | 0·1 | 0·0 | 6·1 | 1·4 | 12·1 | 2·7 |
| 02 | 3 15·5 | 3 16·0 | 3 06·6 | 0·2 | 0·0 | 6·2 | 1·4 | 12·2 | 2·7 |
| 03 | [illegible] | [illegible] | [illegible] | [illegible] | 0·1 | [illegible] | 1·4 | 12·3 | 2·8 |
| 04 | 3 16·0 | 3 16·5 | 3 07·1 | 0·4 | 0·1 | 6·4 | 1·4 | 12·4 | 2·8 |
| 05 | 3 16·3 | 3 16·8 | 3 07·3 | 0·5 | 0·1 | 6·5 | 1·5 | 12·5 | 2·8 |
| 06 | 3 16·5 | 3 17·0 | 3 07·5 | 0·6 | 0·1 | 6·6 | 1·5 | 12·6 | 2·8 |
| 07 | 3 16·8 | 3 17·3 | 3 07·8 | 0·7 | 0·2 | 6·7 | 1·5 | 12·7 | 2·9 |
| 08 | 3 17·0 | 3 17·5 | 3 08·0 | 0·8 | 0·2 | 6·8 | 1·5 | 12·8 | 2·9 |
| 09 | 3 17·3 | 3 17·8 | 3 08·3 | 0·9 | 0·2 | 6·9 | 1·6 | 12·9 | 2·9 |
| 10 | 3 17·5 | 3 18·0 | 3 08·5 | 1·0 | 0·2 | 7·0 | 1·6 | 13·0 | 2·9 |
| 11 | 3 17·8 | 3 18·3 | 3 08·7 | 1·1 | 0·2 | 7·1 | 1·6 | 13·1 | 2·9 |
| 12 | 3 18·0 | 3 18·5 | 3 09·0 | 1·2 | 0·3 | 7·2 | 1·6 | 13·2 | 3·0 |
| 13 | 3 18·3 | 3 18·8 | 3 09·2 | 1·3 | 0·3 | 7·3 | 1·6 | 13·3 | 3·0 |
| 14 | 3 18·5 | 3 19·0 | 3 09·5 | 1·4 | 0·3 | 7·4 | 1·7 | 13·4 | 3·0 |
| 15 | 3 18·8 | 3 19·3 | 3 09·7 | 1·5 | 0·3 | 7·5 | 1·7 | 13·5 | 3·0 |
| 16 | 3 19·0 | 3 19·5 | 3 09·9 | 1·6 | 0·4 | 7·6 | 1·7 | 13·6 | 3·1 |
| 17 | 3 19·3 | 3 19·8 | 3 10·2 | 1·7 | 0·4 | 7·7 | 1·7 | 13·7 | 3·1 |
| 18 | 3 19·5 | 3 20·0 | 3 10·4 | 1·8 | 0·4 | 7·8 | 1·8 | 13·8 | 3·1 |
| 19 | 3 19·8 | 3 20·3 | 3 10·7 | 1·9 | 0·4 | 7·9 | 1·8 | 13·9 | 3·1 |
| 20 | 3 20·0 | 3 20·5 | 3 10·9 | 2·0 | 0·5 | 8·0 | 1·8 | 14·0 | 3·2 |
| 21 | 3 20·3 | 3 20·8 | 3 11·1 | 2·1 | 0·5 | 8·1 | 1·8 | 14·1 | 3·2 |
| 22 | 3 20·5 | 3 21·0 | 3 11·4 | 2·2 | 0·5 | 8·2 | 1·8 | 14·2 | 3·2 |
| 23 | 3 20·8 | 3 21·3 | 3 11·6 | 2·3 | 0·5 | 8·3 | 1·9 | 14·3 | 3·2 |
| 24 | 3 21·0 | 3 21·6 | 3 11·8 | 2·4 | 0·5 | 8·4 | 1·9 | 14·4 | 3·2 |
| 25 | [illegible]1·3 | 3 21·8 | 3 1[illegible] | 2·5 | 0·6 | 8·5 | 1·[illegible] | [illegible]4·5 | 3·3 |
| 2[illegible] | | 3 22·1 | [illegible] | [illegible] | 0·6 | 8·6 | | | 3·3 |
| | | [illegible]22·3 | | | [illegible]6 | [illegible] | | | [illegible]3 |

14^m INCREMENTS AND CORRECTIONS 15^m

| 14^m | SUN PLANETS | ARIES | MOON | v or d | Corr^n | v or d | Corr^n | v or d | Corr^n |
|---|---|---|---|---|---|---|---|---|---|
| s | ° ′ | ° ′ | ° ′ | ′ | ′ | ′ | ′ | ′ | ′ |
| 00 | 3 30·0 | 3 30·6 | 3 20·4 | 0·0 | 0·0 | 6·0 | 1·5 | 12·0 | 2·9 |
| 01 | 3 30·3 | 3 30·8 | 3 20·7 | 0·1 | 0·0 | 6·1 | 1·5 | 12·1 | 2·9 |
| 02 | 3 30·5 | 3 31·1 | 3 20·9 | 0·2 | 0·0 | 6·2 | 1·5 | 12·2 | 2·9 |
| 03 | 3 30·8 | 3 31·3 | 3 21·1 | 0·3 | 0·1 | 6·3 | 1·5 | 12·3 | 3·0 |
| 04 | 3 31·0 | 3 31·6 | 3 21·4 | 0·4 | 0·1 | 6·4 | 1·5 | 12·4 | 3·0 |
| 05 | 3 31·3 | 3 31·8 | 3 21·6 | 0·5 | 0·1 | 6·5 | 1·6 | 12·5 | 3·0 |
| 06 | 3 31·5 | 3 32·1 | 3 21·9 | 0·6 | 0·1 | 6·6 | 1·6 | 12·6 | 3·0 |
| 07 | 3 31·8 | 3 32·3 | 3 22·1 | 0·7 | 0·2 | 6·7 | 1·6 | 12·7 | 3·1 |
| 08 | 3 32·0 | 3 32·6 | 3 22·3 | 0·8 | 0·2 | 6·8 | 1·6 | 12·8 | 3·1 |
| 09 | 3 32·3 | 3 32·8 | 3 22·6 | 0·9 | 0·2 | 6·9 | 1·7 | 12·9 | 3·1 |
| 10 | 3 32·5 | 3 33·1 | 3 22·8 | 1·0 | 0·2 | 7·0 | 1·7 | 13·0 | 3·1 |
| 11 | 3 32·8 | 3 33·3 | 3 23·1 | 1·1 | 0·3 | 7·1 | 1·7 | 13·1 | 3·2 |
| 12 | 3 33·0 | 3 33·6 | 3 23·3 | 1·2 | 0·3 | 7·2 | 1·7 | 13·2 | 3·2 |
| 13 | 3 33·3 | 3 33·8 | 3 23·5 | 1·3 | 0·3 | 7·3 | 1·8 | 13·3 | 3·2 |
| 14 | 3 33·5 | 3 34·1 | 3 23·8 | 1·4 | 0·3 | 7·4 | 1·8 | 13·4 | 3·2 |
| 15 | 3 33·8 | 3 34·3 | 3 24·0 | 1·5 | 0·4 | 7·5 | 1·8 | 13·5 | 3·3 |
| 16 | 3 34·0 | 3 34·6 | 3 24·3 | 1·6 | 0·4 | 7·6 | 1·8 | 13·6 | 3·3 |
| 17 | 3 34·3 | 3 34·8 | 3 24·5 | 1·7 | 0·4 | 7·7 | 1·9 | 13·7 | 3·3 |
| 18 | 3 34·5 | 3 35·1 | 3 24·7 | 1·8 | 0·4 | 7·8 | 1·9 | 13·8 | 3·3 |
| 19 | 3 34·8 | 3 35·3 | 3 25·0 | 1·9 | 0·5 | 7·9 | 1·9 | 13·9 | 3·4 |
| 20 | 3 35·0 | 3 35·6 | 3 25·2 | 2·0 | 0·5 | 8·0 | 1·9 | 14·0 | 3·4 |
| 21 | 3 35·3 | 3 35·8 | 3 25·4 | 2·1 | 0·5 | 8·1 | 2·0 | 14·1 | 3·4 |
| 22 | 3 35·5 | 3 36·1 | 3 25·7 | 2·2 | 0·5 | 8·2 | 2·0 | 14·2 | 3·4 |
| 23 | 3 35·8 | 3 36·3 | 3 25·9 | 2·3 | 0·6 | 8·3 | 2·0 | 14·3 | 3·5 |
| 24 | 3 36·0 | 3 36·6 | 3 26·2 | 2·4 | 0·6 | 8·4 | 2·0 | 14·4 | 3·5 |
| 25 | 3 36·3 | 3 36·8 | [illegible]·4 | 2·5 | 0·6 | 8·5 | 2·1 | [illegible] | 3·5 |
| [illegible] | 3 36·5 | 3 3[illegible] | | [illegible]·6 | 0·6 | 8·6 | [illegible] | | [illegible]5 |
| | [illegible]6·8 | [illegible] | | | [illegible]7 | [illegible] | | | |

| 15^m | SUN PLANETS | ARIES | MOON | v or d | Corr^n | v or d | Corr^n | v or d | Corr^n |
|---|---|---|---|---|---|---|---|---|---|
| s | ° ′ | ° ′ | ° ′ | ′ | ′ | ′ | ′ | ′ | ′ |
| 00 | 3 45·0 | 3 45·6 | 3 34·8 | 0·0 | 0·0 | 6·0 | 1·6 | 12·0 | 3·1 |
| 01 | 3 45·3 | 3 45·9 | 3 35·0 | 0·1 | 0·0 | 6·1 | 1·6 | 12·1 | 3·1 |
| 02 | 3 45·5 | 3 46·1 | 3 35·2 | 0·2 | 0·1 | 6·2 | 1·6 | 12·2 | 3·2 |
| 03 | 3 45·8 | 3 46·4 | 3 35·5 | 0·3 | 0·1 | 6·3 | 1·6 | 12·3 | 3·2 |
| 04 | 3 46·0 | 3 46·6 | 3 35·7 | 0·4 | 0·1 | 6·4 | 1·7 | 12·4 | 3·2 |
| 05 | 3 46·3 | 3 46·9 | 3 35·9 | 0·5 | 0·1 | 6·5 | 1·7 | 12·5 | 3·2 |
| 06 | 3 46·5 | 3 47·1 | 3 36·2 | 0·6 | 0·2 | 6·6 | 1·7 | 12·6 | 3·3 |
| 07 | 3 46·8 | 3 47·4 | 3 36·4 | 0·7 | 0·2 | 6·7 | 1·7 | 12·7 | 3·3 |
| 08 | 3 47·0 | 3 47·6 | 3 36·7 | 0·8 | 0·2 | 6·8 | 1·8 | 12·8 | 3·3 |
| 09 | 3 47·3 | 3 47·9 | 3 36·9 | 0·9 | 0·2 | 6·9 | 1·8 | 12·9 | 3·3 |
| 10 | 3 47·5 | 3 48·1 | 3 37·1 | 1·0 | 0·3 | 7·0 | 1·8 | 13·0 | 3·4 |
| 11 | 3 47·8 | 3 48·4 | 3 37·4 | 1·1 | 0·3 | 7·1 | 1·8 | 13·1 | 3·4 |
| 12 | 3 48·0 | 3 48·6 | 3 37·6 | 1·2 | 0·3 | 7·2 | 1·9 | 13·2 | 3·4 |
| 13 | 3 48·3 | 3 48·9 | 3 37·9 | 1·3 | 0·3 | 7·3 | 1·9 | 13·3 | 3·4 |
| 14 | 3 48·5 | 3 49·1 | 3 38·1 | 1·4 | 0·4 | 7·4 | 1·9 | 13·4 | 3·5 |
| 15 | 3 48·8 | 3 49·4 | 3 38·3 | 1·5 | 0·4 | 7·5 | 1·9 | 13·5 | 3·5 |
| 16 | 3 49·0 | 3 49·6 | 3 38·6 | 1·6 | 0·4 | 7·6 | 2·0 | 13·6 | 3·5 |
| 17 | 3 49·3 | 3 49·9 | 3 38·8 | 1·7 | 0·4 | 7·7 | 2·0 | 13·7 | 3·5 |
| 18 | 3 49·5 | 3 50·1 | 3 39·0 | 1·8 | 0·5 | 7·8 | 2·0 | 13·8 | 3·6 |
| 19 | 3 49·8 | 3 50·4 | 3 39·3 | 1·9 | 0·5 | 7·9 | 2·0 | 13·9 | 3·6 |
| 20 | 3 50·0 | 3 50·6 | 3 39·5 | 2·0 | 0·5 | 8·0 | 2·1 | 14·0 | 3·6 |
| 21 | 3 50·3 | 3 50·9 | 3 39·8 | 2·1 | 0·5 | 8·1 | 2·1 | 14·1 | 3·6 |
| 22 | 3 50·5 | 3 51·1 | 3 40·0 | 2·2 | 0·6 | 8·2 | 2·1 | 14·2 | 3·7 |
| 23 | 3 50·8 | 3 51·4 | 3 40·2 | 2·3 | 0·6 | 8·3 | 2·1 | 14·3 | 3·7 |
| 24 | 3 51·0 | 3 51·6 | 3 40·5 | 2·4 | 0·6 | 8·4 | 2·2 | 14·4 | 3·7 |
| 25 | 3 51·[illegible] | 3 51·9 | 3 40·7 | [illegible] | 0·6 | 8·5 | 2·2 | 14[illegible] | 3·7 |
| 26 | [illegible] | [illegible]2·1 | 3 41·[illegible] | | | 8·6 | 2·2 | | |
| 27 | | | 3 [illegible] | | | [illegible]7 | 2·[illegible] | | |

## ALTITUDE CORRECTION TABLES 0°–35°—MOON

| App. Alt. | 0°–4° Corr$^n$ | 5°–9° Corr$^n$ | 10°–14° Corr$^n$ | 15°–19° Corr$^n$ | 20°–24° Corr$^n$ | 25°–29° Corr$^n$ | 30°–34° Corr$^n$ | App. Alt. |
|---|---|---|---|---|---|---|---|---|
| 00 | 0° 33·8 | 5° 58·2 | 10° 62·1 | 15° 62·8 | 20° 62·2 | 25° 60·8 | 30° 58·9 | 00 |
| 10 | 35·9 | 58·5 | 62·2 | 62·8 | 62·1 | 60·8 | 58·8 | 10 |
| 20 | 37·8 | 58·7 | 62·2 | 62·8 | 62·1 | 60·7 | 58·8 | 20 |
| 30 | 39·6 | 58·9 | 62·3 | 62·8 | 62·1 | 60·7 | 58·7 | 30 |
| 40 | 41·2 | 59·1 | 62·3 | 62·8 | 62·0 | 60·6 | 58·6 | 40 |
| 50 | 42·6 | 59·3 | 62·4 | 62·7 | 62·0 | 60·6 | 58·5 | 50 |
| 00 | 1 44·0 | 6 59·5 | 11 62·4 | 16 62·7 | 21 62·0 | 26 60·5 | 31 58·5 | 00 |
| 10 | 45·2 | 59·7 | 62·4 | 62·7 | 61·9 | 60·4 | 58·4 | 10 |
| 20 | 46·3 | 59·9 | 62·5 | 62·7 | 61·9 | 60·4 | 58·3 | 20 |
| 30 | 47·3 | 60·0 | 62·5 | 62·7 | 61·9 | 60·3 | 58·2 | 30 |
| 40 | 48·3 | 60·2 | 62·5 | 62·7 | 61·8 | 60·3 | 58·2 | 40 |
| 50 | 49·2 | 60·3 | 62·6 | 62·7 | 61·8 | 60·2 | 58·1 | 50 |
| 00 | 2 50·0 | 7 60·5 | 12 62·6 | 17 62·7 | 22 61·7 | 27 60·1 | 32 58·0 | 00 |
| 10 | 50·8 | 60·6 | 62·6 | 62·6 | 61·7 | 60·1 | 57·9 | 10 |
| 20 | 51·4 | 60·7 | 62·6 | 62·6 | 61·6 | 60·0 | 57·8 | 20 |
| 30 | 52·1 | 60·9 | 62·7 | 62·6 | 61·6 | 59·9 | 57·8 | 30 |
| 40 | 52·7 | 61·0 | 62·7 | 62·6 | 61·5 | 59·9 | 57·7 | 40 |
| 50 | 53·3 | 61·1 | 62·7 | 62·6 | 61·5 | 59·8 | 57·6 | 50 |
| 00 | 3 53·8 | 8 61·2 | 13 62·7 | 18 62·5 | 23 61·5 | 28 59·7 | 33 57·5 | 00 |
| 10 | 54·3 | 61·3 | 62·7 | 62·5 | 61·4 | 59·7 | 57·4 | 10 |
| 20 | 54·8 | 61·4 | 62·7 | 62·5 | 61·4 | 59·6 | 57·4 | 20 |
| 30 | 55·2 | 61·5 | 62·8 | 62·5 | 61·3 | 59·6 | 57·3 | 30 |
| 40 | 55·6 | 61·6 | 62·8 | 62·4 | 61·3 | 59·5 | 57·2 | 40 |
| 50 | 56·0 | 61·6 | 62·8 | 62·4 | 61·2 | 59·4 | 57·1 | 50 |
| 00 | 4 56·4 | 9 61·7 | 14 62·8 | 19 62·4 | 24 61·2 | 29 59·3 | 34 57·0 | 00 |
| 10 | 56·7 | 61·8 | 62·8 | 62·3 | 61·1 | 59·3 | 56·9 | 10 |
| 20 | 57·1 | 61·9 | 62·8 | 62·3 | 61·1 | 59·2 | 56·9 | 20 |
| 30 | 57·4 | 61·9 | 62·8 | 62·3 | 61·0 | 59·1 | 56·8 | 30 |
| 40 | 57·7 | 62·0 | 62·8 | 62·2 | 60·9 | 59·1 | 56·7 | 40 |
| 50 | 57·9 | 62·1 | 62·8 | 62·2 | 60·9 | 59·0 | 56·6 | 50 |

| H.P. | L | U | L | U | L | U | L | U | L | U | L | U | L | U | H.P. |
|---|---|---|---|---|---|---|---|---|---|---|---|---|---|---|---|
| 54·0 | 0·3 | 0·9 | 0·3 | 0·9 | 0·4 | 1·0 | 0·5 | 1·1 | 0·6 | 1·2 | 0·7 | 1·3 | 0·9 | 1·5 | 54·0 |
| 54·3 | 0·7 | 1·1 | 0·7 | 1·2 | 0·7 | 1·2 | 0·8 | 1·3 | 0·9 | 1·4 | 1·1 | 1·5 | 1·2 | 1·7 | 54·3 |
| 54·6 | 1·1 | 1·4 | 1·1 | 1·4 | 1·1 | 1·4 | 1·2 | 1·5 | 1·3 | 1·6 | 1·4 | 1·7 | 1·5 | 1·8 | 54·6 |
| 54·9 | 1·4 | 1·6 | 1·5 | 1·6 | 1·5 | 1·6 | 1·6 | 1·7 | 1·6 | 1·8 | 1·8 | 1·9 | 1·9 | 2·0 | 54·9 |
| 55·2 | 1·8 | 1·8 | 1·8 | 1·8 | 1·9 | 1·9 | 1·9 | 1·9 | 2·0 | 2·0 | 2·1 | 2·1 | 2·2 | 2·2 | 55·2 |
| 55·5 | 2·2 | 2·0 | 2·2 | 2·0 | 2·3 | 2·1 | 2·3 | 2·1 | 2·4 | 2·2 | 2·4 | 2·3 | 2·5 | 2·4 | 55·5 |
| 55·8 | 2·6 | 2·2 | 2·6 | 2·2 | 2·6 | 2·3 | 2·7 | 2·3 | 2·7 | 2·4 | 2·8 | 2·4 | 2·9 | 2·5 | 55·8 |
| 56·1 | 3·0 | 2·4 | 3·0 | 2·5 | 3·0 | 2·5 | 3·0 | 2·5 | 3·1 | 2·6 | 3·1 | 2·6 | 3·2 | 2·7 | 56·1 |
| 56·4 | 3·4 | 2·7 | 3·4 | 2·7 | 3·4 | 2·7 | 3·4 | 2·7 | 3·4 | 2·8 | 3·5 | 2·8 | 3·5 | 2·9 | 56·4 |
| 56·7 | 3·7 | 2·9 | 3·7 | 2·9 | 3·8 | 2·9 | 3·8 | 2·9 | 3·8 | 3·0 | 3·8 | 3·0 | 3·9 | 3·0 | 56·7 |
| 57·0 | 4·1 | 3·1 | 4·1 | 3·1 | 4·1 | 3·1 | 4·1 | 3·1 | 4·2 | 3·1 | 4·2 | 3·2 | 4·2 | 3·2 | 57·0 |
| 57·3 | 4·5 | 3·3 | 4·5 | 3·3 | 4·5 | 3·3 | 4·5 | 3·3 | 4·5 | 3·3 | 4·5 | 3·4 | 4·6 | 3·4 | 57·3 |
| 57·6 | 4·9 | 3·5 | 4·9 | 3·5 | 4·9 | 3·5 | 4·9 | 3·5 | 4·9 | 3·5 | 4·9 | 3·5 | 4·9 | 3·6 | 57·6 |
| 57·9 | 5·3 | 3·8 | 5·3 | 3·8 | 5·2 | 3·8 | 5·2 | 3·7 | 5·2 | 3·7 | 5·2 | 3·7 | 5·2 | 3·7 | 57·9 |
| 58·2 | 5·6 | 4·0 | 5·6 | 4·0 | 5·6 | 4·0 | 5·6 | 4·0 | 5·6 | 3·9 | 5·6 | 3·9 | 5·6 | 3·9 | 58·2 |
| 58·5 | 6·0 | 4·2 | 6·0 | 4·2 | 6·0 | 4·2 | 6·0 | 4·2 | 6·0 | 4·1 | 5·9 | 4·1 | 5·9 | 4·1 | 58·5 |
| 58·8 | 6·4 | 4·4 | 6·4 | 4·4 | 6·4 | 4·4 | 6·3 | 4·4 | 6·3 | 4·3 | 6·3 | 4·3 | 6·2 | 4·2 | 58·8 |
| 59·1 | 6·8 | 4·6 | 6·8 | 4·6 | 6·7 | 4·6 | 6·7 | 4·6 | 6·7 | 4·5 | 6·6 | 4·5 | 6·6 | 4·4 | 59·1 |
| 59·4 | 7·2 | 4·8 | 7·1 | 4·8 | 7·1 | 4·8 | 7·1 | 4·8 | 7·0 | 4·7 | 7·0 | 4·7 | 6·9 | 4·6 | 59·4 |
| 59·7 | 7·5 | 5·1 | 7·5 | 5·0 | 7·5 | 5·0 | 7·5 | 5·0 | 7·4 | 4·9 | 7·3 | 4·8 | 7·2 | 4·7 | 59·7 |
| 60·0 | 7·9 | 5·3 | 7·9 | 5·3 | 7·9 | 5·2 | 7·8 | 5·2 | 7·8 | 5·1 | 7·7 | 5·0 | 7·6 | 4·9 | 60·0 |
| 60·3 | 8·3 | 5·5 | 8·3 | 5·5 | 8·2 | 5·4 | 8·2 | 5·4 | 8·1 | 5·3 | 8·0 | 5·2 | 7·9 | 5·1 | 60·3 |
| 60·6 | 8·7 | 5·7 | 8·7 | 5·7 | 8·6 | 5·7 | 8·6 | 5·6 | 8·5 | 5·5 | 8·4 | 5·4 | 8·2 | 5·3 | 60·6 |
| 60·9 | 9·1 | 5·9 | 9·0 | 5·9 | 9·0 | 5·9 | 8·9 | 5·8 | 8·8 | 5·7 | 8·7 | 5·6 | 8·6 | 5·4 | 60·9 |
| 61·2 | 9·5 | 6·2 | 9·4 | 6·1 | 9·4 | 6·1 | 9·3 | 6·0 | 9·2 | 5·9 | 9·1 | 5·8 | 8·9 | 5·6 | 61·2 |
| 61·5 | 9·8 | 6·4 | 9·8 | 6·3 | 9·7 | 6·3 | 9·7 | 6·2 | 9·5 | 6·1 | 9·4 | 5·9 | 9·2 | 5·8 | 61·5 |

### DIP

| Ht. of Eye (m) | Corr$^n$ | Ht. of Eye (ft.) | Ht. of Eye (m) | Corr$^n$ | Ht. of Eye (ft.) |
|---|---|---|---|---|---|
| 2·4 | | 8·0 | 9·5 | | 31·5 |
| | −2·8 | | | −5·5 | |
| 2·6 | | 8·6 | 9·9 | | 32·7 |
| | −2·9 | | | −5·6 | |
| 2·8 | | 9·2 | 10·3 | | 33·9 |
| | −3·0 | | | −5·7 | |
| 3·0 | | 9·8 | 10·6 | | 35·1 |
| | −3·1 | | | −5·8 | |
| 3·2 | | 10·5 | 11·0 | | 36·3 |
| | −3·2 | | | −5·9 | |
| 3·4 | | 11·2 | 11·4 | | 37·6 |
| | −3·3 | | | −6·0 | |
| 3·6 | | 11·9 | 11·8 | | 38·9 |
| | −3·4 | | | −6·1 | |
| 3·8 | | 12·6 | 12·2 | | 40·1 |
| | −3·5 | | | −6·2 | |
| 4·0 | | 13·3 | 12·6 | | 41·5 |
| | −3·6 | | | −6·3 | |
| 4·3 | | 14·1 | 13·0 | | 42·8 |
| | −3·7 | | | −6·4 | |
| 4·5 | | 14·9 | 13·4 | | 44·2 |
| | −3·8 | | | −6·5 | |
| 4·7 | | 15·7 | 13·8 | | 45·5 |
| | −3·9 | | | −6·6 | |
| 5·0 | | 16·5 | 14·2 | | 46·9 |
| | −4·0 | | | −6·7 | |
| 5·2 | | 17·4 | 14·7 | | 48·4 |
| | −4·1 | | | −6·8 | |
| 5·5 | | 18·3 | 15·1 | | 49·8 |
| | −4·2 | | | −6·9 | |
| 5·8 | | 19·1 | 15·5 | | 51·3 |
| | −4·3 | | | −7·0 | |
| 6·1 | | 20·1 | 16·0 | | 52·8 |
| | −4·4 | | | −7·1 | |
| 6·3 | | 21·0 | 16·5 | | 54·3 |
| | −4·5 | | | −7·2 | |
| 6·6 | | 22·0 | 16·9 | | 55·8 |
| | −4·6 | | | −7·3 | |
| 6·9 | | 22·9 | 17·4 | | 57·4 |
| | −4·7 | | | −7·4 | |
| 7·2 | | 23·9 | 17·9 | | 58·9 |
| | −4·8 | | | −7·5 | |
| 7·5 | | 24·9 | 18·4 | | 60·5 |
| | −4·9 | | | −7·6 | |
| 7·9 | | 26·0 | 18·8 | | 62·1 |
| | −5·0 | | | −7·7 | |
| 8·2 | | 27·1 | 19·3 | | 63·8 |
| | −5·1 | | | −7·8 | |
| 8·5 | | 28·1 | 19·8 | | 65·4 |
| | −5·2 | | | −7·9 | |
| 8·8 | | 29·2 | 20·4 | | 67·1 |
| | −5·3 | | | −8·0 | |
| 9·2 | | 30·4 | 20·9 | | 68·8 |
| | −5·4 | | | −8·1 | |
| 9·5 | | 31·5 | 21·4 | | 70·5 |

### MOON CORRECTION TABLE

The correction is in two parts; the first correction is taken from the upper part of the table with argument apparent altitude, and the second from the lower part, with argument H.P., in the same column as that from which the first correction was taken. Separate corrections are given in the lower part for lower (L) and upper (U) limbs. All corrections are to be **added** to apparent altitude, *but 30′ is to be subtracted from the altitude of the upper limb.*

For corrections for pressure and temperature see page A4.

For bubble sextant observations ignore dip, take the mean of upper and lower limb corrections and subtract 15′ from the altitude.

App. Alt. = Apparent altitude = Sextant altitude corrected for index error and dip.

## ALTITUDE CORRECTION TABLES 35°–90°—MOON

| App. Alt. | 35°–39° Corrⁿ | 40°–44° Corrⁿ | 45°–49° Corrⁿ | 50°–54° Corrⁿ | 55°–59° Corrⁿ | 60°–64° Corrⁿ | 65°–69° Corrⁿ | 70°–74° Corrⁿ | 75°–79° Corrⁿ | 80°–84° Corrⁿ | 85°–89° Corrⁿ | App. Alt. |
|---|---|---|---|---|---|---|---|---|---|---|---|---|
| 00 | **35** 56·5 | **40** 53·7 | **45** 50·5 | **50** 46·9 | **55** 43·1 | **60** 38·9 | **65** 34·6 | **70** 30·1 | **75** 25·3 | **80** 20·5 | **85** 15·6 | 00 |
| 10 | 56·4 | 53·6 | 50·4 | 46·8 | 42·9 | 38·8 | 34·4 | 29·9 | 25·2 | 20·4 | 15·5 | 10 |
| 20 | 56·3 | 53·5 | 50·2 | 46·7 | 42·8 | 38·7 | 34·3 | 29·7 | 25·0 | 20·2 | 15·3 | 20 |
| 30 | 56·2 | 53·4 | 50·1 | 46·5 | 42·7 | 38·5 | 34·1 | 29·6 | 24·9 | 20·0 | 15·1 | 30 |
| 40 | 56·2 | 53·3 | 50·0 | 46·4 | 42·5 | 38·4 | 34·0 | 29·4 | 24·7 | 19·9 | 15·0 | 40 |
| 50 | 56·1 | 53·2 | 49·9 | 46·3 | 42·4 | 38·2 | 33·8 | 29·3 | 24·5 | 19·7 | 14·8 | 50 |
| 00 | **36** 56·0 | **41** 53·1 | **46** 49·8 | **51** 46·2 | **56** 42·3 | **61** 38·1 | **66** 33·7 | **71** 29·1 | **76** 24·4 | **81** 19·6 | **86** 14·6 | 00 |
| 10 | 55·9 | 53·0 | 49·7 | 46·0 | 42·1 | 37·9 | 33·5 | 29·0 | 24·2 | 19·4 | 14·5 | 10 |
| 20 | 55·8 | 52·8 | 49·5 | 45·9 | 42·0 | 37·8 | 33·4 | 28·8 | 24·1 | 19·2 | 14·3 | 20 |
| 30 | 55·7 | 52·7 | 49·4 | 45·8 | 41·8 | 37·7 | 33·2 | 28·7 | 23·9 | 19·1 | 14·1 | 30 |
| 40 | 55·6 | 52·6 | 49·3 | 45·7 | 41·7 | 37·5 | 33·1 | 28·5 | 23·8 | 18·9 | 14·0 | 40 |
| 50 | 55·5 | 52·5 | 49·2 | 45·5 | 41·6 | 37·4 | 32·9 | 28·3 | 23·6 | 18·7 | 13·8 | 50 |
| 00 | **37** 55·4 | **42** 52·4 | **47** 49·1 | **52** 45·4 | **57** 41·4 | **62** 37·2 | **67** 32·8 | **72** 28·2 | **77** 23·4 | **82** 18·6 | **87** 13·7 | 00 |
| 10 | 55·3 | 52·3 | 49·0 | 45·3 | 41·3 | 37·1 | 32·6 | 28·0 | 23·3 | 18·4 | 13·5 | 10 |
| 20 | 55·2 | 52·2 | 48·8 | 45·2 | 41·2 | 36·9 | 32·5 | 27·9 | 23·1 | 18·2 | 13·3 | 20 |
| 30 | 55·1 | 52·1 | 48·7 | 45·0 | 41·0 | 36·8 | 32·3 | 27·7 | 22·9 | 18·1 | 13·2 | 30 |
| 40 | 55·0 | 52·0 | 48·6 | 44·9 | 40·9 | 36·6 | 32·2 | 27·6 | 22·8 | 17·9 | 13·0 | 40 |
| 50 | 55·0 | 51·9 | 48·5 | 44·8 | 40·8 | 36·5 | 32·0 | 27·4 | 22·6 | 17·8 | 12·8 | 50 |
| 00 | **38** 54·9 | **43** 51·8 | **48** 48·4 | **53** 44·6 | **58** 40·6 | **63** 36·4 | **68** 31·9 | **73** 27·2 | **78** 22·5 | **83** 17·6 | **88** 12·7 | 00 |
| 10 | 54·8 | 51·7 | 48·2 | 44·5 | 40·5 | 36·2 | 31·7 | 27·1 | 22·3 | 17·4 | 12·5 | 10 |
| 20 | 54·7 | 51·6 | 48·1 | 44·4 | 40·3 | 36·1 | 31·6 | 26·9 | 22·1 | 17·3 | 12·3 | 20 |
| 30 | 54·6 | 51·5 | 48·0 | 44·2 | 40·2 | 35·9 | 31·4 | 26·8 | 22·0 | 17·1 | 12·2 | 30 |
| 40 | 54·5 | 51·4 | 47·9 | 44·1 | 40·1 | 35·8 | 31·3 | 26·6 | 21·8 | 16·9 | 12·0 | 40 |
| 50 | 54·4 | 51·2 | 47·8 | 44·0 | 39·9 | 35·6 | 31·1 | 26·5 | 21·7 | 16·8 | 11·8 | 50 |
| 00 | **39** 54·3 | **44** 51·1 | **49** 47·6 | **54** 43·9 | **59** 39·8 | **64** 35·5 | **69** 31·0 | **74** 26·3 | **79** 21·5 | **84** 16·6 | **89** 11·7 | 00 |
| 10 | 54·2 | 51·0 | 47·5 | 43·7 | 39·6 | 35·3 | 30·8 | 26·1 | 21·3 | 16·5 | 11·5 | 10 |
| 20 | 54·1 | 50·9 | 47·4 | 43·6 | 39·5 | 35·2 | 30·7 | 26·0 | 21·2 | 16·3 | 11·4 | 20 |
| 30 | 54·0 | 50·8 | 47·3 | 43·5 | 39·4 | 35·0 | 30·5 | 25·8 | 21·0 | 16·1 | 11·2 | 30 |
| 40 | 53·9 | 50·7 | 47·2 | 43·3 | 39·2 | 34·9 | 30·4 | 25·7 | 20·9 | 16·0 | 11·0 | 40 |
| 50 | 53·8 | 50·6 | 47·0 | 43·2 | 39·1 | 34·7 | 30·2 | 25·5 | 20·7 | 15·8 | 10·9 | 50 |

| H.P. | L U | L U | L U | L U | L U | L U | L U | L U | L U | L U | L U | H.P. |
|---|---|---|---|---|---|---|---|---|---|---|---|---|
| 54·0 | 1·1 1·7 | 1·3 1·9 | 1·5 2·1 | 1·7 2·4 | 2·0 2·6 | 2·3 2·9 | 2·6 3·2 | 2·9 3·5 | 3·2 3·8 | 3·5 4·1 | 3·8 4·5 | 54·0 |
| 54·3 | 1·4 1·8 | 1·6 2·0 | 1·8 2·2 | 2·0 2·5 | 2·3 2·7 | 2·5 3·0 | 2·8 3·2 | 3·0 3·5 | 3·3 3·8 | 3·6 4·1 | 3·9 4·4 | 54·3 |
| 54·6 | 1·7 2·0 | 1·9 2·2 | 2·1 2·4 | 2·3 2·6 | 2·5 2·8 | 2·7 3·0 | 3·0 3·3 | 3·2 3·5 | 3·5 3·8 | 3·7 4·1 | 4·0 4·3 | 54·6 |
| 54·9 | 2·0 2·2 | 2·2 2·3 | 2·3 2·5 | 2·5 2·7 | 2·7 2·9 | 2·9 3·1 | 3·2 3·3 | 3·4 3·5 | 3·6 3·8 | 3·9 4·0 | 4·1 4·3 | 54·9 |
| 55·2 | 2·3 2·3 | 2·5 2·4 | 2·6 2·6 | 2·8 2·8 | 3·0 2·9 | 3·2 3·1 | 3·4 3·3 | 3·6 3·5 | 3·8 3·7 | 4·0 4·0 | 4·2 4·2 | 55·2 |
| 55·5 | 2·7 2·5 | 2·8 2·6 | 2·9 2·7 | 3·1 2·9 | 3·2 3·0 | 3·4 3·2 | 3·6 3·4 | 3·7 3·5 | 3·9 3·7 | 4·1 3·9 | 4·3 4·1 | 55·5 |
| 55·8 | 3·0 2·6 | 3·1 2·7 | 3·2 2·8 | 3·3 3·0 | 3·5 3·1 | 3·6 3·3 | 3·8 3·4 | 3·9 3·6 | 4·1 3·7 | 4·2 3·9 | 4·4 4·0 | 55·8 |
| 56·1 | 3·3 2·8 | 3·4 2·9 | 3·5 3·0 | 3·6 3·1 | 3·7 3·2 | 3·8 3·3 | 4·0 3·4 | 4·1 3·6 | 4·2 3·7 | 4·4 3·8 | 4·5 4·0 | 56·1 |
| 56·4 | 3·6 2·9 | 3·7 3·0 | 3·8 3·1 | 3·9 3·2 | 3·9 3·3 | 4·0 3·4 | 4·1 3·5 | 4·3 3·6 | 4·4 3·7 | 4·5 3·8 | 4·6 3·9 | 56·4 |
| 56·7 | 3·9 3·1 | 4·0 3·1 | 4·1 3·2 | 4·1 3·3 | 4·2 3·3 | 4·3 3·4 | 4·3 3·5 | 4·4 3·6 | 4·5 3·7 | 4·6 3·8 | 4·7 3·8 | 56·7 |
| 57·0 | 4·3 3·2 | 4·3 3·3 | 4·3 3·3 | 4·4 3·4 | 4·4 3·4 | 4·5 3·5 | 4·5 3·5 | 4·6 3·6 | 4·7 3·6 | 4·7 3·7 | 4·8 3·8 | 57·0 |
| 57·3 | 4·6 3·4 | 4·6 3·4 | 4·6 3·4 | 4·6 3·5 | 4·7 3·5 | 4·7 3·5 | 4·7 3·6 | 4·8 3·6 | 4·8 3·6 | 4·8 3·7 | 4·9 3·7 | 57·3 |
| 57·6 | 4·9 3·6 | 4·9 3·6 | 4·9 3·6 | 4·9 3·6 | 4·9 3·6 | 4·9 3·6 | 4·9 3·6 | 4·9 3·6 | 5·0 3·6 | 5·0 3·6 | 5·0 3·6 | 57·6 |
| 57·9 | 5·2 3·7 | 5·2 3·7 | 5·2 3·7 | 5·2 3·7 | 5·2 3·7 | 5·1 3·6 | 5·1 3·6 | 5·1 3·6 | 5·1 3·6 | 5·1 3·6 | 5·1 3·6 | 57·9 |
| 58·2 | 5·5 3·9 | 5·5 3·8 | 5·5 3·8 | 5·4 3·8 | 5·4 3·7 | 5·4 3·7 | 5·3 3·7 | 5·3 3·6 | 5·2 3·6 | 5·2 3·5 | 5·2 3·5 | 58·2 |
| 58·5 | 5·9 4·0 | 5·8 4·0 | 5·8 3·9 | 5·7 3·9 | 5·6 3·8 | 5·6 3·8 | 5·5 3·7 | 5·5 3·6 | 5·4 3·6 | 5·3 3·5 | 5·3 3·4 | 58·5 |
| 58·8 | 6·2 4·2 | 6·1 4·1 | 6·0 4·1 | 6·0 4·0 | 5·9 3·9 | 5·8 3·8 | 5·7 3·7 | 5·6 3·6 | 5·5 3·5 | 5·4 3·5 | 5·3 3·4 | 58·8 |
| 59·1 | 6·5 4·3 | 6·4 4·3 | 6·3 4·2 | 6·2 4·1 | 6·1 4·0 | 6·0 3·9 | 5·9 3·8 | 5·8 3·6 | 5·7 3·5 | 5·6 3·4 | 5·4 3·3 | 59·1 |
| 59·4 | 6·8 4·5 | 6·7 4·4 | 6·6 4·3 | 6·5 4·2 | 6·4 4·1 | 6·2 3·9 | 6·1 3·8 | 6·0 3·7 | 5·8 3·5 | 5·7 3·4 | 5·5 3·2 | 59·4 |
| 59·7 | 7·1 4·6 | 7·0 4·5 | 6·9 4·4 | 6·8 4·3 | 6·6 4·1 | 6·5 4·0 | 6·3 3·8 | 6·2 3·7 | 6·0 3·5 | 5·8 3·3 | 5·6 3·2 | 59·7 |
| 60·0 | 7·5 4·8 | 7·3 4·7 | 7·2 4·5 | 7·0 4·4 | 6·9 4·2 | 6·7 4·0 | 6·5 3·9 | 6·3 3·7 | 6·1 3·5 | 5·9 3·3 | 5·7 3·1 | 60·0 |
| 60·3 | 7·8 5·0 | 7·6 4·8 | 7·5 4·7 | 7·3 4·5 | 7·1 4·3 | 6·9 4·1 | 6·7 3·9 | 6·5 3·7 | 6·3 3·5 | 6·0 3·2 | 5·8 3·0 | 60·3 |
| 60·6 | 8·1 5·1 | 7·9 5·0 | 7·7 4·8 | 7·6 4·6 | 7·3 4·4 | 7·1 4·2 | 6·9 3·9 | 6·7 3·7 | 6·4 3·4 | 6·2 3·2 | 5·9 2·9 | 60·6 |
| 60·9 | 8·4 5·3 | 8·2 5·1 | 8·0 4·9 | 7·8 4·7 | 7·6 4·5 | 7·3 4·2 | 7·1 4·0 | 6·8 3·7 | 6·6 3·4 | 6·3 3·2 | 6·0 2·9 | 60·9 |
| 61·2 | 8·7 5·4 | 8·5 5·2 | 8·3 5·0 | 8·1 4·8 | 7·8 4·5 | 7·6 4·3 | 7·3 4·0 | 7·0 3·7 | 6·7 3·4 | 6·4 3·1 | 6·1 2·8 | 61·2 |
| 61·5 | 9·1 5·6 | 8·8 5·4 | 8·6 5·1 | 8·3 4·9 | 8·1 4·6 | 7·8 4·3 | 7·5 4·0 | 7·2 3·7 | 6·9 3·4 | 6·5 3·1 | 6·2 2·7 | 61·5 |

## LAT 31°N

| LHA ♈ | Hc | Zn | Hc | Zn | Hc | Zn | Hc | Zn | Hc | Zn | Hc | Zn | Hc | Zn |
|---|---|---|---|---|---|---|---|---|---|---|---|---|---|---|
| | •CAPELLA | | ALDEBARAN | | Diphda | | •FOMALHAUT | | ALTAIR | | •DENEB | | Kochab | |
| 0 | 29 01 | 051 | 26 21 | 086 | 39 52 | 167 | 27 28 | 195 | 28 03 | 263 | 49 04 | 305 | 18 55 | 349 |
| 1 | 29 41 | 051 | 27 12 | 086 | 40 03 | 168 | 27 14 | 196 | 27 12 | 264 | 48 22 | 305 | 18 45 | 349 |
| 2 | 30 22 | 052 | 28 04 | 087 | 40 13 | 169 | 26 59 | 197 | 26 21 | 264 | 47 40 | 305 | 18 35 | 349 |
| 3 | 31 02 | 052 | 28 55 | 087 | 40 22 | 170 | 26 43 | 198 | 25 30 | 265 | 46 58 | 305 | 18 26 | 349 |
| 4 | 31 43 | 052 | 29 46 | 088 | 40 31 | 172 | 26 27 | 199 | 24 39 | 265 | 46 15 | 305 | 18 17 | 350 |
| 5 | 32 23 | 052 | 30 38 | 088 | 40 38 | 173 | 26 10 | 200 | 23 47 | 266 | 45 33 | 305 | 18 08 | 350 |
| 6 | 33 04 | 052 | 31 29 | 089 | 40 43 | 174 | 25 51 | 201 | 22 56 | 267 | 44 51 | 305 | 17 59 | 350 |
| 7 | 33 45 | 053 | 32 21 | 089 | 40 48 | 175 | 25 33 | 202 | 22 05 | 267 | 44 09 | 305 | 17 50 | 350 |
| 8 | 34 26 | 053 | 33 12 | 090 | 40 52 | 177 | 25 13 | 203 | 21 13 | 268 | 43 26 | 305 | 17 42 | 351 |
| 9 | 35 07 | 053 | 34 03 | 090 | 40 54 | 178 | 24 53 | 204 | 20 22 | 268 | 42 44 | 305 | 17 33 | 351 |
| 10 | 35 48 | 053 | 34 55 | 091 | 40 56 | 179 | 24 32 | 205 | 19 30 | 269 | 42 02 | 305 | 17 25 | 351 |
| 11 | 36 29 | 053 | 35 46 | 091 | 40 56 | 180 | 24 10 | 205 | 18 39 | 269 | 41 20 | 305 | 17 17 | 351 |
| 12 | 37 10 | 053 | 36 38 | 092 | 40 55 | 182 | 23 48 | 206 | 17 48 | 270 | 40 38 | 305 | 17 10 | 352 |
| 13 | 37 51 | 053 | 37 29 | 093 | 40 53 | 183 | 23 25 | 207 | 16 56 | 270 | 39 56 | 305 | 17 03 | 352 |
| 14 | 38 33 | 054 | 38 20 | 093 | 40 50 | 184 | 23 01 | 208 | 16 05 | 271 | 39 14 | 305 | 16 55 | 352 |
| | •CAPELLA | | RIGEL | | •Diphda | | FOMALHAUT | | Enif | | •DENEB | | Kochab | |
| 15 | 39 14 | 054 | 17 47 | 112 | 40 45 | 185 | 22 36 | 209 | 39 49 | 256 | 38 32 | 305 | 16 48 | 352 |
| 16 | 39 55 | 054 | 18 35 | 112 | 40 40 | 187 | 22 11 | 210 | 38 59 | 257 | 37 50 | 306 | 16 42 | 353 |
| 17 | 40 37 | 054 | 19 23 | 113 | 40 34 | 188 | 21 45 | 210 | 38 09 | 257 | 37 08 | 306 | 16 35 | 353 |
| 18 | 41 18 | 054 | 20 10 | 113 | 40 26 | 189 | 21 19 | 211 | 37 19 | 258 | 36 27 | 306 | 16 29 | 353 |
| 19 | 42 00 | 054 | 20 57 | 114 | 40 17 | 190 | 20 52 | 212 | 36 28 | 259 | 35 45 | 306 | 16 23 | 353 |
| 20 | 42 42 | 054 | 21 44 | 115 | 40 08 | 192 | 20 25 | 213 | 35 38 | 259 | 35 03 | 306 | 16 17 | 354 |
| 21 | 43 23 | 054 | 22 30 | 115 | 39 57 | 193 | 19 56 | 214 | 34 47 | 260 | 34 22 | 306 | 16 12 | 354 |
| 22 | 44 05 | 054 | 23 17 | 116 | 39 45 | 194 | 19 28 | 214 | 33 56 | 261 | 33 40 | 307 | 16 07 | 354 |
| 23 | 44 47 | 054 | 24 03 | 117 | 39 32 | 195 | 18 58 | 215 | 33 06 | 261 | 32 59 | 307 | 16 02 | 355 |
| 24 | 45 28 | 054 | 24 48 | 117 | 39 18 | 196 | 18 28 | 216 | 32 15 | 262 | 32 18 | 307 | 15 57 | 355 |
| 25 | 46 10 | 054 | 25 34 | 118 | 39 03 | 198 | 17 58 | 217 | 31 24 | 262 | 31 37 | 307 | 15 52 | 355 |
| 26 | 46 52 | 054 | 26 19 | 119 | 38 47 | 199 | 17 27 | 217 | 30 33 | 263 | 30 56 | 307 | 15 48 | 355 |
| 27 | 47 33 | 054 | 27 04 | 120 | 38 30 | 200 | 16 56 | 218 | 29 42 | 263 | 30 15 | 307 | 15 44 | 356 |
| 28 | 48 15 | 054 | 27 49 | 120 | 38 12 | 201 | 16 24 | 219 | 28 51 | 264 | 29 34 | 308 | 15 40 | 356 |
| 29 | 48 57 | 054 | 28 33 | 121 | 37 53 | 202 | 15 51 | 220 | 28 00 | 265 | 28 54 | 308 | 15 37 | 356 |
| | CAPELLA | | BETELGEUSE | | •RIGEL | | Diphda | | •Alpheratz | | DENEB | | •Kochab | |
| 30 | 49 38 | 054 | 30 37 | 100 | 29 17 | 122 | 37 33 | 203 | 65 39 | 273 | 28 13 | 308 | 15 33 | 356 |
| 31 | 50 20 | 054 | 31 28 | 101 | 30 00 | 123 | 37 12 | 204 | 64 48 | 273 | 27 33 | 308 | 15 30 | 357 |
| 32 | 51 01 | 054 | 32 18 | 102 | 30 43 | 123 | 36 50 | 206 | 63 56 | 273 | 26 52 | 309 | 15 27 | 357 |
| 33 | 51 43 | 054 | 33 09 | 102 | 31 26 | 124 | 36 28 | 207 | 63 05 | 274 | 26 12 | 309 | 15 25 | 357 |
| 34 | 52 24 | 053 | 33 59 | 103 | 32 08 | 125 | 36 04 | 208 | 62 14 | 274 | 25 32 | 309 | 15 23 | 358 |
| 35 | 53 05 | 053 | 34 49 | 104 | 32 50 | 126 | 35 40 | 209 | 61 22 | 275 | 24 53 | 309 | 15 20 | 358 |
| 36 | 53 47 | 053 | 35 39 | 104 | 33 32 | 127 | 35 15 | 210 | 60 31 | 275 | 24 13 | 310 | 15 19 | 358 |
| 37 | 54 28 | 053 | 36 29 | 105 | 34 13 | 128 | 34 49 | 211 | 59 40 | 275 | 23 33 | 310 | 15 17 | 358 |
| 38 | 55 09 | 053 | 37 18 | 106 | 34 53 | 128 | 34 22 | 212 | 58 49 | 276 | 22 54 | 310 | 15 16 | 359 |
| 39 | 55 50 | 053 | 38 08 | 106 | 35 33 | 129 | 33 54 | 213 | 57 58 | 276 | 22 15 | 310 | 15 15 | 359 |
| 40 | 56 30 | 052 | 38 57 | 107 | 36 13 | 130 | 33 26 | 214 | 57 06 | 276 | 21 36 | 311 | 15 14 | 359 |
| 41 | 57 11 | 052 | 39 46 | 108 | 36 52 | 131 | 32 57 | 215 | 56 15 | 277 | 20 57 | 311 | 15 13 | 000 |
| 42 | 57 51 | 052 | 40 35 | 108 | 37 30 | 132 | 32 27 | 216 | 55 24 | 277 | 20 18 | 311 | 15 13 | 000 |
| 43 | 58 32 | 051 | 41 24 | 109 | 38 08 | 133 | 31 57 | 217 | 54 33 | 278 | 19 40 | 312 | 15 13 | 000 |
| 44 | 59 12 | 051 | 42 12 | 110 | 38 45 | 134 | 31 26 | 218 | 53 42 | 278 | 19 01 | 312 | 15 13 | 000 |
| | •Dubhe | | POLLUX | | SIRIUS | | •RIGEL | | Diphda | | •Alpheratz | | Schedar | |
| 45 | 14 20 | 025 | 29 10 | 073 | 18 03 | 123 | 39 22 | 135 | 30 54 | 219 | 52 51 | 278 | 54 46 | 327 |
| 46 | 14 41 | 025 | 29 59 | 073 | 18 45 | 124 | 39 58 | 136 | 30 21 | 220 | 52 01 | 279 | 54 18 | 326 |
| 47 | 15 03 | 025 | 30 48 | 074 | 19 28 | 125 | 40 33 | 137 | 29 48 | 220 | 51 10 | 279 | 53 49 | 326 |
| 48 | 15 25 | 026 | 31 38 | 074 | 20 10 | 125 | 41 07 | 138 | 29 15 | 221 | 50 19 | 279 | 53 20 | 325 |
| 49 | 15 48 | 026 | 32 27 | 074 | 20 52 | 126 | 41 41 | 139 | 28 41 | 222 | 49 28 | 280 | 52 50 | 325 |
| 50 | 16 10 | 026 | 33 17 | 075 | 21 33 | 127 | 42 15 | 140 | 28 06 | 223 | 48 38 | 280 | 52 20 | 324 |
| 51 | 16 33 | 027 | 34 07 | 075 | 22 14 | 127 | 42 47 | 142 | 27 30 | 224 | 47 47 | 280 | 51 50 | 324 |
| 52 | 16 56 | 027 | 34 56 | 076 | 22 55 | 128 | 43 18 | 143 | 26 54 | 225 | 46 56 | 281 | 51 20 | 324 |
| 53 | 17 20 | 027 | 35 46 | 076 | 23 35 | 129 | 43 49 | 144 | 26 18 | 226 | 46 06 | 281 | 50 49 | 323 |
| 54 | 17 43 | 027 | 36 36 | 076 | 24 15 | 130 | 44 19 | 145 | 25 41 | 226 | 45 15 | 281 | 50 18 | 323 |
| 55 | 18 07 | 028 | 37 26 | 077 | 24 54 | 130 | 44 48 | 146 | 25 04 | 227 | 44 25 | 282 | 49 47 | 323 |
| 56 | 18 31 | 028 | 38 16 | 077 | 25 33 | 131 | 45 16 | 148 | 24 26 | 228 | 43 35 | 282 | 49 16 | 322 |
| 57 | 18 55 | 028 | 39 06 | 077 | 26 12 | 132 | 45 43 | 149 | 23 47 | 229 | 42 44 | 282 | 48 45 | 322 |
| 58 | 19 20 | 028 | 39 56 | 078 | 26 50 | 133 | 46 10 | 150 | 23 08 | 229 | 41 54 | 283 | 48 13 | 322 |
| 59 | 19 44 | 029 | 40 47 | 078 | 27 27 | 134 | 46 35 | 151 | 22 29 | 230 | 41 04 | 283 | 47 41 | 322 |
| | •Dubhe | | POLLUX | | PROCYON | | •SIRIUS | | RIGEL | | •Hamal | | Schedar | |
| 60 | 20 09 | 029 | 41 37 | 078 | 32 47 | 105 | 28 04 | 134 | 46 59 | 153 | 63 41 | 260 | 47 09 | 321 |
| 61 | 20 34 | 029 | 42 28 | 079 | 33 36 | 106 | 28 41 | 135 | 47 22 | 154 | 62 51 | 261 | 46 37 | 321 |
| 62 | 20 59 | 029 | 43 18 | 079 | 34 26 | 106 | 29 17 | 136 | 47 44 | 155 | 62 00 | 262 | 46 05 | 321 |
| 63 | 21 25 | 030 | 44 09 | 080 | 35 15 | 107 | 29 52 | 137 | 48 05 | 157 | 61 09 | 262 | 45 32 | 321 |
| 64 | 21 50 | 030 | 44 59 | 080 | 36 04 | 108 | 30 27 | 138 | 48 24 | 158 | 60 18 | 263 | 45 00 | 321 |
| 65 | 22 16 | 030 | 45 50 | 080 | 3[illegible] | 108 | 31 01 | 139 | 48 43 | [illegible] | [illegible]9 27 | 264 | 44 27 | 321 |
| [illegible] | 22 42 | 030 | 46 41 | 08[illegible] | [illegible] | [illegible] | 31 34 | 140 | 49 0[illegible] | [illegible] | [illegible]5 | 265 | 43 55 | 320 |
| | [illegible]3 08 | 030 | 47 3[illegible] | [illegible] | [illegible] | [illegible] | [illegible]2 07 | 141 | 49 [illegible] | [illegible] | [illegible] | [illegible]65 | 43 22 | 3[illegible] |
| | [illegible] | 031 | 4[illegible] | [illegible] | [illegible] | [illegible] | [illegible]0 | 142 | [illegible] | [illegible] | [illegible] | [illegible] | 42 4[illegible] | [illegible] |

**LAT 31°N**

| LHA ♈ | Hc | Zn | Hc | Zn | Hc | Zn | Hc | Zn | Hc | Zn | Hc | Zn | Hc | Zn |
|---|---|---|---|---|---|---|---|---|---|---|---|---|---|---|
| | •Dubhe | | REGULUS | | PROCYON | | •SIRIUS | | RIGEL | | ALDEBARAN | | •Mirfak | |
| 90 | 33 38 | 033 | 30 09 | 094 | 55 24 | 133 | 41 07 | 166 | 49 15 | 198 | 65 49 | 238 | 55 18 | 314 |
| 91 | 34 07 | 033 | 31 01 | 094 | 56 01 | 134 | 41 19 | 167 | 48 59 | 199 | 65 05 | 239 | 54 41 | 314 |
| 92 | 34 35 | 033 | 31 52 | 095 | 56 38 | 136 | 41 30 | 168 | 48 41 | 201 | 64 20 | 241 | 54 04 | 314 |
| 93 | 35 03 | 033 | 32 43 | 096 | 57 13 | 137 | 41 40 | 170 | 48 23 | 202 | 63 35 | 242 | 53 27 | 313 |
| 94 | 35 32 | 033 | 33 34 | 096 | 57 47 | 139 | 41 49 | 171 | 48 03 | 203 | 62 49 | 244 | 52 49 | 313 |
| 95 | 36 00 | 033 | 34 25 | 097 | 58 21 | 140 | 41 57 | 172 | 47 42 | 205 | 62 03 | 245 | [illegible] | [illegible] |
| 96 | [illegible] | [illegible] | [illegible] | [illegible] | [illegible] | 142 | 42 03 | 173 | 47 20 | 206 | 61 16 | 246 | 51 34 | 313 |
| 97 | 36 57 | 033 | 36 08 | 098 | 59 24 | 144 | 42 08 | 175 | 46 57 | 207 | 60 29 | 247 | 50 56 | 312 |
| 98 | 37 25 | 033 | 36 58 | 098 | 59 54 | 145 | 42 13 | 176 | 46 32 | 209 | 59 42 | 248 | 50 18 | 312 |
| 99 | 37 53 | 033 | 37 49 | 099 | 60 22 | 147 | 42 16 | 177 | 46 07 | 210 | 58 54 | 249 | 49 40 | 312 |
| 100 | 38 21 | 033 | 38 40 | 100 | 60 49 | 149 | 42 18 | 179 | 45 41 | 211 | 58 06 | 250 | 49 01 | 312 |
| 101 | 38 50 | 033 | 39 31 | 100 | 61 15 | 151 | 42 18 | 180 | 45 14 | 213 | 57 17 | 251 | 48 23 | 312 |
| 102 | 39 18 | 033 | 40 21 | 101 | 61 40 | 153 | 42 18 | 181 | 44 45 | 214 | 56 28 | 252 | 47 45 | 312 |
| 103 | 39 46 | 033 | 41 12 | 102 | 62 02 | 155 | 42 16 | 182 | 44 16 | 215 | 55 39 | 253 | 47 06 | 311 |
| 104 | 40 14 | 033 | 42 02 | 102 | 62 24 | 157 | 42 13 | 184 | 43 46 | 216 | 54 50 | 254 | 46 28 | 311 |
| | •Alkaid | | REGULUS | | Alphard | | •SIRIUS | | RIGEL | | ALDEBARAN | | •CAPELLA | |
| 105 | 16 07 | 042 | 42 52 | 103 | 37 03 | 132 | 42 10 | 185 | 43 16 | 217 | 54 00 | 255 | 64 51 | 314 |
| 106 | 16 41 | 042 | 43 42 | 104 | 37 41 | 133 | 42 05 | 186 | 42 44 | 219 | 53 11 | 256 | 64 14 | 313 |
| 107 | 17 15 | 042 | 44 32 | 104 | 38 18 | 134 | 41 58 | 188 | 42 11 | 220 | 52 21 | 256 | 63 36 | 313 |
| 108 | 17 50 | 043 | 45 22 | 105 | 38 54 | 135 | 41 51 | 189 | 41 38 | 221 | 51 31 | 257 | 62 58 | 312 |
| 109 | 18 25 | 043 | 46 11 | 106 | 39 30 | 136 | 41 42 | 190 | 41 04 | 222 | 50 41 | 258 | 62 20 | 311 |
| 110 | 19 00 | 043 | 47 01 | 107 | 40 06 | 137 | 41 33 | 191 | 40 30 | 223 | 49 50 | 259 | 61 41 | 311 |
| 111 | 19 35 | 043 | 47 50 | 108 | 40 40 | 138 | 41 22 | 193 | 39 54 | 224 | 49 00 | 259 | 61 02 | 310 |
| 112 | 20 11 | 044 | 48 39 | 108 | 41 14 | 139 | 41 10 | 194 | 39 18 | 225 | 48 09 | 260 | 60 23 | 310 |
| 113 | 20 46 | 044 | 49 27 | 109 | 41 47 | 140 | 40 57 | 195 | 38 42 | 226 | 47 19 | 261 | 59 43 | 309 |
| 114 | 21 22 | 044 | 50 16 | 110 | 42 20 | 142 | 40 43 | 196 | 38 04 | 227 | 46 28 | 261 | 59 03 | 309 |
| 115 | 21 58 | 045 | 51 04 | 111 | 42 51 | 143 | 40 28 | 198 | 37 26 | 228 | 45 37 | 262 | 58 23 | 309 |
| 116 | 22 34 | 045 | 51 52 | 112 | 43 22 | 144 | 40 12 | 199 | 36 48 | 229 | 44 46 | 263 | 57 43 | 308 |
| 117 | 23 10 | 045 | 52 40 | 113 | 43 52 | 145 | 39 55 | 200 | 36 09 | 230 | 43 55 | 263 | 57 02 | 308 |
| 118 | 23 47 | 045 | 53 27 | 114 | 44 21 | 146 | 39 37 | 201 | 35 29 | 231 | 43 04 | 264 | 56 22 | 308 |
| 119 | 24 24 | 046 | 54 14 | 115 | 44 49 | 147 | 39 18 | 202 | 34 49 | 232 | 42 13 | 264 | 55 41 | 307 |
| | •Alkaid | | REGULUS | | •Alphard | | SIRIUS | | RIGEL | | ALDEBARAN | | •CAPELLA | |
| 120 | 25 00 | 046 | 55 00 | 116 | 45 16 | 149 | 38 58 | 203 | 34 09 | 232 | 41 21 | 265 | 55 00 | 307 |
| 121 | 25 37 | 046 | 55 46 | 117 | 45 43 | 150 | 38 37 | 205 | 33 28 | 233 | 40 30 | 266 | 54 19 | 307 |
| 122 | 26 15 | 046 | 56 32 | 118 | 46 08 | 151 | 38 15 | 206 | 32 46 | 234 | 39 39 | 266 | 53 38 | 307 |
| 123 | 26 52 | 046 | 57 17 | 119 | 46 32 | 153 | 37 53 | 207 | 32 04 | 235 | 38 48 | 267 | 52 57 | 307 |
| 124 | 27 29 | 047 | 58 02 | 120 | 46 55 | 154 | 37 29 | 208 | 31 22 | 236 | 37 56 | 267 | 52 15 | 306 |
| 125 | 28 07 | 047 | 58 46 | 121 | 47 17 | 155 | 37 04 | 209 | 30 39 | 237 | 37 05 | 268 | 51 34 | 306 |
| 126 | 28 44 | 047 | 59 30 | 123 | 47 38 | 157 | 36 39 | 210 | 29 56 | 237 | 36 13 | 268 | 50 53 | 306 |
| 127 | 29 22 | 047 | 60 13 | 124 | 47 58 | 158 | 36 13 | 211 | 29 13 | 238 | 35 22 | 269 | 50 11 | 306 |
| 128 | 30 00 | 047 | 60 55 | 125 | 48 17 | 159 | 35 46 | 212 | 28 29 | 239 | 34 31 | 269 | 49 30 | 306 |
| 129 | 30 38 | 048 | 61 37 | 127 | 48 34 | 161 | 35 18 | 213 | 27 44 | 240 | 33 39 | 270 | 48 48 | 306 |
| 130 | 31 16 | 048 | 62 17 | 128 | 48 51 | 162 | 34 49 | 214 | 27 00 | 240 | 32 48 | 270 | 48 06 | 306 |
| 131 | 31 54 | 048 | 62 57 | 130 | 49 06 | 164 | 34 20 | 215 | 26 15 | 241 | 31 56 | 271 | 47 25 | 306 |
| 132 | 32 32 | 048 | 63 36 | 132 | 49 20 | 165 | 33 50 | 216 | 25 30 | 242 | 31 05 | 271 | 46 43 | 306 |
| 133 | 33 11 | 048 | 64 14 | 133 | 49 32 | 167 | 33 19 | 217 | 24 44 | 243 | 30 13 | 272 | 46 01 | 306 |
| 134 | 33 49 | 048 | 64 51 | 135 | 49 43 | 168 | 32 47 | 218 | 23 58 | 243 | 29 22 | 272 | 45 20 | 306 |
| | •Alkaid | | ARCTURUS | | SPICA | | •Alphard | | SIRIUS | | BETELGEUSE | | •CAPELLA | |
| 135 | 34 28 | 049 | 19 08 | 079 | 14 00 | 112 | 49 53 | 170 | 32 15 | 219 | 40 44 | 251 | 44 38 | 306 |
| 136 | 35 06 | 049 | 19 59 | 079 | 14 47 | 113 | 50 02 | 171 | 31 42 | 220 | 39 55 | 252 | 43 56 | 306 |
| 137 | 35 45 | 049 | 20 49 | 079 | 15 34 | 114 | 50 09 | 173 | 31 09 | 221 | 39 06 | 253 | 43 15 | 306 |
| 138 | 36 24 | 049 | 21 40 | 080 | 16 21 | 114 | 50 15 | 174 | 30 35 | 222 | 38 16 | 254 | 42 33 | 306 |
| 139 | 37 02 | 049 | 22 30 | 080 | 17 08 | 115 | 50 19 | 176 | 30 00 | 223 | 37 27 | 254 | 41 51 | 306 |
| 140 | 37 41 | 049 | 23 21 | 081 | 17 55 | 115 | 50 22 | 177 | 29 25 | 224 | 36 37 | 255 | 41 10 | 306 |
| 141 | 38 20 | 049 | 24 12 | 081 | 18 41 | 116 | 50 24 | 179 | 28 49 | 225 | 35 48 | 256 | 40 28 | 306 |
| 142 | 38 59 | 049 | 25 03 | 082 | 19 27 | 117 | 50 24 | 180 | 28 13 | 225 | 34 58 | 256 | 39 47 | 306 |
| 143 | 39 38 | 049 | 25 54 | 082 | 20 13 | 117 | 50 23 | 182 | 27 36 | 226 | 34 08 | 257 | 39 05 | 306 |
| 144 | 40 17 | 049 | 26 45 | 083 | 20 58 | 118 | 50 21 | 184 | 26 59 | 227 | 33 18 | 258 | 38 24 | 306 |
| 145 | 40 56 | 049 | 27 36 | 083 | 21 44 | 119 | 50 17 | 185 | 26 21 | 228 | 32 27 | 258 | 37 43 | 307 |
| 146 | 41 35 | 049 | 28 27 | 084 | 22 28 | 119 | 50 12 | 187 | 25 43 | 229 | 31 37 | 259 | 37 01 | 307 |
| 147 | 42 14 | 049 | 29 18 | 084 | 23 13 | 120 | 50 05 | 188 | 25 04 | 229 | 30 46 | 259 | 36 20 | 307 |
| 148 | 42 53 | 049 | 30 09 | 084 | 23 57 | 121 | 49 57 | 190 | 24 25 | 230 | 29 56 | 260 | 35 39 | 307 |
| 149 | 43 32 | 049 | 31 00 | 085 | 24 41 | 122 | 49 48 | 191 | 23 45 | 231 | 29 05 | 261 | 34 58 | 307 |
| | Alkaid | | •ARCTURUS | | SPICA | | •Alphard | | PROCYON | | BETELGEUSE | | •CAPELLA | |
| 150 | 44 11 | 049 | 31 52 | 085 | 25 25 | 122 | 49 37 | 193 | 48 01 | 239 | 28 14 | 261 | 34 17 | 307 |
| 151 | 44 50 | 049 | 32 43 | 086 | 26 08 | 123 | 49 25 | 194 | 47 16 | 240 | 27 23 | 262 | 33 36 | 307 |
| 152 | 45 29 | 049 | 33 34 | 086 | 26 51 | 124 | 49 12 | 196 | 46 31 | 241 | 26 32 | 262 | 32 55 | 308 |
| 153 | 46 08 | 049 | 34 26 | 087 | 27 34 | 125 | 48 57 | 197 | 45 46 | 242 | 25 41 | 263 | 32 15 | 308 |
| 154 | 46 47 | 049 | 35 17 | 087 | 28 16 | 125 | 48 42 | 199 | 45 00 | 243 | 24 50 | 264 | 31 34 | 308 |
| 155 | 47 26 | 049 | 36 08 | 088 | [illegible] | 126 | 48 25 | 200 | [illegible] | 244 | 23 59 | 264 | 30 53 | [illegible] |
| [illegible] | 48 05 | 049 | 37 00 | [illegible] | [illegible] | 127 | 48 06 | 201 | [illegible] | [illegible] | 23 08 | 265 | 30 13 | [illegible] |
| [illegible] | 48 44 | 049 | [illegible] | [illegible] | [illegible] | [illegible] | 47 47 | 203 | [illegible] | [illegible] | 22 17 | 265 | [illegible] | [illegible] |
| [illegible] | [illegible] | 049 | [illegible] | [illegible] | [illegible] | [illegible] | 47 26 | [illegible] | [illegible] | [illegible] | [illegible] | 266 | [illegible] | [illegible] |
| [illegible] | [illegible] | 049 | [illegible] | [illegible] | [illegible] | [illegible] | [illegible] | [illegible] | [illegible] | [illegible] | [illegible] | [illegible] | [illegible] | [illegible] |

## LAT 31°N

| LHA ♈ | Hc | Zn | Hc | Zn | Hc | Zn | Hc | Zn | Hc | Zn | Hc | Zn | Hc | Zn |
|---|---|---|---|---|---|---|---|---|---|---|---|---|---|---|
| | •VEGA | | Alphecca | | ARCTURUS | | •SPICA | | REGULUS | | •POLLUX | | Dubhe | |
| 180 | 12 31 | 052 | 43 24 | 081 | 57 26 | 103 | 43 18 | 151 | 57 53 | 240 | 35 06 | 284 | 57 48 | 347 |
| 181 | 13 12 | 052 | 44 15 | 081 | 58 16 | 104 | 43 42 | 152 | 57 08 | 241 | 34 16 | 285 | 57 36 | 347 |
| 182 | 13 53 | 053 | 45 05 | 082 | 59 06 | 105 | 44 06 | 153 | 56 22 | 242 | 33 27 | 285 | 57 24 | 346 |
| 183 | 14 34 | 053 | 45 56 | 082 | 59 55 | 106 | 44 28 | 155 | 55 37 | 243 | 32 37 | 285 | 57 11 | 345 |
| 184 | 15 15 | 054 | 46 47 | 083 | 60 45 | 107 | 44 50 | 156 | 54 50 | 245 | 31 48 | 286 | 56 57 | 344 |
| 185 | 15 56 | 054 | 47 38 | 083 | 61 34 | 108 | 45 10 | 157 | 54 04 | 246 | 30 58 | 286 | 56 43 | 343 |
| 186 | 16 38 | 054 | 48 30 | 083 | 62 23 | 109 | 45 29 | 159 | 53 17 | 247 | 30 09 | 287 | 56 28 | 343 |
| 187 | 17 20 | 055 | 49 21 | 084 | 63 11 | 110 | 45 48 | 160 | 52 29 | 247 | 29 20 | 287 | 56 12 | 342 |
| 188 | 18 02 | 055 | 50 12 | 084 | 64 00 | 111 | 46 05 | 161 | 51 42 | 248 | 28 30 | 287 | 55 56 | 341 |
| 189 | 18 44 | 055 | 51 03 | 085 | 64 48 | 112 | 46 21 | 163 | 50 54 | 249 | 27 41 | 288 | 55 39 | 341 |
| 190 | 19 27 | 056 | 51 54 | 085 | 65 35 | 113 | 46 35 | 164 | 50 06 | 250 | 26 53 | 288 | 55 22 | 340 |
| 191 | 20 09 | 056 | 52 45 | 086 | 66 22 | 114 | 46 49 | 165 | 49 17 | 251 | 26 04 | 288 | 55 04 | 339 |
| 192 | 20 52 | 056 | 53 37 | 086 | 67 09 | 116 | 47 01 | 167 | 48 28 | 252 | 25 15 | 289 | 54 46 | 339 |
| 193 | 21 35 | 057 | 54 28 | 086 | 67 55 | 117 | 47 12 | 168 | 47 39 | 253 | 24 26 | 289 | 54 27 | 338 |
| 194 | 22 18 | 057 | 55 19 | 087 | 68 40 | 119 | 47 22 | 170 | 46 50 | 253 | 23 38 | 290 | 54 08 | 338 |
| | •Kochab | | VEGA | | Rasalhague | | •ANTARES | | SPICA | | •REGULUS | | Dubhe | |
| 195 | 44 36 | 010 | 23 01 | 057 | 24 42 | 090 | 14 02 | 133 | 47 31 | 171 | 46 01 | 254 | 53 48 | 337 |
| 196 | 44 45 | 010 | 23 45 | 058 | 25 34 | 090 | 14 39 | 134 | 47 38 | 173 | 45 11 | 255 | 53 27 | 336 |
| 197 | 44 53 | 010 | 24 28 | 058 | 26 25 | 091 | 15 16 | 135 | 47 44 | 174 | 44 21 | 256 | 53 07 | 336 |
| 198 | 45 02 | 009 | 25 12 | 058 | 27 16 | 091 | 15 52 | 135 | 47 49 | 175 | 43 31 | 256 | 52 45 | 335 |
| 199 | 45 10 | 009 | 25 56 | 059 | 28 08 | 092 | 16 28 | 136 | 47 52 | 177 | 42 41 | 257 | 52 24 | 335 |
| 200 | 45 18 | 009 | 26 40 | 059 | 28 59 | 092 | 17 04 | 137 | 47 54 | 178 | 41 51 | 258 | 52 02 | 334 |
| 201 | 45 25 | 008 | 27 24 | 059 | 29 51 | 093 | 17 39 | 137 | 47 55 | 180 | 41 01 | 258 | 51 39 | 334 |
| 202 | 45 32 | 008 | 28 08 | 060 | 30 42 | 094 | 18 14 | 138 | 47 54 | 181 | 40 10 | 259 | 51 16 | 333 |
| 203 | 45 39 | 008 | 28 53 | 060 | 31 33 | 094 | 18 48 | 139 | 47 53 | 183 | 39 20 | 260 | 50 53 | 333 |
| 204 | 45 46 | 007 | 29 37 | 060 | 32 25 | 095 | 19 21 | 140 | 47 49 | 184 | 38 29 | 260 | 50 30 | 333 |
| 205 | 45 52 | 007 | 30 22 | 060 | 33 16 | 095 | 19 54 | 140 | 47 45 | 186 | 37 38 | 261 | 50 06 | 332 |
| 206 | 45 58 | 006 | 31 07 | 061 | 34 07 | 096 | 20 27 | 141 | 47 39 | 187 | 36 48 | 262 | 49 42 | 332 |
| 207 | 46 04 | 006 | 31 52 | 061 | 34 58 | 096 | 20 59 | 142 | 47 32 | 189 | 35 57 | 262 | 49 17 | 331 |
| 208 | 46 09 | 006 | 32 37 | 061 | 35 49 | 097 | 21 31 | 143 | 47 24 | 190 | 35 06 | 263 | 48 53 | 331 |
| 209 | 46 14 | 005 | 33 22 | 061 | 36 40 | 098 | 22 02 | 143 | 47 14 | 191 | 34 15 | 263 | 48 28 | 331 |
| | •Kochab | | VEGA | | Rasalhague | | •ANTARES | | SPICA | | •REGULUS | | Dubhe | |
| 210 | 46 19 | 005 | 34 07 | 062 | 37 31 | 098 | 22 32 | 144 | 47 03 | 193 | 33 23 | 264 | 48 03 | 330 |
| 211 | 46 23 | 005 | 34 52 | 062 | 38 22 | 099 | 23 02 | 145 | 46 51 | 194 | 32 32 | 265 | 47 37 | 330 |
| 212 | 46 27 | 004 | 35 38 | 062 | 39 13 | 099 | 23 31 | 146 | 46 38 | 196 | 31 41 | 265 | 47 11 | 330 |
| 213 | 46 30 | 004 | 36 23 | 062 | 40 04 | 100 | 24 00 | 147 | 46 24 | 197 | 30 50 | 266 | 46 45 | 330 |
| 214 | 46 34 | 003 | 37 09 | 063 | 40 54 | 101 | 24 27 | 147 | 46 08 | 198 | 29 59 | 266 | 46 19 | 329 |
| 215 | 46 36 | 003 | 37 54 | 063 | 41 45 | 101 | 24 55 | 148 | 45 51 | 200 | 29 07 | 267 | 45 53 | 329 |
| 216 | 46 39 | 003 | 38 40 | 063 | 42 35 | 102 | 25 21 | 149 | 45 33 | 201 | 28 16 | 267 | 45 26 | 329 |
| 217 | 46 41 | 002 | 39 26 | 063 | 43 25 | 103 | 25 48 | 150 | 45 14 | 202 | 27 24 | 268 | 45 00 | 329 |
| 218 | 46 43 | 002 | 40 12 | 063 | 44 15 | 103 | 26 13 | 151 | 44 54 | 204 | 26 33 | 268 | 44 33 | 328 |
| 219 | 46 45 | 001 | 40 58 | 064 | 45 05 | 104 | 26 37 | 152 | 44 33 | 205 | 25 42 | 269 | 44 06 | 328 |
| 220 | 46 46 | 001 | 41 44 | 064 | 45 55 | 105 | 27 01 | 153 | 44 10 | 206 | 24 50 | 269 | 43 39 | 328 |
| 221 | 46 46 | 001 | 42 30 | 064 | 46 45 | 106 | 27 25 | 154 | 43 47 | 208 | 23 59 | 270 | 43 11 | 328 |
| 222 | 46 47 | 000 | 43 16 | 064 | 47 34 | 106 | 27 47 | 155 | 43 23 | 209 | 23 07 | 270 | 42 44 | 328 |
| 223 | 46 47 | 000 | 44 03 | 064 | 48 24 | 107 | 28 09 | 155 | 42 58 | 210 | 22 16 | 271 | 42 16 | 328 |
| 224 | 46 47 | 359 | 44 49 | 064 | 49 13 | 108 | 28 30 | 156 | 42 31 | 211 | 21 24 | 271 | 41 49 | 327 |
| | DENEB | | VEGA | | •ALTAIR | | ANTARES | | •SPICA | | Denebola | | •Dubhe | |
| 225 | 24 34 | 051 | 45 35 | 064 | 19 29 | 091 | 28 50 | 157 | 42 04 | 212 | 43 19 | 261 | 41 21 | 327 |
| 226 | 25 14 | 051 | 46 22 | 065 | 20 21 | 092 | 29 09 | 158 | 41 36 | 214 | 42 28 | 261 | 40 53 | 327 |
| 227 | 25 54 | 051 | 47 08 | 065 | 21 12 | 092 | 29 28 | 159 | 41 07 | 215 | 41 37 | 262 | 40 25 | 327 |
| 228 | 26 34 | 051 | 47 55 | 065 | 22 03 | 093 | 29 46 | 160 | 40 38 | 216 | 40 46 | 263 | 39 57 | 327 |
| 229 | 27 14 | 052 | 48 41 | 065 | 22 55 | 093 | 30 03 | 161 | 40 07 | 217 | 39 55 | 263 | 39 29 | 327 |
| 230 | 27 55 | 052 | 49 28 | 065 | 23 46 | 094 | 30 19 | 162 | 39 36 | 218 | 39 04 | 264 | 39 01 | 327 |
| 231 | 28 35 | 052 | 50 15 | 065 | 24 37 | 094 | 30 34 | 163 | 39 04 | 219 | 38 13 | 264 | 38 33 | 327 |
| 232 | 29 16 | 052 | 51 01 | 065 | 25 29 | 095 | 30 49 | 164 | 38 31 | 220 | 37 22 | 265 | 38 05 | 327 |
| 233 | 29 56 | 052 | 51 48 | 065 | 26 20 | 096 | 31 02 | 165 | 37 58 | 221 | 36 30 | 266 | 37 36 | 327 |
| 234 | 30 37 | 053 | 52 35 | 065 | 27 11 | 096 | 31 15 | 166 | 37 24 | 222 | 35 39 | 266 | 37 08 | 327 |
| 235 | 31 18 | 053 | 53 21 | 065 | 28 02 | 097 | 31 27 | 167 | 36 49 | 223 | 34 48 | 267 | 36 40 | 327 |
| 236 | 31 59 | 053 | 54 08 | 065 | 28 53 | 097 | 31 38 | 168 | 36 13 | 224 | 33 56 | 267 | 36 11 | 327 |
| 237 | 32 40 | 053 | 54 55 | 065 | 29 44 | 098 | 31 47 | 169 | 35 37 | 225 | 33 05 | 268 | 35 43 | 327 |
| 238 | 33 22 | 053 | 55 42 | 065 | 30 35 | 098 | 31 57 | 170 | 35 00 | 226 | 32 14 | 268 | 35 15 | 327 |
| 239 | 34 03 | 054 | 56 29 | 065 | 31 26 | 099 | 32 05 | 171 | 34 23 | 227 | 31 22 | 269 | 34 46 | 327 |
| | •DENEB | | ALTAIR | | Nunki | | •ANTARES | | SPICA | | ARCTURUS | | •Alkaid | |
| 240 | 34 44 | 054 | 32 17 | 100 | 19 10 | 139 | 32 12 | 172 | 33 45 | 228 | 63 35 | 250 | 59 02 | 316 |
| 241 | 35 26 | 054 | 33 07 | 100 | 19 43 | 140 | 32 18 | 174 | 33 07 | 229 | 62 47 | 251 | 58 27 | 316 |
| 242 | 36 07 | 054 | 33 58 | 101 | 20 16 | 141 | 32 24 | 175 | 32 28 | 230 | 61 58 | 252 | 57 50 | 315 |
| 243 | 36 49 | 054 | 34 48 | 102 | 20 48 | 141 | 32 28 | 176 | 31 49 | 230 | 61 09 | 253 | 57 14 | 315 |
| 244 | 37 31 | 054 | 35 39 | 102 | 21 20 | 142 | 32 31 | 177 | 31 09 | 231 | 60 20 | 254 | 56 37 | 314 |
| 245 | 38 13 | 054 | 36 29 | [illegible] | 21 51 | 143 | 32 34 | [illegible] | 30 28 | 232 | 59 30 | [illegible] | 56 00 | 314 |
| [illegible]46 | 38 55 | 055 | 37 [illegible] | [illegible] | 22 22 | 144 | 32 35 | [illegible] | [illegible] 47 | 233 | 58 40 | [illegible] | [illegible] 23 | 314 |
| [illegible] | 39 37 | 055 | [illegible] | [illegible] | [illegible] 52 | 145 | 32 [illegible] | [illegible] | [illegible] | 234 | 57 5[illegible] | [illegible] | [illegible] | 313 |
| [illegible] | [illegible] 19 | 055 | [illegible] | [illegible] | [illegible] | 145 | [illegible] | [illegible] | [illegible] | 235 | 57 [illegible] | [illegible] | [illegible] | 313 |
| [illegible] | [illegible] | 0[illegible] | [illegible] | [illegible] | [illegible] | 146 | [illegible] | [illegible] | [illegible] | [illegible]5 | [illegible] | [illegible] | [illegible] | [illegible]3 |

**LAT 31°N**

| LHA ♈ | Hc Zn | Hc Zn | Hc Zn | Hc Zn | Hc Zn | Hc Zn | Hc Zn |
|---|---|---|---|---|---|---|---|
| | •DENEB | ALTAIR | •Nunki | ANTARES | ARCTURUS | •Alkaid | Kochab |
| 270 | 55 45 054 | 56 08 125 | 31 14 166 | 28 35 203 | 38 16 271 | 39 57 311 | 40 49 345 |
| 271 | 56 26 054 | 56 49 126 | 31 26 167 | 28 14 204 | 37 25 271 | 39 18 311 | 40 36 344 |
| 272 | 57 08 053 | 57 30 128 | 31 37 168 | 27 52 205 | 36 33 272 | 38 39 311 | 40 22 344 |
| 273 | 57 49 053 | 58 11 129 | 31 48 169 | 27 30 206 | 35 42 272 | 38 00 311 | 40 08 344 |
| 274 | 58 30 053 | 58 50 130 | 31 [illegible] 170 | [illegible] | 34 51 273 | 37 21 311 | 39 54 344 |
| 275 | 59 11 052 | 59 29 132 | 32 06 171 | 26 43 208 | 33 59 273 | 36 42 311 | 39 39 344 |
| 276 | 59 51 052 | 60 07 133 | 32 14 172 | 26 19 209 | 33 08 274 | 36 03 311 | 39 25 344 |
| 277 | 60 32 052 | 60 44 135 | 32 20 173 | 25 54 210 | 32 17 274 | 35 25 311 | 39 10 343 |
| 278 | 61 12 051 | 61 20 137 | 32 26 174 | 25 28 211 | 31 25 275 | 34 46 311 | 38 55 343 |
| 279 | 61 52 051 | 61 55 138 | 32 31 175 | 25 01 211 | 30 34 275 | 34 07 312 | 38 41 343 |
| 280 | 62 32 050 | 62 28 140 | 32 35 176 | 24 34 212 | 29 43 276 | 33 29 312 | 38 26 343 |
| 281 | 63 11 050 | 63 01 142 | 32 38 177 | 24 06 213 | 28 52 276 | 32 50 312 | 38 11 343 |
| 282 | 63 50 049 | 63 32 144 | 32 40 178 | 23 38 214 | 28 01 277 | 32 12 312 | 37 55 343 |
| 283 | 64 29 048 | 64 02 146 | 32 41 179 | 23 09 215 | 27 10 277 | 31 34 312 | 37 40 343 |
| 284 | 65 07 048 | 64 30 148 | 32 41 180 | 22 39 216 | 26 19 278 | 30 56 312 | 37 25 343 |
| | •Alpheratz | Enif | ALTAIR | •ANTARES | ARCTURUS | •Alkaid | Kochab |
| 285 | 24 49 070 | 46 36 110 | 64 57 150 | 22 09 216 | 25 28 278 | 30 18 312 | 37 09 342 |
| 286 | 25 37 070 | 47 24 111 | 65 22 152 | 21 38 217 | 24 37 279 | 29 40 313 | 36 54 342 |
| 287 | 26 25 071 | 48 12 112 | 65 46 154 | 21 07 218 | 23 46 279 | 29 02 313 | 36 38 342 |
| 288 | 27 14 071 | 48 59 113 | 66 07 156 | 20 35 219 | 22 55 279 | 28 24 313 | 36 22 342 |
| 289 | 28 03 071 | 49 46 114 | 66 27 159 | 20 02 220 | 22 05 280 | 27 47 313 | 36 06 342 |
| 290 | 28 51 072 | 50 33 115 | 66 45 161 | 19 29 220 | 21 14 280 | 27 09 313 | 35 50 342 |
| 291 | 29 40 072 | 51 20 116 | 67 01 163 | 18 56 221 | 20 23 281 | 26 32 314 | 35 34 342 |
| 292 | 30 29 072 | 52 06 117 | 67 14 166 | 18 22 222 | 19 33 281 | 25 55 314 | 35 18 342 |
| 293 | 31 18 073 | 52 52 118 | 67 26 168 | 17 47 222 | 18 42 282 | 25 18 314 | 35 02 342 |
| 294 | 32 07 073 | 53 37 119 | 67 35 171 | 17 12 223 | 17 52 282 | 24 41 314 | 34 46 342 |
| 295 | 32 57 073 | 54 22 120 | 67 42 173 | 16 37 224 | 17 02 283 | 24 04 315 | 34 30 342 |
| 296 | 33 46 074 | 55 06 121 | 67 47 176 | 16 01 225 | 16 12 283 | 23 28 315 | 34 14 342 |
| 297 | 34 36 074 | 55 50 122 | 67 49 179 | 15 25 225 | 15 22 284 | 22 51 315 | 33 58 342 |
| 298 | 35 25 075 | 56 33 123 | 67 49 181 | 14 48 226 | 14 32 284 | 22 15 315 | 33 41 342 |
| 299 | 36 15 075 | 57 16 125 | 67 47 184 | 14 11 227 | 13 42 284 | 21 39 316 | 33 25 342 |
| | •Mirfak | Alpheratz | •FOMALHAUT | ALTAIR | Rasalhague | •Alphecca | Kochab |
| 300 | 11 21 038 | 37 04 075 | 16 10 141 | 67 42 186 | 51 44 249 | 32 30 284 | 33 09 342 |
| 301 | 11 53 038 | 37 54 076 | 16 43 142 | 67 35 189 | 50 56 250 | 31 40 284 | 32 53 342 |
| 302 | 12 25 039 | 38 44 076 | 17 14 142 | 67 26 192 | 50 07 251 | 30 50 285 | 32 36 342 |
| 303 | 12 57 039 | 39 34 076 | 17 45 143 | 67 15 194 | 49 18 252 | 30 00 285 | 32 20 341 |
| 304 | 13 30 039 | 40 24 077 | 18 16 144 | 67 01 197 | 48 29 253 | 29 11 285 | 32 04 342 |
| 305 | 14 03 040 | 41 14 077 | 18 46 145 | 66 45 199 | 47 40 254 | 28 21 286 | 31 47 342 |
| 306 | 14 36 040 | 42 04 077 | 19 16 145 | 66 28 201 | 46 51 254 | 27 32 286 | 31 31 342 |
| 307 | 15 09 040 | 42 54 078 | 19 45 146 | 66 08 204 | 46 01 255 | 26 43 287 | 31 15 342 |
| 308 | 15 43 041 | 43 45 078 | 20 13 147 | 65 46 206 | 45 11 256 | 25 53 287 | 30 58 342 |
| 309 | 16 16 041 | 44 35 078 | 20 41 148 | 65 23 208 | 44 21 257 | 25 04 287 | 30 42 342 |
| 310 | 16 50 041 | 45 25 079 | 21 08 148 | 64 58 210 | 43 31 257 | 24 15 288 | 30 26 342 |
| 311 | 17 24 042 | 46 16 079 | 21 35 149 | 64 31 212 | 42 41 258 | 23 26 288 | 30 10 342 |
| 312 | 17 59 042 | 47 06 079 | 22 01 150 | 64 03 214 | 41 51 259 | 22 37 289 | 29 54 342 |
| 313 | 18 33 042 | 47 57 080 | 22 26 151 | 63 33 216 | 41 00 259 | 21 49 289 | 29 38 342 |
| 314 | 19 08 043 | 48 47 080 | 22 51 152 | 63 02 218 | 40 10 260 | 21 00 289 | 29 21 342 |
| | •Mirfak | Hamal | Diphda | •FOMALHAUT | ALTAIR | •VEGA | Kochab |
| 315 | 19 43 043 | 22 46 076 | 17 25 125 | 23 15 153 | 62 29 220 | 59 46 295 | 29 05 342 |
| 316 | 20 18 043 | 23 36 076 | 18 07 125 | 23 38 153 | 61 56 222 | 58 59 295 | 28 49 342 |
| 317 | 20 54 044 | 24 26 076 | 18 49 126 | 24 01 154 | 61 21 223 | 58 12 295 | 28 34 342 |
| 318 | 21 29 044 | 25 16 077 | 19 31 127 | 24 23 155 | 60 45 225 | 57 25 295 | 28 18 342 |
| 319 | 22 05 044 | 26 06 077 | 20 12 127 | 24 44 156 | 60 08 227 | 56 39 295 | 28 02 342 |
| 320 | 22 41 044 | 26 56 078 | 20 52 128 | 25 05 157 | 59 30 228 | 55 52 295 | 27 46 342 |
| 321 | 23 17 045 | 27 47 078 | 21 33 129 | 25 25 158 | 58 51 230 | 55 05 295 | 27 31 342 |
| 322 | 23 53 045 | 28 37 078 | 22 13 130 | 25 44 159 | 58 12 231 | 54 18 295 | 27 15 342 |
| 323 | 24 29 045 | 29 27 079 | 22 52 130 | 26 02 160 | 57 31 232 | 53 32 295 | 27 00 343 |
| 324 | 25 06 045 | 30 18 079 | 23 31 131 | 26 20 160 | 56 50 234 | 52 45 295 | 26 44 343 |
| 325 | 25 43 046 | 31 09 080 | 24 10 132 | 26 37 161 | 56 09 235 | 51 58 295 | 26 29 343 |
| 326 | 26 19 046 | 31 59 080 | 24 48 133 | 26 53 162 | 55 26 236 | 51 11 295 | 26 14 343 |
| 327 | 26 56 046 | 32 50 081 | 25 25 133 | 27 08 163 | 54 43 237 | 50 25 295 | 25 58 343 |
| 328 | 27 34 046 | 33 41 081 | 26 03 134 | 27 22 164 | 54 00 239 | 49 38 295 | 25 43 343 |
| 329 | 28 11 046 | 34 31 081 | 26 39 135 | 27 36 165 | 53 15 240 | 48 51 295 | 25 29 343 |
| | •Mirfak | Hamal | Diphda | •FOMALHAUT | ALTAIR | •VEGA | Kochab |
| 330 | 28 48 047 | 35 22 082 | 27 15 136 | 27 49 166 | 52 31 241 | 48 05 295 | 25 14 343 |
| 331 | 29 26 047 | 36 13 082 | 27 51 137 | 28 01 167 | 51 46 242 | 47 18 295 | 24 59 343 |
| 332 | 30 03 047 | 37 04 083 | 28 26 137 | 28 12 168 | 51 00 243 | 46 32 295 | 24 44 344 |
| 333 | 30 41 047 | 37 55 083 | 29 01 138 | 28 22 169 | 50 14 244 | 45 45 295 | 24 30 344 |
| 334 | 31 19 047 | 38 46 084 | 29 34 139 | 28 32 170 | 49 28 245 | 44 59 296 | 24 16 344 |
| 335 | 31 56 047 | 39 38 08[illegible] | [illegible]0 08 140 | 28 40 17[illegible] | [illegible]8 41 246 | 44 12 [illegible] | 24 01 344 |
| [illegible] | 32 34 048 | 40 29 [illegible] | [illegible]0 141 | 28 48 [illegible] | [illegible] 54 247 | 43 26 [illegible] | [illegible] 47 344 |
| | [illegible] 12 048 | 4[illegible] | [illegible] 142 | 28 5[illegible] | [illegible] 247 | 42 [illegible] | [illegible] 344 |
| | [illegible] 048 | | [illegible]43 | 29 [illegible] | [illegible]48 | [illegible] | [illegible] |
| | | | | [illegible] | | | |

## TABLE 5—CORRECTION FOR PRECESSION AND NUTATION

| L.H.A. ♈ | North latitudes | | | | | | | | | | |
|---|---|---|---|---|---|---|---|---|---|---|---|
| | N. 89° | N. 80° | N. 70° | N. 60° | N. 50° | N. 40° | N. 20° | 0° | S. 20° | S. 40° | S[illegible] |
| | | | | | | | | **1986** | | | |
| ° | ′ ° | ′ ° | ′ ° | ′ ° | ′ ° | ′ ° | ′ ° | ′ ° | ′ ° | ′ | |
| 0 | 0 — | 0 — | 1 030 | 1 040 | 1 050 | 1 060 | 1 060 | 1 070 | 1 070 | 1 0[illegible] | |
| 30 | 0 — | 1 030 | 1 050 | 1 050 | 1 060 | 1 060 | 1 070 | 1 070 | 1 060 | 1 06[illegible] | |
| 60 | 0 — | 1 060 | 1 060 | 1 070 | 1 070 | 1 070 | 1 070 | 1 070 | 1 070 | 1 060 | |
| 90 | 0 — | 1 080 | 1 080 | 1 080 | 1 080 | 1 080 | 1 080 | 1 080 | 1 080 | 1 080 | 0 |
| 120 | 0 — | 1 100 | 1 100 | 1 100 | 1 100 | 1 100 | 1 100 | 1 100 | 1 100 | 1 100 | 0 |
| 150 | 0 — | 1 120 | 1 120 | 1 110 | 1 110 | 1 110 | 1 110 | 1 110 | 1 110 | 1 120 | [illegible] |
| 180 | 0 — | 1 150 | 1 130 | 1 130 | 1 120 | 1 120 | 1 110 | 1 110 | 1 120 | 1 12[illegible] | |
| 210 | 0 — | 0 — | 1 150 | 1 140 | 1 130 | 1 120 | 1 120 | 1 110 | 1 110 | 1 [illegible] | |
| 240 | 0 — | 0 — | 0 — | 0 — | 1 130 | 1 120 | 1 110 | 1 110 | 1 110 | 1 [illegible] | |
| 270 | 0 — | 0 — | 0 — | 0 — | 0 — | 1 100 | 1 100 | 1 100 | 1 100 | 1 10[illegible] | |
| 300 | 0 — | 0 — | 0 — | 0 — | 0 — | 1 080 | 1 080 | 1 080 | 1 080 | 1 080 | |
| 330 | 0 — | 0 — | 0 — | 0 — | 1 050 | 1 060 | 1 070 | 1 070 | 1 070 | 1 070 | [illegible] |
| 360 | 0 — | 0 — | 1 030 | 1 040 | 1 050 | 1 060 | 1 060 | 1 070 | 1 070 | 1 060 | 1 [illegible] |
| | | | | | | | | **1987** | | | |
| 0 | 1 350 | 1 010 | 1 030 | 1 050 | 1 050 | 2 060 | 2 070 | 2 070 | 2 070 | 2 [illegible] | |
| 30 | 1 020 | 1 040 | 1 050 | 1 060 | 2 060 | 2 060 | 2 070 | 2 070 | 2 070 | 1 [illegible] | |
| 60 | 1 050 | 1 060 | 1 070 | 2 070 | 2 070 | 2 070 | 2 080 | 2 070 | 2 070 | 1 0[illegible] | |
| 90 | 1 080 | 1 080 | 1 080 | 2 090 | 2 090 | 2 090 | 2 090 | 2 090 | 2 090 | 1 080 | |
| 120 | 1 110 | 1 110 | 1 100 | 2 100 | 2 100 | 2 100 | 2 100 | 2 100 | 2 100 | 1 110 | [illegible] |
| 150 | 1 140 | 1 130 | 1 120 | 2 110 | 2 110 | 2 110 | 2 110 | 2 110 | 2 110 | 1 120 | 1 |
| 180 | 1 170 | 1 150 | 1 140 | 1 130 | 2 120 | 2 120 | 2 110 | 2 110 | 2 120 | 2 120 | 1 [illegible] |
| 210 | 1 200 | 1 180 | 1 150 | 1 140 | 1 130 | 1 120 | 2 120 | 2 110 | 2 110 | 2 120 | 2 |
| 240 | 1 230 | 1 210 | 1 180 | 1 140 | 1 130 | 1 120 | 2 110 | 2 110 | 2 110 | 2 110 | |
| 270 | 1 260 | 1 250 | 0 — | 0 — | 1 100 | 1 100 | 2 100 | 2 090 | 2 090 | 2 09[illegible] | |
| 300 | 1 290 | 1 300 | 0 — | 0 — | 1 070 | 1 070 | 2 080 | 2 080 | 2 080 | 2 0[illegible] | |
| 330 | 1 320 | 1 340 | 1 010 | 1 040 | 1 050 | 1 060 | 2 070 | 2 070 | 2 070 | 2 [illegible] | |
| 360 | 1 350 | 1 010 | 1 030 | 1 050 | 1 050 | 2 060 | 2 070 | 2 070 | 2 070 | 2 [illegible] | |
| | | | | | | | | **1988** | | | |
| 0 | 1 000 | 1 020 | 1 030 | 2 050 | 2 050 | 2 060 | 3 070 | 3 070 | 3 070 | 3 060 | 2 |
| 30 | 1 030 | 1 040 | 2 050 | 2 060 | 2 060 | 3 070 | 3 070 | 3 070 | 3 070 | 2 060 | 2 [illegible] |
| 60 | 1 060 | 2 060 | 2 070 | 2 070 | 3 070 | 3 080 | 3 080 | 3 080 | 2 070 | 2 060 | 1 [illegible] |
| 90 | 1 080 | 2 090 | 2 090 | 2 090 | 3 090 | 3 090 | 3 090 | 3 090 | 2 090 | 1 080 | [illegible] |
| 120 | 1 110 | 2 110 | 2 100 | 2 100 | 3 100 | 3 100 | 3 100 | 3 100 | 2 100 | 1 110 | |
| 150 | 1 140 | 2 130 | 2 120 | 2 120 | 3 110 | 3 110 | 3 110 | 3 110 | 3 110 | 2 12[illegible] | |
| 180 | 1 170 | 1 150 | 2 140 | 2 130 | 2 120 | 3 120 | 3 110 | 3 110 | 3 120 | 2 [illegible] | |
| 210 | 1 200 | 1 180 | 1 160 | 1 140 | 2 130 | 2 120 | 3 110 | 3 110 | 3 110 | 3 [illegible] | |
| 240 | 1 230 | 1 210 | 1 180 | 1 140 | 1 130 | 2 120 | 2 110 | 3 110 | 3 100 | 3 [illegible] | |
| 270 | 1 260 | 1 260 | 0 — | 0 — | 1 100 | 1 100 | 2 090 | 3 090 | 3 090 | 3 09[illegible] | |
| 300 | 1 290 | 1 310 | 0 — | 1 040 | 1 060 | 1 070 | 2 080 | 3 080 | 3 080 | 3 080 | |
| 330 | 1 330 | 1 350 | 1 020 | 1 040 | 2 050 | 2 060 | 3 070 | 3 070 | 3 070 | 3 070 | [illegible] |
| 360 | 1 000 | 1 020 | 1 030 | 2 050 | 2 050 | 2 060 | 3 070 | 3 070 | 3 070 | 3 060 | 2 [illegible] |

## TABLE 6—CORRECTION (*Q*) FOR *POLARIS*

| LHA ♈ | *Q* | LHA ♈ | *Q* | LHA ♈ | *Q* | LHA ♈ | *Q* | LHA ♈ | *Q* | LHA ♈ | *Q* | LHA ♈ | *Q* | LHA ♈ | *Q* |
|---|---|---|---|---|---|---|---|---|---|---|---|---|---|---|---|
| ° ′ | ′ | ° ′ | ′ | ° ′ | ′ | ° ′ | ′ | ° ′ | ′ | ° ′ | ′ | ° ′ | ′ | ° ′ | ′ |
| 359 40 | | 84 18 | | 118 16 | | 150 19 | | 205 44 | | 276 27 | | 308 39 | | 342 18 | |
| | −40 | | −30 | | −4 | | +22 | | +48 | | +22 | | −4 | | −30 |
| 1 49 | | 85 49 | | 119 28 | | 151 40 | | 222 23 | | 277 48 | | 309 51 | | 343 49 | |
| | −41 | | −29 | | −3 | | +23 | | +47 | | +21 | | −5 | | −31 |
| 4 06 | | 87 18 | | 120 40 | | 153 02 | | 228 31 | | 279 08 | | 311 03 | | 345 23 | |
| | −42 | | −28 | | −2 | | +24 | | +46 | | +20 | | −6 | | −32 |
| 6 33 | | 88 46 | | 121 52 | | 154 25 | | 232 45 | | 280 27 | | 312 15 | | 346 59 | |
| | −43 | | −27 | | −1 | | +25 | | +45 | | +19 | | −7 | | −33 |
| 9 14 | | 90 13 | | 123 03 | | 155 49 | | 236 13 | | 281 45 | | 313 27 | | 348 37 | |
| | −44 | | −26 | | 0 | | +26 | | +44 | | +18 | | −8 | | −34 |
| 12 12 | | 91 37 | | 124 16 | | 157 14 | | 239 14 | | 283 03 | | 314 40 | | 350 18 | |
| | −45 | | −25 | | +1 | | +27 | | +43 | | +17 | | −9 | | −35 |
| 15 37 | | 93 01 | | 125 27 | | 158 41 | | 241 56 | | 284 19 | | 315 52 | | 352 02 | |
| | −46 | | −24 | | +2 | | +28 | | +42 | | +16 | | −10 | | −36 |
| 19 48 | | 94 23 | | 126 39 | | 160 10 | | 244 25 | | 285 35 | | 317 06 | | 353 50 | |
| | −47 | | −23 | | +3 | | +29 | | +41 | | +15 | | −11 | | −37 |
| 25 51 | | 95 45 | | 127 51 | | 161 40 | | 246 44 | | 286 51 | | 318 19 | | 355 41 | |
| | −48 | | −22 | | +4 | | +30 | | +40 | | +14 | | −12 | | −38 |
| 42 16 | | 97 05 | | 129 03 | | 163 12 | | 248 54 | | 288 06 | | 319 33 | | 357 38 | |
| | −47 | | −21 | | +5 | | +31 | | +39 | | +13 | | −13 | | −39 |
| 48 19 | | 98 24 | | 130 15 | | 164 47 | | 250 58 | | 289 21 | | 320 47 | | 359 40 | |
| | −46 | | −20 | | +6 | | +32 | | +38 | | +12 | | −14 | | −40 |
| 52 30 | | 99 43 | | 131 27 | | 166 23 | | 252 56 | | 290 35 | | 322 02 | | 1 49 | |
| | −45 | | −19 | | +7 | | +33 | | +37 | | +11 | | −15 | | −41 |
| 55 55 | | 101 01 | | 132 40 | | 168 02 | | 254 49 | | 291 48 | | 323 17 | | 4 06 | |
| | −44 | | −18 | | +8 | | +34 | | +36 | | +10 | | −16 | | −42 |
| 58 53 | | 102 18 | | 133 52 | | 169 44 | | 256 38 | | 293 02 | | 324 33 | | 6 33 | |
| | −43 | | −17 | | +9 | | +35 | | +35 | | +9 | | −17 | | −43 |
| 61 34 | | 103 34 | | 135 05 | | 171 29 | | 258 23 | | 294 15 | | 325 49 | | 9 14 | |
| | −42 | | −16 | | +10 | | +36 | | +34 | | +8 | | −18 | | −44 |
| 64 01 | | 104 50 | | 136 19 | | 173 18 | | 260 05 | | 295 27 | | 327 06 | | 12 12 | |
| | −41 | | −15 | | +11 | | +37 | | +33 | | +7 | | −19 | | −45 |
| 66 18 | | 106 05 | | 137 32 | | 175 11 | | 261 44 | | 296 40 | | 328 24 | | 15 37 | |
| | −40 | | −14 | | +12 | | +38 | | +32 | | +6 | | −20 | | −46 |
| 68 27 | | 107 20 | | 138 46 | | 177 09 | | 263 20 | | 297 52 | | 329 43 | | 19 48 | |
| | −39 | | −13 | | +13 | | +39 | | +31 | | +5 | | −21 | | −47 |
| 70 29 | | 108 34 | | 140 01 | | 179 13 | | 264 55 | | 299 04 | | 331 02 | | 25 51 | |
| | −38 | | −12 | | +14 | | +40 | | +30 | | +4 | | −22 | | −48 |
| 72 26 | | 109 48 | | 141 16 | | 181 23 | | 266 27 | | 300 16 | | 332 22 | | 42 16 | |
| | −37 | | −11 | | +15 | | +41 | | +29 | | +3 | | −23 | | −47 |
| 74 17 | | 111 01 | | 142 32 | | 183 42 | | 267 57 | | 301 28 | | 333 44 | | 48 19 | |
| | −36 | | −10 | | +16 | | +42 | | +28 | | +2 | | −24 | | −46 |
| 76 05 | | 112 15 | | 143 48 | | 186 11 | | 269 26 | | 302 40 | | 335 06 | | 52 30 | |
| | −35 | | −9 | | +17 | | +43 | | +27 | | +1 | | −25 | | −45 |
| 77 49 | | 113 27 | | 145 04 | | 188 53 | | 270 53 | | 303 51 | | 336 30 | | 55 55 | |
| | −34 | | −8 | | +18 | | +44 | | +26 | | 0 | | −26 | | −44 |
| 79 30 | | 114 40 | | 146 22 | | 191 54 | | 272 18 | | 305 04 | | 337 54 | | 58 53 | |
| | −33 | | −7 | | +19 | | +45 | | +25 | | −1 | | −27 | | −43 |
| 81 08 | | 115 52 | | 147 40 | | 195 22 | | 273 42 | | 306 15 | | 339 21 | | 61 34 | |
| | −32 | | −6 | | +20 | | +46 | | +24 | | −2 | | −28 | | −42 |
| 82 44 | | 117 04 | | 148 59 | | 199 36 | | 275 05 | | 307 27 | | 340 49 | | 64 01 | |
| | −31 | | −5 | | +21 | | +47 | | +23 | | −3 | | −29 | | −41 |
| 84 18 | | 118 16 | | 150 19 | | 205 44 | | 276 27 | | 308 39 | | 342 18 | | 66 18 | |

The above table, which does *not* include refraction, gives the quantity *Q* to be applied to the corrected sextant altitude of *Polaris* to give the latitude of the observer. In critical cases ascend.

*Polaris:* Mag. 2·1, SHA 325° 56′, Dec. N 89° 12′·0

## DECLINATION (0°-14°) SAME NAME AS LATITUDE

| 9° | | | 10° | | | 11° | | | 12° | | | 13° | | | |
|---|---|---|---|---|---|---|---|---|---|---|---|---|---|---|---|
| Hc | d | Z | Hc | d | Z | Hc | d | Z | Hc | d | Z | Hc | d | Z | LHA |
| ° ′ | ′ | ° | ° ′ | ′ | ° | ° ′ | ′ | ° | ° ′ | ′ | ° | ° ′ | ′ | ° | |
| 21 43 | +30 | 93 | 22 13 | +30 | 92 | 22 43 | +29 | 91 | 23 12 | +28 | 90 | 23 40 | +29 | 89 | 290 |
| 20 52 | 30 | 92 | 21 22 | 29 | 91 | 21 51 | 29 | 90 | 22 20 | 29 | 89 | 22 49 | 28 | 88 | 289 |
| 20 01 | 29 | 91 | 20 30 | 30 | 91 | 21 00 | 29 | 90 | 21 29 | 29 | 89 | 21 58 | 28 | 88 | 288 |
| 19 09 | 30 | 91 | 19 39 | 29 | 90 | 20 08 | 29 | 89 | 20 37 | 29 | 88 | 21 06 | 29 | 87 | 287 |
| 18 18 | 29 | 90 | 18 47 | 30 | 90 | 19 17 | 29 | 89 | 19 46 | 29 | 88 | 20 15 | 28 | 87 | 286 |
| 17 26 | +30 | 90 | 17 56 | +29 | 89 | 18 25 | +30 | 88 | 18 55 | +29 | 87 | 19 24 | +28 | 86 | 285 |
| 16 35 | 30 | 89 | 17 05 | 29 | 88 | 17 34 | 29 | 88 | 18 03 | 29 | 87 | 18 32 | 29 | 86 | 284 |
| 15 44 | 29 | 89 | 16 13 | 30 | 88 | 16 43 | 29 | 87 | 17 12 | 29 | 86 | 17 41 | 29 | 85 | 283 |
| 14 52 | 30 | 88 | 15 22 | 29 | 87 | 15 51 | 30 | 87 | 16 21 | 29 | 86 | 16 50 | 29 | 85 | 282 |
| 14 01 | 29 | 88 | 14 30 | 30 | 87 | 15 00 | 29 | 86 | 15 29 | 30 | 85 | 15 59 | 28 | 84 | 281 |
| 13 09 | +30 | 87 | 13 39 | +30 | 86 | 14 09 | +29 | 86 | 14 38 | +29 | 85 | 15 07 | +29 | 84 | 280 |
| 12 18 | 30 | 87 | 12 48 | 30 | 86 | 13 18 | 29 | 85 | 13 47 | 29 | 84 | 14 16 | 29 | 83 | 279 |
| 11 27 | 30 | 86 | 11 57 | 29 | 85 | 12 26 | 30 | 85 | 12 56 | 29 | 84 | 13 25 | 29 | 83 | 278 |
| 10 35 | 30 | 86 | 11 05 | 30 | 85 | 11 35 | 30 | 84 | 12 05 | 29 | 83 | 12 34 | 30 | 82 | 277 |
| 09 44 | 30 | 85 | 10 14 | 30 | 84 | 10 44 | 30 | 84 | 11 14 | 29 | 83 | 11 43 | 30 | 82 | 276 |
| 08 53 | +30 | 85 | 09 23 | +30 | 84 | 09 53 | +30 | 83 | 10 23 | +29 | 82 | 10 52 | +30 | 81 | 275 |
| 08 02 | 30 | 84 | 08 32 | 30 | 83 | 09 02 | 30 | 83 | 09 32 | 30 | 82 | 10 02 | 29 | 81 | 274 |
| 07 10 | 31 | 84 | 07 41 | 30 | 83 | 08 11 | 30 | 82 | 08 41 | 30 | 81 | 09 11 | 30 | 80 | 273 |
| 06 19 | 31 | 83 | 06 50 | 30 | 82 | 07 20 | 30 | 82 | 07 50 | 30 | 81 | 08 20 | 30 | 80 | 272 |
| 05 28 | 31 | 83 | 05 59 | 30 | 82 | 06 29 | 31 | 81 | 07 00 | 30 | 80 | 07 30 | 30 | 79 | 271 |
| 04 37 | +31 | 82 | 05 08 | +30 | 81 | 05 38 | +31 | 81 | 06 09 | +30 | 80 | 06 39 | +31 | 79 | 270 |
| 03 46 | 31 | 82 | 04 17 | 31 | 81 | 04 48 | 30 | 80 | 05 18 | 31 | 79 | 05 49 | 30 | 78 | 269 |
| 02 55 | 31 | 81 | 03 26 | 31 | 80 | 03 57 | 31 | 80 | 04 28 | 30 | 79 | 04 58 | 31 | 78 | 268 |
| 02 05 | 31 | 81 | 02 36 | 31 | 80 | 03 07 | 30 | 79 | 03 37 | 31 | 78 | 04 08 | 31 | 77 | 267 |
| 01 14 | 31 | 80 | 01 45 | 31 | 79 | 02 16 | 31 | 79 | 02 47 | 31 | 78 | 03 18 | 31 | 77 | 266 |
| 00 23 | +32 | 80 | 00 55 | +31 | 79 | 01 26 | +31 | 78 | 01 57 | +31 | 77 | 02 28 | +31 | 76 | 265 |
| −0 27 | 31 | 79 | 00 04 | 31 | 78 | 00 35 | 32 | 78 | 01 07 | 31 | 77 | 01 38 | 32 | 76 | 264 |
| −1 18 | 32 | 79 | −0 46 | 31 | 78 | −0 15 | 32 | 77 | 00 17 | 31 | 76 | 00 48 | 32 | 75 | 263 |
| −2 08 | 32 | 78 | −1 36 | 31 | 77 | −1 05 | 32 | 76 | −0 33 | 32 | 76 | −0 01 | 31 | 75 | 262 |
| −2 58 | 31 | 78 | −2 27 | 32 | 77 | −1 55 | 32 | 76 | −1 23 | 32 | 75 | −0 51 | 32 | 74 | 261 |
| −3 49 | +32 | 77 | −3 17 | +32 | 76 | −2 45 | +33 | 75 | −2 12 | +32 | 75 | −1 40 | +32 | 74 | 260 |
| −4 39 | 33 | 77 | −4 06 | 32 | 76 | −3 34 | 32 | 75 | −3 02 | 32 | 74 | −2 30 | 33 | 73 | 259 |
| −5 29 | 33 | 76 | −4 56 | 32 | 75 | −4 24 | 33 | 74 | −3 51 | 32 | 74 | −3 19 | 33 | 73 | 258 |
| −6 19 | 33 | 76 | −5 46 | 33 | 75 | −5 13 | 32 | 74 | −4 41 | 33 | 73 | −4 08 | 33 | 72 | 257 |
| | | 104 | −6 36 | 33 | 74 | −6 03 | 33 | 73 | −5 30 | 33 | 72 | −4 57 | 33 | 72 | 256 |
| | | | | | | | | 105 | −6 19 | +34 | 72 | −5 45 | +33 | 71 | 255 |
| | | | | | | | | | | | 106 | −6 34 | 34 | 70 | 254 |

N. Lat. { LHA greater than 180° Zn = Z
LHA less than 180° Zn = 360 − Z }

## DECLINATION (15°-29°) CONTRARY NAME TO LATITUDE

| | 15° | | | 16° | | | 21° | | | 22° | | | |
|---|---|---|---|---|---|---|---|---|---|---|---|---|---|
| LHA | Hc | d | Z | Hc | d | Z | Hc | d | Z | Hc | d | Z | LHA |
| 52 | 22 07 | 41 | 125 | 21 26 | 42 | 126 | 17 57 | 43 | 129 | 17 14 | 42 | 130 | 308 |
| 51 | 22 49 | 42 | 126 | 22 07 | 41 | 126 | 18 36 | 42 | 130 | 17 54 | 43 | 131 | 309 |
| 50 | 23 31 | -42 | 126 | 22 49 | -43 | 127 | 19 15 | -43 | 131 | 18 32 | -43 | 132 | 310 |
| 49 | 24 12 | 42 | 127 | 23 30 | 43 | 128 | 19 54 | 43 | 132 | 19 11 | 44 | 132 | 311 |
| 48 | 24 53 | 43 | 128 | 24 10 | 43 | 129 | 20 33 | 45 | 132 | 19 48 | 44 | 133 | 312 |
| 47 | 25 33 | 43 | 129 | 24 50 | 43 | 129 | 21 10 | 44 | 133 | 20 26 | 45 | 134 | 313 |
| 46 | 26 13 | 43 | 129 | 25 30 | 44 | 130 | 21 48 | 45 | 134 | 21 03 | 45 | 134 | 314 |
| 45 | 26 53 | -44 | 130 | 26 09 | -45 | 131 | 22 25 | -46 | 134 | 21 39 | -45 | 135 | 315 |
| 44 | 27 32 | 44 | 131 | 26 48 | 45 | 132 | 23 01 | 46 | 135 | 22 15 | 46 | 136 | 316 |
| 43 | 28 11 | 45 | 132 | 27 26 | 45 | 132 | 23 37 | 46 | 136 | 22 51 | 46 | 137 | 317 |
| 42 | 28 49 | 45 | 133 | 28 04 | 46 | 133 | 24 13 | 47 | 137 | 23 26 | 47 | 138 | 318 |
| 41 | 29 27 | 46 | 133 | 28 41 | 46 | 134 | 24 48 | 47 | 138 | 24 01 | 48 | 138 | 319 |
| 40 | 30 04 | -47 | 134 | 29 17 | -46 | 135 | 25 22 | -47 | 138 | 24 35 | -48 | 139 | 320 |
| 39 | 30 40 | 46 | 135 | 29 54 | 47 | 136 | 25 56 | 48 | 139 | 25 08 | 48 | 140 | 321 |
| 38 | 31 17 | 48 | 136 | 30 29 | 47 | 137 | 26 29 | 48 | 140 | 25 41 | 49 | 141 | 322 |
| 37 | 31 52 | 48 | 137 | 31 04 | 48 | 138 | 27 02 | 49 | 141 | 26 13 | 49 | 142 | 323 |
| 36 | 32 27 | 48 | 138 | 31 39 | 49 | 138 | 27 34 | 49 | 142 | 26 45 | 50 | 142 | 324 |
| 35 | 33 01 | -49 | 139 | 32 12 | -48 | 139 | 28 06 | -50 | 143 | 27 16 | -50 | 143 | 325 |
| 34 | 33 35 | 49 | 140 | 32 46 | 50 | 140 | 28 37 | 51 | 144 | 27 46 | 50 | 144 | 326 |
| 33 | 34 08 | 50 | 141 | 33 18 | 50 | 141 | 29 07 | 51 | 144 | 28 16 | 51 | 145 | 327 |
| 32 | 34 40 | 50 | 142 | 33 50 | 50 | 142 | 29 37 | 52 | 145 | 28 45 | 51 | 146 | 328 |
| 31 | 35 12 | 51 | 143 | 34 21 | 50 | 143 | 30 05 | 51 | 146 | 29 14 | 52 | 147 | 329 |
| 30 | 35 43 | -51 | 144 | 34 52 | -51 | 144 | 30 34 | -52 | 147 | 29 42 | -53 | 148 | 330 |
| 29 | 36 13 | 51 | 145 | 35 22 | 52 | 145 | 31 01 | 52 | 148 | 30 09 | 53 | 149 | 331 |
| 28 | 36 43 | 52 | 146 | 35 51 | 53 | 146 | 31 28 | 53 | 149 | 30 35 | 53 | 150 | 332 |
| 27 | 37 11 | 52 | 147 | 36 19 | 53 | 147 | 31 54 | 53 | 150 | 31 01 | 54 | 151 | 333 |
| 26 | 37 39 | 53 | 148 | 36 46 | 53 | 148 | 32 19 | 53 | 151 | 31 26 | 54 | 152 | 334 |
| 25 | 38 06 | -53 | 149 | 37 13 | -54 | 149 | 32 44 | -54 | 152 | 31 50 | -55 | 153 | 335 |
| 24 | 38 33 | 54 | 150 | 37 39 | 54 | 150 | 33 08 | 55 | 153 | 32 13 | 55 | 154 | 336 |
| 23 | 38 58 | 54 | 151 | 38 04 | 55 | 152 | 33 31 | 55 | 154 | 32 36 | 56 | 155 | 337 |
| 22 | 39 22 | 54 | 152 | 38 28 | 55 | 153 | 33 53 | 56 | 155 | 32 57 | 55 | 156 | 338 |
| 21 | 39 46 | 55 | 153 | 38 51 | 55 | 154 | 34 14 | 56 | 156 | 33 18 | 56 | 157 | 339 |
| 20 | 40 09 | -56 | 154 | 39 13 | -55 | 155 | 34 34 | -56 | 157 | 33 38 | -56 | 158 | 340 |
| 19 | 40 31 | 56 | 156 | 39 35 | 56 | 156 | 34 54 | 57 | 158 | 33 57 | 56 | 159 | 341 |
| 18 | 40 51 | 56 | 157 | 39 55 | 56 | 157 | 35 12 | 56 | 159 | 34 16 | 57 | 160 | 342 |
| 17 | 41 11 | 57 | 158 | 40 14 | 56 | 158 | 35 30 | 57 | 160 | 34 33 | 57 | 161 | 343 |
| 16 | 41 30 | 57 | 159 | 40 33 | 57 | 160 | 35 47 | 58 | 162 | 34 49 | 57 | 162 | 344 |
| 15 | 41 48 | -58 | 160 | 40 50 | -57 | 161 | 36 03 | -58 | 163 | 35 05 | -58 | 163 | 345 |

N. Lat. { LHA greater than 180° Zn = Z
LHA less than 180° Zn = 360 − Z }

## TABLE III. — Correction to Tabulated Altitude for Minutes of Declination

| 38 | 39 | 40 | 41 | 42 | 43 | 44 | 45 | 46 | 47 | 48 | 49 | 50 | 51 | 52 | 53 | 54 | 55 | 56 | 57 | 58 | 59 | 60 | d ′ |
|---|---|---|---|---|---|---|---|---|---|---|---|---|---|---|---|---|---|---|---|---|---|---|---|
| | 0 | 0 | 0 | 0 | 0 | 0 | 0 | 0 | 0 | 0 | 0 | 0 | 0 | 0 | 0 | 0 | 0 | 0 | 0 | 0 | 0 | 0 | 0 |
| | | 1 | 1 | 1 | 1 | 1 | 1 | 1 | 1 | 1 | 1 | 1 | 1 | 1 | 1 | 1 | 1 | 1 | 1 | 1 | 1 | 1 | 1 |
| | 1 | 1 | 1 | 1 | 1 | 1 | 2 | 2 | 2 | 2 | 2 | 2 | 2 | 2 | 2 | 2 | 2 | 2 | 2 | 2 | 2 | 2 | 2 |
| 2 | 2 | 2 | 2 | 2 | 2 | 2 | 2 | 2 | 2 | 2 | 2 | 2 | 3 | 3 | 3 | 3 | 3 | 3 | 3 | 3 | 3 | 3 | 3 |
| 3 | 3 | 3 | 3 | 3 | 3 | 3 | 3 | 3 | 3 | 3 | 3 | 3 | 3 | 3 | 4 | 4 | 4 | 4 | 4 | 4 | 4 | 4 | 4 |
| | | 3 | 3 | 4 | 4 | 4 | 4 | 4 | 4 | 4 | 4 | 4 | 4 | 4 | 4 | 4 | 5 | 5 | 5 | 5 | 5 | 5 | 5 |
| | 4 | 4 | 4 | 4 | 4 | 4 | 4 | 5 | 5 | 5 | 5 | 5 | 5 | 5 | 5 | 5 | 6 | 6 | 6 | 6 | 6 | 6 | 6 |
| 4 | 5 | 5 | 5 | 5 | 5 | 5 | 5 | 5 | 5 | 6 | 6 | 6 | 6 | 6 | 6 | 6 | 6 | 7 | 7 | 7 | 7 | 7 | 7 |
| 5 | 5 | 5 | 5 | 6 | 6 | 6 | 6 | 6 | 6 | 6 | 7 | 7 | 7 | 7 | 7 | 7 | 7 | 7 | 8 | 8 | 8 | 8 | 8 |
| | 6 | 6 | 6 | 6 | 6 | 7 | 7 | 7 | 7 | 7 | 7 | 8 | 8 | 8 | 8 | 8 | 8 | 8 | 9 | 9 | 9 | 9 | 9 |
| | | 7 | 7 | 7 | 7 | 7 | 8 | 8 | 8 | 8 | 8 | 8 | 8 | 9 | 9 | 9 | 9 | 9 | 10 | 10 | 10 | 10 | 10 |
| | 7 | 7 | 8 | 8 | 8 | 8 | 8 | 8 | 9 | 9 | 9 | 9 | 9 | 10 | 10 | 10 | 10 | 10 | 10 | 11 | 11 | 11 | 11 |
| 8 | 8 | 8 | 8 | 8 | 9 | 9 | 9 | 9 | 9 | 10 | 10 | 10 | 10 | 10 | 11 | 11 | 11 | 11 | 11 | 12 | 12 | 12 | 12 |
| 8 | 8 | 9 | 9 | 9 | 9 | 10 | 10 | 10 | 10 | 10 | 11 | 11 | 11 | 11 | 11 | 12 | 12 | 12 | 12 | 13 | 13 | 13 | 13 |
| | 9 | 9 | 10 | 10 | 10 | 10 | 10 | 11 | 11 | 11 | 11 | 12 | 12 | 12 | 12 | 13 | 13 | 13 | 13 | 14 | 14 | 14 | 14 |
| | | 10 | 10 | 10 | 11 | 11 | 11 | 12 | 12 | 12 | 12 | 12 | 13 | 13 | 13 | 14 | 14 | 14 | 14 | 14 | 15 | 15 | 15 |
| | 10 | 11 | 11 | 11 | 11 | 12 | 12 | 12 | 13 | 13 | 13 | 13 | 14 | 14 | 14 | 14 | 15 | 15 | 15 | 15 | 16 | 16 | 16 |
| 11 | 11 | 11 | 12 | 12 | 12 | 12 | 13 | 13 | 13 | 14 | 14 | 14 | 14 | 15 | 15 | 15 | 16 | 16 | 16 | 16 | 17 | 17 | 17 |
| | 12 | 12 | 12 | 13 | 13 | 13 | 14 | 14 | 14 | 14 | 15 | 15 | 15 | 16 | 16 | 16 | 16 | 17 | 17 | 17 | 18 | 18 | 18 |
| | | 13 | 13 | 13 | 14 | 14 | 14 | 15 | 15 | 15 | 16 | 16 | 16 | 16 | 17 | 17 | 17 | 18 | 18 | 18 | 19 | 19 | 19 |
| | 13 | 13 | 14 | 14 | 14 | 15 | 15 | 15 | 16 | 16 | 16 | 17 | 17 | 17 | 18 | 18 | 18 | 19 | 19 | 19 | 20 | 20 | 20 |
| 13 | 14 | 14 | 14 | 15 | 15 | 15 | 16 | 16 | 16 | 17 | 17 | 18 | 18 | 18 | 19 | 19 | 19 | 20 | 20 | 20 | 21 | 21 | 21 |
| 14 | 14 | 15 | 15 | 15 | 16 | 16 | 16 | 17 | 17 | 18 | 18 | 18 | 19 | 19 | 19 | 20 | 20 | 21 | 21 | 21 | 22 | 22 | 22 |
| | 15 | 15 | 16 | 16 | 16 | 17 | 17 | 18 | 18 | 18 | 19 | 19 | 20 | 20 | 20 | 21 | 21 | 21 | 22 | 22 | 23 | 23 | 23 |
| | | 16 | 16 | 17 | 17 | 18 | 18 | 18 | 19 | 19 | 20 | 20 | 20 | 21 | 21 | 22 | 22 | 22 | 23 | 23 | 24 | 24 | 24 |
| | 16 | 17 | 17 | 18 | 18 | 18 | 19 | 19 | 20 | 20 | 20 | 21 | 21 | 22 | 22 | 22 | 23 | 23 | 24 | 24 | 25 | 25 | 25 |
| 16 | 17 | 17 | 18 | 18 | 19 | 19 | 20 | 20 | 20 | 21 | 21 | 22 | 22 | 23 | 23 | 23 | 24 | 24 | 25 | 25 | 26 | 26 | 26 |
| | 18 | 18 | 18 | 19 | 19 | 20 | 20 | 21 | 21 | 22 | 22 | 22 | 23 | 23 | 24 | 24 | 25 | 25 | 26 | 26 | 27 | 27 | 27 |
| | | 19 | 19 | 20 | 20 | 21 | 21 | 21 | 22 | 22 | 23 | 23 | 24 | 24 | 25 | 25 | 26 | 26 | 27 | 27 | 28 | 28 | 28 |
| | | 19 | 20 | 20 | 21 | 21 | 22 | 22 | 23 | 23 | 24 | 24 | 25 | 25 | 26 | 26 | 27 | 27 | 28 | 28 | 29 | 29 | 29 |
| 19 | 20 | 20 | 20 | 21 | 22 | 22 | 22 | 23 | 24 | 24 | 24 | 25 | 26 | 26 | 26 | 27 | 28 | 28 | 28 | 29 | 30 | 30 | 30 |
| 20 | 20 | 21 | 21 | 22 | 22 | 23 | 23 | 24 | 24 | 25 | 25 | 26 | 26 | 27 | 27 | 28 | 28 | 29 | 29 | 30 | 30 | 31 | 31 |
| | 21 | 21 | 22 | 22 | 23 | 23 | 24 | 25 | 25 | 26 | 26 | 27 | 27 | 28 | 28 | 29 | 29 | 30 | 30 | 31 | 31 | 32 | 32 |
| | | 22 | 23 | 23 | 24 | 24 | 25 | 25 | 26 | 26 | 27 | 28 | 28 | 29 | 29 | 30 | 30 | 31 | 31 | 32 | 32 | 33 | 33 |
| | 22 | 23 | 23 | 24 | 24 | 25 | 26 | 26 | 27 | 27 | 28 | 28 | 29 | 29 | 30 | 31 | 31 | 32 | 32 | 33 | 33 | 34 | 34 |
| 22 | 23 | 23 | 24 | 24 | 25 | 26 | 26 | 27 | 27 | 28 | 29 | 29 | 30 | 30 | 31 | 32 | 32 | 33 | 33 | 34 | 34 | 35 | 35 |
| | 23 | 24 | 25 | 25 | 26 | 26 | 27 | 28 | 28 | 29 | 29 | 30 | 31 | 31 | 32 | 32 | 33 | 34 | 34 | 35 | 35 | 36 | 36 |
| | | 25 | 25 | 26 | 27 | 27 | 28 | 28 | 29 | 30 | 30 | 31 | 31 | 32 | 33 | 33 | 34 | 35 | 35 | 36 | 36 | 37 | 37 |
| | | 25 | 26 | 27 | 27 | 28 | 28 | 29 | 30 | 30 | 31 | 32 | 32 | 33 | 34 | 34 | 35 | 35 | 36 | 37 | 37 | 38 | 38 |
| | 25 | 26 | 27 | 27 | 28 | 29 | 29 | 30 | 31 | 31 | 32 | 32 | 33 | 34 | 34 | 35 | 36 | 36 | 37 | 38 | 38 | 39 | 39 |
| 25 | 26 | 27 | 27 | 28 | 29 | 29 | 30 | 31 | 31 | 32 | 33 | 33 | 34 | 35 | 35 | 36 | 37 | 37 | 38 | 39 | 39 | 40 | 40 |
| | 27 | 27 | 28 | 29 | 29 | 30 | 31 | 31 | 32 | 33 | 33 | 34 | 35 | 36 | 36 | 37 | 38 | 38 | 39 | 40 | 40 | 41 | 41 |
| | | 28 | 29 | 29 | 30 | 31 | 32 | 32 | 33 | 34 | 34 | 35 | 36 | 36 | 37 | 38 | 38 | 39 | 40 | 41 | 41 | 42 | 42 |
| | 28 | 29 | 29 | 30 | 31 | 32 | 32 | 33 | 34 | 34 | 35 | 36 | 37 | 37 | 38 | 39 | 39 | 40 | 41 | 42 | 42 | 43 | 43 |
| 28 | 29 | 29 | 30 | 31 | 32 | 32 | 33 | 34 | 34 | 35 | 36 | 37 | 37 | 38 | 39 | 40 | 40 | 41 | 42 | 43 | 43 | 44 | 44 |
| | 29 | 30 | 31 | 32 | 32 | 33 | 34 | 34 | 35 | 36 | 37 | 38 | 38 | 39 | 40 | 40 | 41 | 42 | 43 | 44 | 44 | 45 | 45 |
| | | 31 | 31 | 32 | 33 | 34 | 34 | 35 | 36 | 37 | [illegible] | 38 | 39 | 40 | [illegible] | 41 | 42 | 43 | 44 | 44 | 45 | 46 | 46 |
| | | | 32 | | | 34 | | | 37 | [illegible] | | | 40 | [illegible] | | [illegible] | 43 | | | 45 | | | 47 |

# Index